The Brown Reader

50 Writers Remember College Hill

Edited by Judy Sternlight

SIMON & SCHUSTER

New York London Toronto Sydney New Delhi

Simon & Schuster

1230 Avenue of the Americas

New York, NY 10020

Compilation and preface copyright © 2014 by Brown University

First Simon & Schuster trade paperback edition May 2014

SIMON & SCHUSTER and colophon are registered trademarks of Simon & Schuster, Inc.

For information about special discounts for bulk purchases, please contact Simon & Schuster Special Sales at 1-866-506-1949 or business@simonandschuster.com.

The Simon & Schuster Speakers Bureau can bring authors to your live event. For more information or to book an event, contact the Simon & Schuster Speakers Bureau at 1-866-248-3049 or visit our website at www.simonspeakers.com.

Cover design by Abby Weintraub

Manufactured in the United States of America

1 3 5 7 9 10 8 6 4 2

Library of Congress Cataloging-in-Publication Data is available.

ISBN 978-1-4767-6519-8
ISBN 978-1-4767-6520-4 (ebook)

Page 305 constitutes an extension of this copyright page.

Contents

Preface

JUDY STERNLIGHT

In anticipation of Brown University's 250th anniversary, I returned to Providence at the start of 2013 to discuss the creation of this anthology with members of the Brown community. We talked about some of the remarkable writers whose voices, opinions, and life choices had been influenced by this singular Ivy League institution (and how some of those students had influenced the university right back), and we agreed that a collection of original pieces by these alums, recalling their college days, would be a great way to commemorate Brown's sestercentennial.

Being back at Brown for the first time since my graduation in 1982 was fascinating and surreal. I discovered that some favorite landmarks—Jake's coffee shop on Thayer Street where I used to study, and the funky vintage clothing stores where I'd found silk bed jackets and rainbow-striped stilettos to enhance my waif look—were long gone. I recognized the outlines of College Hill, but some of the renovated buildings clashed with my expectations. Still, I found touchstones everywhere: the Rock, the John Hay Library, and Carrie Tower appeared just as I remembered them. And there was a vital energy in the people I encountered on my stroll through campus that filled me with a profound sense of recognition.

When I caught sight of the Ashamu Dance Studio in Lyman Hall—bang! I time-traveled back to Julie Strandberg's modern dance class. I was a skinny dancer, warming up to a recording of Vivaldi (or a pair of live drummers) as Julie, graceful and muscular, drifted among us, calmly adjusting our positions as we stretched. The studio was brand-new in 1979 and the sprung wood floor still smelled fresh.

Sunshine poured through the big, square windows, warming the floorboards under my bare toes. Names and bodies and faces came rushing back.

I was rehearsing a duet with my future housemate Barbara to the song "Planet Claire" by the B-52s. We wore one-sleeved, polka-dotted unitards (mine purple, Barbara's pink) and our synchronized New Wave piece was greeted with raucous applause at the annual Faunce House dance concert . . . One year later, a performance at Faunce House would find me in despair; I had just split up with my rock-musician, law-school-bound boyfriend when I was cast as an old cockney hag in George Bernard Shaw's *Major Barbara*. I chose to embrace the misery, blackening my teeth with theatrical wax to match my raggedy costume, while sharing a dressing room with actresses in beautiful gowns.

My years at Brown were filled with dramatic mood swings. But while I was emoting up and down, I was also learning. I focused intensely on the performing arts from practical, technical, historical, and philosophical vantage points but I also explored psychology, sociology, and creative writing, and learned the art of collaboration through Production Workshop, the thriving student-run theater.

Some students were very adventurous, taking full advantage of the freedom of the New Curriculum (a system that has been described as Escher-like) and the option of Satisfactory/No Credit (S/NC); they took big chances in studying subjects they knew little about or combined disparate interests into cohesive paths of study. Examples in *The Brown Reader* include Christine Montross, who combined poetry and medicine; Brian Christian, who paired his computer science background with creative writing; and Marie Myung-Ok Lee, who concentrated in economics, fell in love with a US history class, and ultimately became a novelist.

My common thread was a keen interest in human behavior and a passion for storytelling. This dual focus, which intensified in my classes at Brown, would one day help me to navigate the various stages of my career in theater, communications, and publishing. At

Brown, I learned from gifted professors, but I was also inspired by the independence and idiosyncrasies of my classmates. This gave me a lifelong hunger to work with bright and intuitive people who are experts at different things—which is one of the greatest rewards of being a book editor.

In January 2013, as I peered through the windows of Ashamu, I imagined class after class of Theatre Arts concentrators moving through that airy, sunlit studio over the years, pursuing their dreams, while I was off living my life in New York, forging my own path to good storytelling.

Working on this anthology has given me the chance to collaborate with an extraordinary group of writers and creative artists whose essays invite us to see the world—and Brown—through their eyes, over the past few decades. Alternately hilarious, poignant, subversive, and thought provoking, the cumulative effect of these pieces, as one early reader told me, is a kind of love letter to the humanities.

Filled with vivid historical details from the past sixty years, *The Brown Reader* takes an intimate look at what these students' academic passions were, where they lived, what they thought of the food at the Ratty, whom they fell in love with, and how they engaged with what was happening in the world around them. At the same time, it follows the sweep of Brown's evolution over the years, as the university responded to student protests and changing times, initiated new programs and policies, and fostered what Donald Antrim calls "a philosophy of education that embraces agency and autonomy: You are among mentors and your peers, the University seems to be saying to its students, and you are nevertheless independent, singular, autodidacts in a way . . ."

Some of the recollections in this anthology shed negative light on Brown at different points in time, while others offer rave reviews or poke fun at the school. This lack of whitewashing—a willingness to convey the bitter and the sweet, the outrageous and the very personal—strikes me as an especially Brunonian approach that should resonate with anyone who has spent time at the school. I was surprised by the number of transfer students who landed in this collection. But it's an indication of how many of us carefully chose Brown, and sometimes fought hard to get there.

Limited by time, space, and authors' prior commitments, we knew it would be impossible to include all of the professional writers who deserved a place in this collection. Our aim was to gather a diverse sampling of recollections from writers who attended the university from the 1950s to the present—inviting them to help articulate (as Jeffrey Eugenides puts it) "what makes Brown Brown."

Because of our focus on professional writers, readers will see an emphasis on the humanities and arts in this anthology and few pieces on science, mathematics, or sports. We regret this omission but hope that these contributions will invite each reader to revisit—or anticipate—their coming-of-age years.

Marilynne Robinson writes, "I have come more and more to realize that the trust I placed in Brown was very graciously answered by the trust Brown placed in me." We each took away something different. And whether we realized right away what we had learned or it took some time to discover it, our educational journeys at Brown continued to shape us long after we had walked through the Van Wickle Gates at commencement.

THE BROWN AESTHETIC

The Brown aesthetic, if we can call it that, is a very loose translation, I would argue, of the New Curriculum: more loose-limbed, more playful, more interdisciplinary, harder to define, at its worst silly (in 1974, my freshman roommate attended a lecture by Buckminster Fuller about the spiritual properties of the geodesic dome and spent all of November chanting in a teepee) and at its best mind-bending, life-altering, culture-challenging.

—**David Shields** ('78)

Brown remains to this day the environment where I met more original, driven, creative people at higher density than any other place I have ever been.

—**Ayad Akhtar** ('93)

I met [Nathanael] West at Brown after he transferred from Tufts in '23. He advanced daring notions. One of them was that we ought to disguise ourselves with ticking aprons and walk into the John Hay Library, where there was an elephant folio of Hogarth. We'd carry table legs. West's idea was to nail the folio onto the table legs, and if anyone stopped us, we'd say we were moving a coffee table. I pointed out to him the nails would spoil the volume, so we dropped the scheme. Who wants a Hogarth folio with nail holes?

—**S. J. Perelman** ('25)

In Brunensis Speramus

SEAN KELLY

Sun Under Cloud Cover

JEFFREY EUGENIDES

The Princeton Reader: It was my senior year rowing lightweight crew. Our last regatta of the season, on beautiful Lake Carnegie, was against Harvard, and boy, did we want to beat those Harvard guys!

The Cornell Reader: It was the middle of winter. My boyfriend had just dumped me. I was failing applied math. I went out to the Gorge and stared down at the beautiful black pit.

The Harvard Reader: One thing we liked to do after meetings at the *Crimson* was go for a drink at Grendel's and try to guess whose initials were carved into the bar. Was "J.A." James Agee or John Ashbery? Was "B.B." Bruce Babbitt or Benazir Bhutto? We could do that for hours!

The Brown Reader: There was this guy freshman year named Ted Zimmerman. He had a beard already, which impressed me. He liked to listen to free jazz—Anthony Braxton, people like that—while warming a brandy snifter of Courvoisier over a big hippie candle. I thought it was pretty cool to have a brandy snifter in your dorm room. Or brandy, even. Ted was into Nietzsche, too, the late, poetic stuff. Whenever he said something, even if it was about his toaster oven, he'd say, "Thus spake Zimmerman."

I'd never met anyone like Ted before. I used to stop by his dorm room to talk to him, but he never seemed interested. Finally, he explained why. "You're just blah," he said. "In fact, that's what I'm

4

going to call you from now on. Blah." After that, whenever Ted Zimmerman saw me, he'd say, "Hello, Blah." I loved that about college. That people were willing to be rude to your face, but in a charming and even friendly way. Finally, when we were seniors, Ted came up to me and used my real name.

"Why aren't you calling me Blah anymore?" I asked.

"Because you aren't Blah anymore," he said. "You were Blah when you came to Brown. But you're not Blah now."

The Columbia Reader: Oh, God, I don't even remember. It wasn't like I spent any time on *campus*. That would have been twee. I was in the city, man! Why would I go to some dorm party and suck foam out of a keg when I could go downtown to the Mudd Club? My whole time at Columbia I never ate once in the cafeteria. I'm pretty proud about that. Seriously. If I was hungry I just went home and had Rosaria cook me something. Do you remember that time we got wasted and stuck those cold cuts to the walls and Rosaria came at us with that spoon? That spoon was terrifying! And then she's chasing Whoogie around the dining table and Whoogie's going, "*Señora! Por favor! Señora!*" That was hilarious!

The Cornell Reader: This was before they put up the protective fence. In those days, you could lean over the railing and stare down into the Gorge. It called to me. It said, "Your boyfriend's going to be so sorry."

The Brown Reader: Yeah, I knew John-John. I was in a play with him. Senior year. *Short Eyes* by Miguel Piñero. Ever see that? "Short eyes" is what they call child molesters in prison. Worst thing you can be. In the play, the molester's white, and the rest of the cast, the other prisoners, are people of color. Most of us had never acted before. The director recruited us. Came over to the frat and asked if we wanted to be in it. She needed big guys, she said, and we were all on the football team, so.

I got to play this cool dude named Iceman. And I had this three-page monologue where I had to jerk off to Jane Fonda. "Janie! Janie, baby. Come get this long dick big black buck fuckin'!" I can still remember the lines. You ever see *Barbarella*? Jane Fonda in *Barbarella* was like my Stanislavksi Method.

Anyway, it's opening night, and guess who's in the audience, because Kennedy's in the play? Right. Jackie O. She's there to see her little boy. So before the show, when we're in the dressing room, I say to John, "Hey, John, I was thinking of changing my monologue tonight. You know, I don't have to jerk off to Jane Fonda. Not *tonight*." And Kennedy just stood there, until he got it. And then he goes, "No way! No way, man!" And we all broke up.

John-John was really cool. I remember I asked him once if he wanted to be an actor—because he was *good*. He had the looks, too. No doubt. But he said he didn't think acting gave enough back to society. That's what he told me.

When he died in that plane crash, oh my God—I still can't believe that. To have all that going for you, the lineage, and that photo of him saluting his father's casket, *to be part of history*, to get married to a beautiful woman and then crash your plane into the ocean? That just overturned my whole conception of things. I thought, *John-John's dead and I'm alive? John-John never got to have kids, and I do? He never got to live his life, and I do? How is that even possible?*

The Dartmouth Reader: My dad went here, sir. And my grandfather. Yes, sir. They both played intramural lacrosse, as do I. I have especially enjoyed the intramural sport program during my time here at Dartmouth. It allows students such as myself, who have a deep and abiding interest in athletics, and who believe that athletic competition is "character-building"—but who, for one reason or another, such as the fact that my legs are slightly different lengths, sir, which makes it harder to run—to still get out there on the field and work up a sweat. Also, the air in New Hampshire is pollution-free, which I appreciate from a pulmonary standpoint. Yes, sir. Premed. My dad was a physician also. And my grandfather. I'm not sure, sir. I guess I'd like to open up a small family practice, maybe even right here in Hanover. But the economic realities of today are different from those of olden times. For instance, malpractice insurance is just crazy! My father says the lawyers are going to drive all the doctors out of business until there's no one left to perform heart bypasses on the lawyers, so then the lawyers will all die and it'll be safe to practice medicine again! He was just kidding about that, though, of course. My point is, as much as I would like to open a small family practice, the financial reality going forward is that I'm probably gravitating toward anesthesiology, due to the high income and the regular schedule. I'd like to have a family of my own someday, sir. Three or four kids. That's correct, sir. Future Dartmouth grads. I could field a whole squad.

The Brown Reader: New Curriculum? More like No Curriculum. I didn't take a single history course at Brown. No math. No science. The only thing I know about the Hundred Years' War is how long it took. But this is the middle-aged me talking. When I came to Brown, what the New Curriculum said to me was, "Hey, you're an adult now. You're in charge of your own education. We're not going to tell you what to do." That resonated with me. There are downsides, sure. But I knew what I wanted to do when I arrived at Brown. A lot of kids did. That's what makes Brown Brown. I knew what I wanted to do and I just went for it. And as the poet said, in the end that made all the difference. Excuse me? The Hundred Years' War took 116 years? You see? That's exactly what I'm talking about.

The Yale Reader: Like who *didn't* Harold Bloom ask to take a bath? Any woman he taught, sooner or later he'd go, "My dear, wouldn't it be more relaxing to discuss Miltonic prosody in a nice warm bath?" Yeah, sure. If you could find a tub big enough.

The Brown Reader: I couldn't leave Dave. I just couldn't.

Earlier that night, around five p.m., we'd met downtown, as arranged, to swallow one tab of blotter acid each. After that, we wandered around, waiting for it to take effect. Nothing seemed to be happening at first—and then something definitely was.

We went into a doughnut shop. We sat by a hissing radiator, listening to it as though to music. Someone had put a Styrofoam cup over the valve to catch the spray.

That, too, seemed full of significance.

Our thoughts circled back on themselves. Dave and I kept trying to articulate our branching, circular revelations. Finally, we came up with a metaphor. "It's like Escher!"

We meant the way figures in an Escher drawing seem to be simultaneously ascending and descending the same stairway.

Things got easier after that. Whenever we turned a corner and had a brainstorm about the nature of time or the industrial grid, we relied on our shorthand. We said, "Escher!"

Around ten p.m., the drug began to wear off. Tired of exploring, we went back up to College Hill. There was a party that night at French House, where Dave lived. When we got there, we were scared to go in. We stood outside, looking in the windows at all the people who weren't tripping and who could never understand the state we were in.

Finally, we went in, anyway.

Almost immediately, we ran into Marie. Marie was a tall, beautiful, sad-looking girl who, until recently, had gone out with a friend of mine. Now they'd broken up and she was available. I'd been flirting with her for weeks. I had a sense that something might happen between us. When she came up to me at the party and smiled, I knew I was right.

But I couldn't leave Dave. I just couldn't.

We didn't tell Marie we were tripping. That was our little secret. What we did, instead, was we both took Marie up to Dave's room.

We sat on either side of her, on the couch. I wasn't feeling the least bit horny.

When we were downtown, Dave had put a cookie into his mouth, experimentally, to see if he could eat it, but he couldn't, and so he'd taken the cookie out again.

That was how I was feeling sexually.

Still, we were strangely uninhibited. That was why we began massaging Marie's feet. We took off her shoes and socks and got really into it. I tried to figure out where Marie's acupressure points were, concentrating with my eyes closed, as though I could sense them through my fingers. I was perfectly content. I would have done that all night long. But all of a sudden, in a high-pitched yet commanding voice, Dave spoke up.

"Marie," he said, as though acknowledging the obvious, "these pants have got to come off."

I froze. I stopped massaging Marie's feet, and waited.

Calmly, Marie undid the clasp of her jeans and pulled them off.

Right about now you're thinking that this isn't an appropriate contribution to *The Brown Reader*. But just wait. Dave, that impresario, turned out the lights. He put a Mozart piano concerto on the record player, leaving the stackholder up so the record would repeat. We pulled his mattress onto the floor. For the next hour, while the Mozart played, the three of us rolled around on the mattress, trying not to fall off. The mattress wasn't very big, though, and we did fall off, usually Dave or me, at which point we clambered back onto it as if it were a life raft.

In the middle of all this activity, the door opened and Dave's roommate Karl came in. He didn't turn on the light, but he could see what we were doing. I expected him to turn and leave. Instead, he said in an angry voice, "I'm going to bed!"

Karl took off his shirt and pants and got into his own bed across the room. He turned his face to the wall. Dave, Marie, and I waited a minute or two, and then we went at it again.

Every time the Mozart record ended, the mechanism returned the needle to the beginning, and the music started up again.

We were surprised, a half hour later, when Karl jumped out of bed and stormed out of the room. We'd forgotten he was there.

I feel bad about that now (sorry, Karl). But at the time, I didn't.

Here's the point I want to make. I've been trying to fix on a single moment, among all the moments of my time on College Hill, that most clearly symbolizes what it meant to be at Brown. I had wonderful professors and met wonderful people and took wonderful classes, but as I sit here right now, thinking, that night is what comes back to me. To be on the long slow descent of a hallucinogenic drug, to be confused about your sexuality, not sure if you're A/C or D/C, to be starfished on the floor in a novel and rather shocking physical constellation, to be engaged in naughtiness sure to prove memorable, to be so unknown to yourself that self-discovery seems impossible and yet, conversely, right around the corner, to be with your best friend and your new girlfriend at the same time and to not be able to know who was who, to be doing all this in a place called French House, with the window open, and dawn coming up, a bird beginning to sing, and, most of all, to know that all this funny business has to end soon because you have some serious studying to do tomorrow, Proust to read in the original (Dave), Horatian epodes to translate (me), a ten-page paper on competitive interactions among coral reef fish (Marie)—to be up all night in the darkness of your youth but to be ready for the day to come, to be like the sun on our collegiate seal, under cloud cover but breaking through, just wait, breaking through to shine on and on—that was what going to Brown felt like to me.

The U. Penn Reader: We always get the short end of the stick. I'm sick of it. Like how many times have I had to explain, yes, the University of Pennsylvania is not a state school. It's private, one of the oldest colleges in the nation, and it's part of the Ivy League, douchebag.

Like, if you were doing one of these remembrance things for, say, Brown, you could write whatever you wanted. You could just sit down and play with yourself and write about whatever came to mind. You could just be *creative*.

Ooh, look at me! I went to *Brow-wwwn*!

You can't do that here. Not at Penn. Penn doesn't have an identity like that, so we have to work a little harder. But Brown? You could just talk about any stupid, nasty thing you did at college and act proud about it.

Brown? *Please*. Don't get me started.

Train Rides

LOIS LOWRY

I can still remember the comfortable upholstered chair, molded to the shape of countless teenagers, in the library of the private school for girls I attended in Brooklyn Heights. To its left were the shelves containing college catalogs. In 1954, I was a sixteen-year-old high school senior and I settled myself into that chair every chance I got. I pored over those catalogs, examining the photographs of campus landmarks (picturing myself in a Jonathan Logan dress and Capezio slippers, standing in front of the Sir Christopher Wren Building at William and Mary, or the Thompson Library at Vassar). Reading the small print, I was able to inform my classmate Stephanie, who owned a palomino horse, that there was a college in Virginia that would allow her to house Chico there. I carefully assessed the liberal arts requirements at various colleges (I had managed to avoid both chemistry and physics during my high school years and was eager to find a school that would let me continue that avoidance).

College counseling, to the best of my recollection, consisted of my telling my English teacher that I wanted to go to Brown—actually, to Pembroke, as the women's college within Brown University was then called. She was enthusiastic about my writing and had told me that I stood a pretty good chance of actually becoming a writer. She leafed through the Pembroke catalog, glanced at the writing courses offered, and agreed that it looked like a good choice.

I filled out the application papers and sent them in. Perhaps I should have consulted my parents. Instead I presented it to them as a fait accompli. My mother looked startled and nervous at my announcement. My father? He said something like "Over my dead body."

My father was a military man, an army colonel accustomed to underlings (including his wife and children) obeying his commands. But when he ordered me to attend Penn State the following fall, I could not bring myself to reply with the expected "Yessir." My older sister, a home economics major, was a junior at Penn State. I had visited her there, had glimpsed her sorority-centered life, and wanted no part of it.

Although we lived at that time in New York, our military life had taken us around the world, and my parents had selected Pennsylvania as their permanent legal residence. At sixteen, I had no knowledge of the finances of a college education. Looking back, I realize now that our Pennsylvania residency would have made tuition at Penn State considerably less costly than "some highfalutin college" (my father's words) in Rhode Island.

So we embarked on a protracted battle, my father and I. He was terse, adamant, logical. I was surly, arrogant, and adolescent.

But amazingly, I won. I won because two letters arrived from Brown. The first accepted me into the class of 1958. And the second offered me a scholarship. I remember my father's puzzled look as he read the second letter and realized that some credentialed committee had found his sullen younger daughter worthy in some way he didn't entirely understand. During the summer he was transferred to Washington, DC, and we left our New York home. In the fall of 1954 he drove me and a set of Samsonite luggage filled with my belongings to Union Station and put me on a train for the long ride to a city he had never seen and would never visit. I settled into my seat and flipped through the pages of *Mademoiselle*, glancing up occasionally to watch the landscape of my own past slide by. The train made a stop in Philadelphia, where I had once attended an aunt's wedding and seen a movie, *Our Vines Have Tender Grapes*, when I was eight. Next stop, New York, where with a friend during the presidential campaign in the fall of 1952 I skipped school in order to follow Eisenhower's motorcade from the Battery to Times Square. Then Hartford: not far from where I had, the previous year, attended a spring dance at Choate, wearing a blue taffeta strapless dress that I had borrowed from my sister's closet without her knowledge. Finally New London, where a classmate was perhaps at that very moment unpacking her own Samsonite at Connecticut College. The bits and pieces of my past all slipped away, and only Providence lay ahead.

Actually, Providence in 1954 was something of a wasteland; that fall, downtown buildings were still stained by Hurricane Carol, which had flooded the city at the beginning of September. I noticed the remnants of the hurricane damage when I arrived but didn't pay much attention. My thoughts were already up that hill, a hill I had seen only once before, on the bitter cold day the previous winter that I had visited Brown—also by train, also alone—as an applicant. That day, in an attempt at sophistication, I had worn high-heeled shoes, clearly a mistake, I had realized, navigating the hill. But the tough walking had not dimmed my enthusiasm, and College Hill had loomed since then, throughout the days of bitter arguments with my father, as the one place I wanted to be, the place where my intellectual life would begin.

I wrote to my parents once a week. I told them that I had been exempted from the required "Freshman Composition," that I had fulfilled the foreign language requirement through a proficiency test in French, and that I had passed the required swimming test. I did not tell them that I, along with every other freshman girl, had been photographed naked. (We were told—and we believed, preposterous though it now seems—that the college needed those photos to monitor our posture. The scandal of that crackpot untruth was finally revealed in the seventies.)

My parents, even without being alerted to the so-called posture pictures, probably envisioned a dissolute future for the daughter who had steadfastly refused to embrace the cheery hugs-and-giggles existence of her sister, who that fall was among the nominees for Penn State's homecoming queen. I fulfilled their every dread. Brown did its part in luring me to the dark side by distributing free packets of cigarettes—colorful little five-packs of Winstons. Their slogan was "Winstons taste good like a cigarette should!" We who were grammar purists knew that it should say "as," not "like," but we didn't let faulty grammar keep us from scooping up the freebies and quickly becoming addicted. Classrooms were well supplied with small ashtrays and we became adept at arranging our notebooks, pens, cigarettes, and ashtrays on the small, flat desklike surfaces that unfolded from the arm of each chair.

By the time I went home for Thanksgiving I had mastered the deep disdainful inhale and its follow-up, a slow, smoky exhale, reeking with attitude. I was also, by then, quoting T. S. Eliot a lot, especially *Prufrock*. Ah, the degradation of ideals. The futility of it all.

A poetry text from that time—still in my bookcase today—contains a page with a small, singed circle caused by a dropped ash. It also has, in my adolescent handwriting, notes in the margins (embarrassingly, I misspelled *humorous* and *judgment*) along with the name of my new boyfriend in a decorative penciled circle. Scribbled beside the lines of Auden's "For the Time Being" I see that I expressed shock, by a row of question marks and exclamation points—!!!! ????—at my professor's commenting on what he called "the Christian myth." *Myth?* Did that mean that Professor Andrew Sabol did not believe in the Presbyterian doctrine that I had been raised on? !!!!!! ?????

Well, if he called it a myth, then so would I. Did I dare disturb the universe? Darn right. I did so during Thanksgiving vacation at my grandparents' dinner table, somewhere between the saying of grace and the serving of turkey. Silence ensued. I may have murmured, as a follow-up, that I should have been a pair of ragged claws scuttling across the floors of silent seas.

In retrospect I wonder how my family tolerated me when I was seventeen and a freshman at Brown. I wonder why they didn't bonk me over the head with a carton of Winstons, stab me with one of my own knitting needles (because yes, I had taken up knitting, too: endless misshapen argyle socks for a boyfriend), or strangle me with the sleeve of the hideous army-surplus trench coat I had taken to wearing as a statement of some sort.

They were waiting, I guess, for me to get beyond it. My grades—which were sent to parents in those years—reassured them that I was a good student, getting top grades even in the required courses (yes! Required courses in those days! But to my relief, not physics or chemistry). I yawned (and knitted and smoked) through courses in math and political science in order to qualify for my *real* academic life—the life of a would-be writer, the reason I had gone to Brown.

Newly eighteen, in the fall of my sophomore year, I was admitted to Professor Charles Philbrick's short-story writing seminar, an upper-level course intended for serious students of writing. On the first day, when I entered a smallish room and peered through the smoky haze, I saw a group of students, all male, slouched in chairs around a table. I instinctively pulled the folds of my too-big crummy trench coat tighter to conceal my schoolgirl outfit of plaid skirt and cashmere sweater. It wouldn't have mattered. No one cared what I wore, or how I looked, or what fraternity party I had attended over the weekend (or that I had discreetly looked the other way while my drunken date, walking me back to the dorm, vomited into someone's rhododendrons on Prospect Street).

They only cared about what I thought. And what I wrote.

I remember the names of only two of those students and I will not use them here. But one was older, an army veteran; he had served in Korea and emulated Mailer and James Jones in his writing. The other was a Roth/Malamud wannabe, a brooding Jewish boy from New York. Some years later I came across a novel by him (in his author photo he was wearing an ascot) on a remainder table in San Diego.

And I remember Charles Philbrick with great gratitude. As part of the course, we had private meetings with the professor in his office. He had rosy cheeks and an easy smile. Did he smoke a pipe, or have I imagined that detail, along with a tweed jacket? What I know with certainty is that he was never dismissive. He always approached my work—shallow, schoolgirlish stories modeled on Salinger—seriously.

He told me gently that although I needed to *experience* more, there was time for that, and that after time had passed, if I kept thinking, and reading, and writing, and observing—I could be a writer. Each time I left his office and walked back to my dorm, it was in a state of exhilaration, of a yearning for experience, almost giddy with a love of language and its possibilities.

My final story for that course was called "Train Ride." Although Professor Philbrick was intrigued and impressed by it—and gave me an A for the course—it was a pretentious story with substantial flaws and credibility issues. But it was a first for me. It was different from the sardonic, sophomoric work I had been producing all semester.

Though I am suffused with embarrassment relating this, here is the plot of "Train Ride." A man, taking his dog with him, has gone out onto a deserted Canadian lake in his small motorboat, to fish. Thick weeds have somehow become entangled in his motor, and when he is unable to disentangle them from the boat, he goes into the water to try. But the same thick material gets caught around his feet and legs; the boat begins to drift away from him, and while the dog watches from the boat, the man is trapped there, unable to pull himself free.

While he struggles, a passenger train makes its way along the side of the lake. Three unrelated passengers, all men, glance through the train windows and see the boat, the dog, and the head of the struggling man.

I'll stop there. It's enough to explain that each fictional observer has his own past, his own agenda (all of it meticulously recorded by the writer), and his own way of deciphering what is taking place on the lake, though it holds little interest for any of them; as the train ride continues and the lake recedes behind them, their thoughts turn to other things.

The end.

But it wasn't, not for me. It was the beginning of my awareness of the connections of things: how the Auden poem called "Musée des Beaux Arts," which I had studied the previous semester, had told me something about man's disinterest (my smudged pencil note in the margin says "important moments unattended"); and now I connected that to Professor Downing's art history class and the Brueghel painting of the death of Icarus, when, with melted wings, the boy falls from the sky and no one notices; and both of those were connected to things I had studied in Professor Church's psychology class, and to the Greek tragedians I had examined with Professor Luck in classics, and . . . and . . . It was as if the small colored squares of a Rubik's Cube had suddenly fallen into the correct slots and created a finished, organized whole.

It was the start of my becoming an educated person with a beginning understanding of the complex and personal purpose of education. It was an awakening thirst for communication and understanding that has never left me.

When I next boarded the train in Providence for the long ride home, I was still wearing the grubby trench coat, with the same old voluminous striped scarf around my neck. I knew that my mother would once again roll her eyes in despair when she saw my fashion statement, such a sad contrast to my sister's trim tweed suits and high-heeled shoes. But I was growing up. I would shed my disguises in the years to come, and my adolescent posturing would dissipate like the smoke from the Winstons that I would eventually discard as well. I would become a writer. Professor Philbrick, so tactful and patient, had told me that I would, and it was true.

Invisible Histories

ROWAN RICARDO PHILLIPS

I was in the yellow leaf of my senior year at Swarthmore College. And now, as I neared the very end of that stage in my life, I had little idea of, and even less interest in, what the role and purpose of graduate school was to be. I'd had my college experience, three years at Swarthmore and one year at Oxford, and my expectations for graduate school were not extravagant; I pictured myself in a classroom and then in the library and then repeat. That's it. (For those of you unfamiliar with Swarthmore, this reflects a particular type of "Swattie" intensity that's difficult to describe to others. Whether it's based on nature or nurture, I don't know.)

Poetry had become something of deep and inherent importance to me: a nonnegotiable vocation. I felt that studying it as a discipline and knowing its history inside and out would suit my temperament and aid my growth, however slow, as a writer. What did I expect from graduate school? I wanted to read as much about poetry as was possible; I hoped for good mentoring and I wanted to write a dissertation. I had applied and been admitted to doctoral programs and so I was spending much of March and into April visiting English graduate programs. The way things worked out, Brown was to be my final trip.

From Philadelphia it was a wink of a flight—a small climb and descent of a small airplane, its FASTEN SEAT BELTS sign turning on, then off, then on again in comically quick succession to mark the beginning, middle, and end of the flight—and there I was, in Providence, running my index finger along the return ticket in my back pocket with the vaguest of plans to crash at a grad student's place. My mind wasn't in it, but the tickets had already been purchased and sent to me so I had come out of courtesy, even though I had already made up my mind to attend another program. I'd stay at Brown only as long as was necessary—to be polite. And as soon as I could escape, I'd take that feather-drop of a flight back to Philadelphia to enjoy what was left of my quickly fading undergraduate life.

Brown. I savored the word as my cab passed the state house and its lonely air of unaccompanied prominence in the Providence sky, as it crossed the garlanded, newly moved river and slowly climbed College Street toward the dead end of the Van Wickle Gates. I thought about how strange this feeling was—of being there and not being there. I might as well have been on the moon.

I decided to go to Brown that same day.

In short, I decided to go to Brown because of Michael S. Harper and the late Dean Bernard Bruce, both of whom encouraged me to think of the university as something more than an institution, to recognize that it was (and is) a deep canvas, a palimpsest, on which unseen history and institutional history and personal history come together to form something unique, something beautiful and needful, a song still forming, for the listeners and the singers.

As bildungsroman and adventurish as this may first sound I can assure you that it wasn't. Dean Bruce was as personable, sharp, and full of conviction, as generous of mind and spirit, as any dean I have ever met in my life. And Harper's poetry I already knew very well, and in knowing it well I held a deep astonishment for the man and for the nuances of his work, its chiasmatic braiding of the personal and the historical and, similarly, the ethical and the aesthetic. While at Swarthmore I had absorbed not only his work but also the deep and distinctive finish of his voice from a dusty cassette recording tucked deep in a cabinet in McCabe Library. The recording was of a reading he had given at Swarthmore in the midseventies. Listening to a great poet's work in solitude, as I did for a month in my dorm, you fall into a deep pocket of understanding, your ear heightens its capacity for empathy, your mind makes a deal with your heart. I didn't, while listening, know this. And I came to Brown with no expectation of meeting him. In my youth, I imagined that great poets graced their universities like the ghost of Hamlet's father, grand diaphanous avatars who descended on rare occasions to instruct and delight. I was very wrong about this.

"Do you know who that is?"

We're back to my first day at Brown.

Harper had taken it upon himself to spend the entire day with me, showing me the campus, his office, introducing me to Dean Bruce, talking, talking, talking, me listening, listening, listening. They cracked jokes and at times became deadly serious; mentioning book after book, Harper pulled copies of these works—seemingly from the air—and handed them to me, this while grilling me on what I knew. It was a lot to take in (and a hell of a lot to carry), but it appealed to me intuitively as the way I wanted to learn, and grow up: balancing academic rigors with this off-the-grid instruction and challenge; the squared mind rounding its edges and beginning to spin. It caught me off guard and with a particular type of slow, and then sudden, burn that I would learn to sustain throughout the years I would be there.

"Do you know who that is?"

We were entering the Rockefeller Library for the first time and Harper gestured with his large hand toward a painting on the far left of the entryway.

I didn't know who that was.

"I have something for you then."

I had already received more books than I could carry back onto the plane with me, on that return flight that my mind was pushing farther back in the week. But each book, each manuscript and letter he showed me had a history behind it, a story and a mission for the entrusted reader. In less than a day, Michael Harper had become my righteous American Dr. Johnson: a *Lives of the Poets* enlivened. Five, six years of this: How could I turn that down?

I always think about Brown from the outside in. I can't tell you the name of a single dorm or dining hall and I barely know any of the traditions. But Brown, after the six years I spent there, is an inalienable part of me. Life as a Brown graduate student is a particular experience; you're generally there longer than an entire entering class of undergraduates. The campus flickers between real and metaphorical, the walls between town and gown erode after barely a year, and you end up knowing Providence as well as Brown and Brown as poorly as Providence. It's alarmingly easy to feel uprooted. I was fortunate to have a few important anchors protecting me from this. Two of them were Harper and Bruce and the other two turned out to be the Rockefeller and John Hay Libraries, both of which I probably spent more time in than I did in all my various Providence apartments (and that one apartment in Pawtucket) combined.

"Do you know who that is?"

As I passed through the door to the Rock, entering and exiting day after day and year after year, Inman Page's stern portrait was always there to greet me and bid me adieu, vigilant and austere in burnt siennas, maroons, and brown hues. Page was one of the first two black graduates of Brown (along with George Washington Milford).

In 1877, Page was elected to give the commencement oration for his class, which garnered praise from the *Providence Journal*. Painted by Richard Yarde, the portrait of Page was based on a photo of the scholar as a young man. I took up the habit of nodding to the portrait each time I entered or left the library—a quick nod and a futile attempt at eye contact. Inman Page was always looking out the door, gazing, rather intently, onto Prospect Street.

At the close of my first year at Brown, as I saw my first Providence summer widen and empty the campus, I received that thing that Harper had promised to show me when he first introduced me to that portrait. It was a copy of the literary magazine the *Carleton Miscellany*. I open it now and see the black inscription still clear as an inked fingerprint on the first page:

Michael S. Harper
6 25 97
For Rowan from MSH—
'every goodbye ain't gone'

Volume 18, no. 3, of the winter 1980 issue, coedited by Harper and John Wright, would mark the end of the magazine with a special final issue dedicated to a Ralph Ellison festival hosted by Brown at Harper's initiative during the first week of classes, September 19–21, 1979. The magazine, an influential publication in its day, sang a swan song all too familiar to many of us who work in or follow the arts.

> With this issue of *The Miscellany* we are forced to take a rest. After much discussion, the Administration of the College has decided that, in a time of budgetary constraint, the magazine, because of its small circulation, will have to bow to other needs of the College. This is a very sad time for many of us as the lineage of *The Miscellany* is a long and noble one.

The issue, some of which is available online in Carleton College's digital collection, is a veritable feast of Ellisonia: essays by R. W. B. Lewis, Robert Stepto, Nathan A. Scott, Leon Forrest, and another of Harper's ex-students, the late Melvin Dixon, along with three essays by Ellison, including one of his more famous ones, "Going to the Territory."

Facing the table of contents is a picture of Ralph Ellison lecturing. He's clearly in the Rockefeller. And on the wall behind him is Richard Yarde's portrait of Inman Page. It turns out that, after a successful but peripatetic career in education, Page settled down in Oklahoma, where in 1922 he accepted a position as the principal of Oklahoma City's Douglass High School, where he taught a student by the name of Ralph Ellison, who graduated with honors. As is well-known, Harper and Ellison would become great friends. And the knowledge that the mentor of the latter was the first black graduate of the institution where the former now taught, a knowledge that worked on "the lower frequencies" of institutional memory and history, became acknowledgment with Page's portrait and Ellison's essay "Portrait of Inman Page."

Sitting outside in the summer heat, tucked under the shade of the Rockefeller Library, mere feet from Yarde's portrait of Page there in the interior, I closely read Ellison's reflection on this vivid coincidence he found awaiting him at Brown—a coincidence that, in terms of its power and resonance, clearly affected him.

In the wake of an exhausting first year in the PhD program, I had a renewed sense of why we learn and what an academic institution like Brown can teach us—not just from the brilliant and smooth surfaces of its known and acknowledged self but also, importantly, from the folds, fissures, cracks, and sutures of its unknown and unacknowledged self.

It would have been easy to overlook the Page portrait or to note with Pavlovian good intentions the "firstness" of Page's status as a graduate as a reason for its conception. Likewise, this final issue of the *Carleton Miscellany* could be overlooked as easily as the portrait. For although they are matters of history, their poignancy comes from the initiative and participation of people willing to make a difference in the order and hierarchies through which we understand historical connections at places as varied as Douglass High School and Brown University. And this type of action, toward a greater, smarter good, marked my time at Brown. It marked how I was taught and strove to teach, how I read, researched, and wrote. We don't have to be poor passing facts, after all.

You can hear it in Ellison's concluding words as he thanked Brown's administration and Michael S. Harper and his assistants, and referenced the complex union between Brown in particular and American history in general—a union from which vital parts of our overlooked past rise up and take their rightful places, adding voices that are necessary to our understanding and experience of the present day.

In the time since I left Brown, Page's portrait has been moved to the John Hay Library, which was my second home away from home on campus. I like to think that, among the rare books and manuscripts, the special collections and university archives, Inman E. Page feels at least somewhat at home, as he is one of the rarest and most special aspects of our school.

Did Harper and Bruce know that this was waiting for me? Likely. The library became more than a library for me that day. The Rock was now another Rock, one of many. What other mysteries did it hold, I wondered. There's an old song that goes, "I ran to the rocks to hide my face, the rocks cried out no hiding place, ain't no hiding place here."

When history becomes personal, as opposed to institutional, the hiding places that may have been there before—namely a studious distance between you and the subject—can transmogrify into something more raw, inchoate, and all but impossible to ignore. These sublime, kaleidoscopic, and fissured relationships to Brown also, of course, have their tenebrous side.

I still remember opening—for the first time—the final report of the 2003–2007 special committee convened to research and write *Slavery and Justice: Report of the Brown University Steering Committee on Slavery and Justice.* While fully expecting to have my worst fears confirmed, I never expected that Brown's centuries-old history in the slave trade could really pierce my skin. But then, having barely turned the first reading page, there it was—the historical tragedy turning personal with those 109 out of 196 stolen Africans dying in the festering hold of the Brown brothers' brigantine, the *Sally* (which was fitted out for its adventure in 1764, the same year that the College of Rhode Island was founded). The survivors, sickly, emaciated, and bringing far less of a profit than was expected, were all sold for a song to cut the traders' losses, all sold on a twelve-mile-by-twelve-mile island in the middle of the Caribbean Sea called Antigua, where my parents and their parents and their parents and their parents saw the first light of this world.

Thus, despite the early ambivalence of my first arrival there, Brown and I have been tied together by a terribly long cord. I sometimes wonder, given the nightmare of this coincidence and my subsequent joy of having studied there, whether we were not always destined to be a part of each other's lives, my personal history braiding with Brown's public history and leaving such a complex tapestry behind. But the ties that bind us have proved to be strong even in their most broken places.

Bartleby at Brown

JINCY WILLETT KORNHAUSER

When I was young, I assumed that education happened on a strict timeline, a series of steps ending with some kind of advanced degree. After climbing onto the conveyer belt in kindergarten, I had little to do with the process. All I had to do was not fall off. Although I was not in any sense an active, engaged learner, high grades and standardized test scores came easily to me. Learning really had nothing to do with it; performance was all. Then I was seventeen, a class of 1968 freshman at Colby, at which point grades and scores became more challenging; by then, I was sick of performing and still profoundly incurious about the subject matter of my classes. Eventually, sporting a GPA of 1.6, I bailed in 1966 and started work as a secretary at Brown.

I had worked there in previous summers—I started with J. Walter Wilson (the man, not the building) and then found work in other departments. Brown was like home to me. I had lived on campus in the late 1940s while my dad earned his math degree and we lived in Brown Town, a collection of Quonset huts in Aldrich-Dexter Field that were specially constructed for returning GIs and their families.

I was comfortable at Brown, and now, what a relief it was to work from nine to five. I could go home and read whatever I wanted to and not have to prove to anybody that I had done it or remember anything I didn't think worth remembering. I loved working; the people were nice and the tasks so dull that I could perform them without great thought and with zero anxiety. My mind could wander at will. I wasn't a student anymore; I was a townie, and that was just swell. After a few years, I left Brown and became a legal secretary downtown, dabbling in paralegal work. The pay was better and the work marginally interesting.

Then it wasn't.

Slowly I came to realize that I was spending my days typing and perfecting paragraphs and bullet points that no one would ever read, sentences that existed only to be filed away against the contingency that someday they would be of use. *Enclosed please find [some stultifying legal document]*. (And there was that silent desperate *please* . . .)

The job began to haunt me. I could live with being a paper pusher, and boredom wasn't the issue, not really, since I could always daydream while working. It was all those words mummified in dusty cabinets, cabinets shunted into cluttered storerooms. One day, when I was twenty-seven, I was strolling down Westminster Street on my lunch break and heard something odd. I was talking to myself. Not that there's anything wrong with that, except I was practically yelling.

That's one wretched character, I thought, as though observing myself from across the street. *What's her problem?* I had no idea. I'd have had more luck seeing inside her head if she *had* been across the street.

At the time, when I wasn't transcribing Dictabelts, I read constantly, sometimes two or three junk novels in a day. But occasionally I'd dip into something worthwhile. And so it came to pass that one evening I read "Bartleby, the Scrivener."

If you Google "life-changing books," you'll find no end of lists: *Madame Bovary*; *The Confessions of St. Augustine*; *The Collected Poems of Wilfred Owen*. My life was changed by a short story about a scrivener, the nineteenth-century equivalent of a legal secretary, who has been debilitated by years toiling in the dead letter room of a Washington post office. "Conceive a man by nature and misfortune prone to a pallid hopelessness, can any business seem more fitted to heighten it than that of continually handling these dead letters and assorting them for the flames?" He recovers from a nervous collapse, takes work for a master of chancery on Wall Street, shuts down entirely, and thereafter refuses to copy another word. He stares at the office wall and will not be moved, except, in the end, by the people who take him away. I read this story and understood it completely. I had to change my life.

This sounds histrionic, but it is true.

Until I read "Bartleby," I had not even considered going back to college. Now, suddenly, I knew I had to. I can't explain this intuitive leap: returning to school had nothing to do with career aspirations. This was 1976; workers weren't forced to go back to school simply to remain employable. I'm not the sort of person to whom such things happen, but "Bartleby" spoke to me. It was just as Hector, that great teacher in Alan Bennett's *The History Boys*, describes:

> The best moments in reading are when you come across something—a thought, a feeling, a way of looking at things—that you'd thought special, particular to you, and here it is, set down by someone else. A person you've never met, maybe even someone long dead. And it's as if a hand has come out and taken yours.

I just had to learn. If I didn't, I'd be lost. There was suddenly so much to know.

Because I lived in Providence and was unwilling to move, I applied only to Brown. The RUE program was pretty new at that time. Had it not been for RUE, I doubt that I would have been admitted. For RUE students, admission didn't depend on SAT scores (some of us had never taken the SAT). I don't know if my ancient high school grades were factored in, and of course my college record was horrible. Perhaps there was an element of self-selection to it, as though the very act of applying showed we were suitably imaginative. And I have no idea if RUE admissions standards have changed since 1975. If they have—if it's harder to get in now than it was back then—I must count myself doubly lucky, to be the age I am now, to have taken that leap when I did.

Resumed Undergraduate Education allows people to learn when they're good and ready. Not all high school graduates are ready. I certainly wasn't. And many more can't afford the time or money or both; they've started families, joined the armed services, gone to work to support themselves. Studies show that older undergraduates acquit themselves well scholastically, on par with and sometimes exceeding the performance of younger students. Maybe it's because we're not distracted by social anxiety. Or maybe it's because we're so grateful to be there, at a full stop, learning.

I hope the RUE program continues to flourish. I've made more of my life than I would have, thanks to RUE and to Herman Melville.

Indirection

DONALD ANTRIM

I wasn't a writer in college. I wasn't much of a student. My father was a literature professor, but never mind about that. I acted in plays. This meant staying up late and, for me, a reduced attention to the family business of academics. I had romantic fantasies of an artistic life and getting laid, and I had financial aid and an afternoon job in the John Hay Library.

I didn't much like going to work. Three days a week, I dragged myself up the Hay's grand marble exterior stairs, through the big pocket front doors, and across the main hall to the reference desk. After checking in, I got right out of there. I might say, to whoever stood behind the desk that day, "Hey, why don't I take care of some of these?" then roll a cart of books into the ancient elevator, press the button, and ascend toward higher realms of procrastination and avoidance, the Harris Collection of American Poetry and Plays. I remember the Harris Collection as low aisles of army-green shelves rising from a glass tile floor. You could reach up and touch the ceiling. Typically, the stacks were dark when the elevator door opened. The building's windows were sealed over, as they are today, and you had to find the switch and turn the lights on. The switch made a loud click that could be heard up and down. The light was dim and glaring but bright enough to read by. I did some reshelving.

The Harris Collection is comprehensive and exhaustive; it rivals the Library of Congress collections in its field. Bound books, loose pamphlets, newspaper clippings, broadsides, posters, various letterpress chapbooks—I wandered the stacks and read Elizabeth Bishop and George Oppen, John Berryman, David Ignatow, Richard Hugo, Denise Levertov, L. E. Sissman. I liked David Godine books, and I developed a thing for Black Sparrow first editions, numbered in pencil and featuring silkscreens and watercolors tipped in at the front.

And there were the vanity books, they were everywhere, the self-published song cycles of retired admirals and widowed grandmothers and civic leaders with ambitions toward beauty. It was not good poetry, but, in being included, it somehow became important. Who knew that so much was written in America? Who knew how deeply poetry mattered?

I read for music, for rigor and perspective and form; and I rehearsed and directed plays and thought endlessly about dramatic narrative and comic speed and concrete blocking onstage, about acting and entertainment; and, at a certain point, I noticed that I always carried poetry with me into the theater. I read it sitting in the house during rehearsals and I read it backstage in the green room during shows. I didn't become a poet in the end, but that's neither here nor there. I got my education without looking for it.

A boy in a library, making his way into literature—it's not an unusual story. Looking back, it seems to me that the story in this case is institutional as well as personal. It's a Brown story. Brown's adherence to the liberal, open, hippie curriculum expresses a philosophy of education that embraces agency and autonomy: You are among mentors and your peers, the university seems to be saying to its students, and you are nevertheless independent, singular, autodidacts in a way, and your lives will be made of everything you didn't know you were looking for, what you couldn't imagine you might find.

Bending the Letter

BRIAN CHRISTIAN

Coming from a tiny high school with a technical emphasis, I looked to college as a time of freedom—freedom to explore and experiment. My application essay took Frost and (via Emerson) raised the ante: "To take the path less traveled is not enough. Go where there is no path, and leave a trail." There must have been something in that mandate that struck a chord, as every school that admitted me except for one offered me the ability to go against their own rules: to waive core requirements, take classes pass/fail, and design my own major if I wanted. The other university, instead, made it clear that *every* student could do these things. And so my decision was made.

I soon found myself bending what few rules there were. In my second semester, I discovered that a computer science requirement conflicted with a music theory class I was desperate to take. My solution: register for both, by submitting a separate form for each and hoping no one noticed. No one did.

When my first-year advisor heard about my plans, he was furious. "I cannot condone this," he said, suddenly brusque and intimidating, his Austrian accent heightening the effect. "I refuse to sign off on this." When I explained that in fact he already had, he disowned me as his advisee. But the registrar never reversed my double booking, and through hijinks reminiscent of the restaurant scene in *Mrs. Doubtfire*, I managed to get As in both.

Much of the rest of my Brown trajectory was characterized by a similar combination of ambition, overoptimism, stubbornness, and wiles.

That year I also leapfrogged Fiction I (which was enrolled by a crapshoot lottery) and landed directly into Fiction II (which required a portfolio) when my Meiklejohn peer advisor told me the secret truth: *every* freshman assumed (as I had) that their work wasn't good enough to get them into Fiction II, and so didn't apply. Even as Fiction I turned students away in droves, Fiction II enrolled 100 percent of the students who applied, and still had empty seats.

The message stuck with me: Life isn't linear. And competition is fiercest where everyone else is aiming. The result is that often, as Timothy Ferriss puts it, "Doing the unrealistic is easier than doing the realistic." I never forgot that.

Third semester I wrote my heart out on an application to an upper-level nonfiction workshop and got one of the few spots traditionally reserved for seniors. Fourth semester I slipped into a poetry seminar and took a seat while the professor, who knew the head count was wrong, admonished, "Anyone not registered for this class, please leave." I stayed. After my third week of clinging to the course like a barnacle, he signed me on as an overload.

I took it Satisfactory/No Credit and, unable to handle a fifth course atop four degree requirements, sheepishly offered two poems in lieu of a final paper. I barely passed. But the course was my gateway drug to poetry, and it bent the arc of my life. The deep irony, as I see it, is that virtually all of the life-defining academic experiences I had at Brown, and in particular the ones that led to my becoming a writer, were made possible by the anachronistically and almost embarrassingly old-school pencil-and-paper registration system that existed virtually unchanged from the 1960s into the '00s, a system that no longer exists. Current undergraduates are spared the half-hour wait in University Hall to hand over their pink carbon paper. It's important to note, though, what is lost.

In the digital Brown, Fiction II is only available to Literary Arts concentrators. Introduction to Creative Nonfiction has strict grade-level caps. Registering for two classes at the same hour is, of course, not possible, nor is registering for two sections of the same class (which I also did).

My very thesis represents an academic possibility now closed to current Brown undergraduates. The creative writing faculty was at the time a slightly secessionist part of the English department, and one of the ways that their separatism manifested itself was through a special initiative called the Capstone Program, through which anyone who applied and was accepted—not just English majors—could write their thesis with the creative writing faculty.

When the faculties finally separated in 2005, the plug was pulled on the Capstone Program, which was no longer needed (the argument went) as a stand-in for the "real" Literary Arts honors thesis that was now available in its own proper major. I was narrowly grandfathered in.

It was with a wry smile that I read a 2012 *Brown Daily Herald* article discussing the archaic predigital registration system, a system so discombobulated that "students could register for classes that met at the same time." A wry smile, and a sincere concern.

I can't help wondering if the Brown of 2013 into which current high school seniors will matriculate is as perfect a fit for students like me as the Brown of 2002 was. "The old system did not enforce enrollment restrictions such as concentrations or pre-requisites," the article continued. In many ways the things most characteristic of my Brown education are now impossible, relics of an earlier and looser age. The trappings of twentieth-century Brown hung on just long enough into the twenty-first for me to get away with what I did.

The other day I was talking with an old classmate, now in law school. "If there were a button that you could press to make all of the law currently on the books perfectly and completely enforced, any lawyer will tell you that pressing that button would destroy society," he said. The problem is that computerizing any process, unless done with great care, is the equivalent of pushing that button. Computers are tyrannical, Orwellian in precisely this way by design; any programmer will tell you that "exceptions" are what computers make when they crash.

But many of the great things in life come by way of exceptions.

Junior year, my friend Maggie and I went around campus with chalk and a copy of Neruda's *Book of Questions*. "DOES SMOKE TALK WITH THE CLOUDS?" we wrote on Caswell dormitory. (Some anonymous chalker later replied: "NO.") An admitted student by the name of Andrew happened to be visiting campus that day and photographed the chalkings, which delighted him. The school seemed to be literally overflowing with creativity, he thought, and decided to matriculate that fall. He and I became close friends, long before either of us discovered our chalk connection.

Maggie and I were inscribing—I remember the line— "WOULDN'T IT BE BEST TO OUTLAW INTERPLANETARY KISSES?" on the MacMillan patio when we were accosted by a campus security guard.

"What are you guys up to?" he demanded.

"It's Pablo Neruda!" we exclaimed, showing him the book.

"Okay, well . . . If it's poetry . . ."

We seemed to know what we were doing. For poetry, he made an exception.

That was part of the promise that Brown offered me. I hope it will continue to make that promise: That incoming students will continue to find ways to bend the letter of Brown's law to more perfectly uphold its spirit. And that Brown will continue to make exceptions for them to do so.

There is one thing—in particular—that gives me hope.

> In memoriam, we will leave the laws
> you've broken broken.
> —Ben Lerner (AB '01, MFA '03)

The day of my Campus Dance, the final huzzah before I was to be booted into the allegedly "real" world I'd heard so much about, with thousands of alumni pouring into campus from all corners of the globe, Andrew, our friend Blair, and I grabbed a copy of another book of poems: *A Thousand Devils* by K. Silem Mohammad, a weird, manic, mischievous book.

We passed the book around as we strolled the campus. "DO THE WORDS 'MERCANTILE CORNFROG' MEAN ANYTHING TO YOU?" I chalked on the mathematics department, posing for a picture.

"I'M MAJORLY MAC LOW, SO YOU'RE IN GOOD SUS-PENDERS," Andrew wrote on the Watson Institute, the corner of Charlesfield and Thayer.

We scoured the book first for delight, and then gradually for reso-nance. "THE CHALKBOARD IS WOBBLING IN A NEW WAY," wrote Blair on one of the wings of Hegeman.

I found one that seemed a perfect disciplinary fit for the Medi-cal Research Laboratory and, hoisted up onto Andrew's shoulders, strained to inscribe it across the top of the building's "Whispering Arch": "RED ALERT! A PHYLUM IS COLLAPSING—"

On the stairs to the theater: "WHAT I KNOW IS SHORT-CIRCUITED SEEMING // BUSTED IN LIGHT OF UP-TO-DATE SILENCE." Something in that seemed about right for a commencement. Last, the Neruda again—"DOES SMOKE TALK WITH THE CLOUDS?"—this time on the steps to my first-year room in Hope.

Within minutes our work was being undone. As we walked back across campus we spotted Brown security officers glumly, lethargi-cally sponging "MERCANTILE CORNFROG" from the bricks. It was okay. We hadn't expected our work to last long on the campus's day of highest visibility. (I thought about a group of Zen monks I had seen that semester, constructing an incredibly elaborate sand mandala in the Watson Institute lobby, slowly and with utmost care carrying it outside, and then, with equal care, tilting their intricate design into the Providence River.) Anything writ water-soluble may as well be writ in water itself.

We dressed up for the dance. Night fell, the festoons of light glowed, and the throngs convened. Our work was gone. Brown was back to its pristine self. And then we spotted it:

"RED ALERT! A PHYLUM IS COLLAPSING—"

Perhaps no one had noticed it above the Whispering Arch. Perhaps its message was just relevant enough for its host building. Perhaps it was simply too high to reach.

I stayed in Providence into the summer, sending my creative writing prize money to an old flame's parents as sublet rent, and spending the oppressive, humid summer weeks estivating and mourning and bringing iced coffee from Bagel Gourmet down the hill to translate poems in the air-conditioned nooks of the Athenaeum. Curiously, the chalking remained through the first of the summer thundershowers, then the second, protected by its archway. Clearly it had been seen by security and faculty and staff by this point; somehow it had survived them too. But it was fading and I knew the elements would have at it soon enough. I drove west in August of '06 to Seattle to start my MFA.

I visited Brown in March of '07. It was still there. Andrew phoned me when he returned for class that September. Not only was it still there: it was *sharper* than when any of us had last seen it. It had been *rewritten*.

Two thousand eight; 2009; 2010. I gradually forgot about it. I returned in May of '11 for my five-year reunion. There, incredibly, it was.

"RED ALERT! A PHYLUM IS COLLAPSING—"

What could possibly enable a writing in chalk to last five *years*? Whose hands have touched it up? I have, to this day, never found out who has been maintaining the message—just as they presumably cannot know who first put it there. (Or where it came from: amazingly neither Google nor Amazon seems to know the line is Mohammad's.) Maybe this essay will make the first half of that introduction.

I went back through Providence just this year, the winter of '13, now seven years after my own graduation. Finding a parking space on Waterman, I walked past the greenhouse toward Lincoln Field. A living palimpsest, its own faded and faint iterations beneath itself.

"RED ALERT! A PHYLUM IS COLLAPSING—" It stands as a kind of testament to my time at Brown:

What I took to be endless was fleeting.

What I took to be ephemeral continues.

CAMPUS LIFE

The closest I ever came to an orgy . . . was at a student dance at Brown around 1922. I did not suspect it was an orgy until three days later; in fact, at the time it seemed to me decorous to the point of torpor and fully consonant with the high principles of the Brown Christian Association, under whose auspices it was held. Attired in a greenish Norfolk jacket . . . I spent the evening buffeting about in the stag line, prayerfully beseeching the underclassmen I knew for permission to cut in on their women and tread a few measures of the Camel Walk. At frequent intervals, noisily advertising an overpowering thirst, I retired to a cloakroom with several other blades and choked down a minute quantity of gin, warmed to body heat, from a pocket flask. Altogether, it was a strikingly commonplace experience . . .

—**S. J. Perelman** ('25)

I loved the fact that the bucolic Brown campus was in the middle of this very gritty city with tremendous sort of ethnic legacies, and corrupt or quasi-corrupt politicians and an active mob, and diners literally on the wrong side of the tracks. As a young journalist there was a lot to observe on the margins of campus and beyond campus.

—**David Corn** ('81)

A Campus Tour:
My Life in Poetry at Brown

NICOLE COOLEY

The Rock

On the first floor of the Rockefeller Library, in the reference section, I sat alone in a wooden study carrel, Cotgrave's *Dictionarie of the French and English Tongues* from 1611 open on my lap. I loved the book's age, loved its dustiness, its smell, the way its pages threatened to crumble in my fingers, and the fact that, more than 350 years after it was written, I could hold it in my hands.

For hours, with the help of the ancient dictionary, I worked through French poems. I read and reread the dizains—dense ten-line poems—by the Renaissance poet Maurice Scève, who was the subject of my undergraduate comparative literature thesis. I wrote list after list, French and English, side by side. The words of the poems were objects I could touch, stones I could slip into my pockets. Translating was crossing a bridge into another world. Every word I wrote was a step across, from French to English, from my childhood to my life as an adult.

Learning to read and speak French for the first time at Brown as a freshman had brought me to poetry in a new way. I loved the range of French classes, from "The Inaccessible Object of Desire" to "Nerval, Baudelaire, Valery" to "Four French Poets of the Renaissance." I took as many French poetry classes as I could.

I was nineteen, and I believed I'd found my most sacred space: the Brown library—those carrels in the reference section full of my beloved dictionaries.

The Henry Moore Statue on the Green

We gathered there, on top of it, on its blackened bronze, on the grass surrounding it, with our books of poems, our notebooks, our pens, our imported French cigarettes. The Henry Moore was a destination and a gathering place. The bronze statue, given to the university in 1974, was our place for poetry.

As young poets at Brown, we took ourselves too seriously in all the best ways. We wanted to be intellectuals. We read Herbert Marcuse, Jacques Derrida, French feminist theory. It was the mideighties but we fashioned ourselves as characters from Jean-Luc Godard's films about the student revolutions in Paris in 1968 that none of us had experienced. We'd seen glimpses of the era in semiotics classes, and that was enough.

Sitting on the Henry Moore, with our packs of Gitanes cigarettes, in our thrift shop coats, we talked urgently about poetry and politics. We were eighteen, we were nineteen, we were twenty. We felt both unbelievably young and unbearably old and we were neither, in the way that you can only experience that contradiction at the end of your childhood and the beginning of your adulthood.

On Meeting Street

My friend, a graduate student in creative writing, wanted to show me his latest poetry project: he had written poems all over his car. A large, used Oldsmobile, faded blue, his car was covered in letters, in language, on the hood, the doors, the trunk, the windshield, and the wheels. As we stood on Meeting Street in the late-afternoon fall sunshine and he showed me his MFA-project car that he was turning in instead of a paper manuscript, instead of typed-up poems, I understood poetry in a whole new way. Poetry was a force of pure liberation. Poetry was absolute freedom.

French House

I started French at Brown as soon as I arrived and in my sophomore year I moved off campus to French House. To be accepted, you had to pass an interview in French conducted by current residents. On East Manning Street, behind Brown's campus, French House consisted of two houses, beautiful stone buildings. The rooms, full of dark wood, were large, with high ceilings. The biggest and most important part of living in French House was French Dinner, served twice a week, a meal during which we were only allowed to speak French. When I moved into French House, I was the weakest French speaker in the group. To practice, I read French poems out loud, Baudelaire, Rimbaud, Valéry. If I read enough poetry, I believed I could do the practical things: I could speak in French at dinner.

The IHOP on Thayer Street

My freshman year, the International House of Pancakes across from campus was where I wrote all my poems. The waitstaff would let me sit in a booth all day, with a bottomless pot of coffee, the restaurant's claim to fame, and the occasional buttered muffin or piece of toast. The IHOP was where I began my lifelong love of writing in ugly places, preferring diners and doughnut shops to luxurious cafés. In the IHOP, the pressure was off. I watched the spinning glass cylinder of pies and read and scribbled in my notebook and didn't care if the poem I wrote was good or not.

That spring, I was taking a poetry workshop with Philip Levine— later to become the poet laureate and a winner of the Pulitzer Prize— who was teaching at Brown for one semester. Writing classes at Brown required an admission test: you showed up on the first day of class and did a writing exercise in a blue exam book and later found out if—based on the quality of that work—you were admitted. On the first day of Phil's class, he told everyone who showed up that they could stay in the class. Our class was composed not only of under-graduates but also a professor from the psychology department and a songwriter who played his poems on his guitar.

Phil encouraged us to write about what mattered to us, to think about how we could explore the most important things in our lives in our own poems. In the IHOP, I hunkered down and wrote my family secrets, my deepest fears and wishes, the stories of the people I'd loved who were dead and gone.

The Rare Book Bindery at the John Hay Library

My job on campus was saving rare books of poems.

In the basement of the John Hay Library, I assisted master book-binder Daniel Knowlton, constructing covers out of wood and card-board and vellum for volumes in the John Hay's collection. Most of what was wheeled down on carts to the bindery was poetry, as the John Hay has one of the largest collections of rare American poetry books in the nation.

I loved my job. I smoothed down vellum, cut out cardboard to fit around each book, and learned to use the iron letterpress to stamp out words in gold. I folded and refolded pink marbled papers.

The object, as Mr. Knowlton explained it, was to make the box that held each book as beautiful as the text inside. The best part: before I made each box I read a little of the book to determine how the box might reflect the book's content. In cool silence, I sat at a desk in the bindery and imagined: What kind of box should Wanda Coleman get? Or William Blake? Or Allen Ginsberg?

The Blue Room

Before it was beautifully renovated, the Blue Room was a coffee-house with grimy windows, unwashed walls, and a slanting floor that made everyone's chairs scrape loudly over the tiles. And of course I loved it; the Blue Room fit all my teenage fantasies of a place where writers would gather and dramatic events would occur. The light was bad, the music full of static. When my first college boyfriend broke up with me there one night, over Styrofoam cups of coffee, I thought, in the midst of my sadness, *This is a good place for the end of a relationship. If we were to break up in a French movie, it would have to take place here.* And, in fact, I met my French tutor there each Thursday morning and we drilled verb tenses for French conversation.

Pembroke Hall

I attended the poetry reading with a fellow student from my poetry workshop, and we were two of only three people in the audience. The poet was Robert Mezey.

For me, it was a perfect date; after the reading, the Q & A with the poet was an intimate conversation. Robert Mezey talked to us, the three young poets in the room. He asked us about our work, shared his writing process with us. It was a wonderful evening.

Years later, the boy who had brought me to the reading would die in the bombing over Lockerbie, in the terrorist act that killed four Brown students. I would always remember that evening, sitting beside him in the classroom, sharing the spirit of poetry.

Michael Harper's Office

Professor Harper gave us index cards in an envelope at the end of each poetry workshop class. I'd wait to open my envelope until I was halfway down the stairs of the classroom building, where my fellow writing students could not see me. I'd pull the cards out of the envelope like they were winning lottery tickets.

"Poems to write" was the heading on each card and Professor Harper tailored the assignments to suit each of us and our backgrounds. That spring, Michael Harper wanted me to write a poem titled "Huey Long." He wanted me to write a poem called "The Rhetoric of Women's Poetry: A Polemic." Neither was even remotely like the poems I'd been writing for his class. He challenged us to write in new ways and to break our writing habits.

I was twenty years old, so I would beg for reasons. I wanted him to explain the lists of titles to me. I wanted secrets, shortcuts, clues to fix the careful poems I'd been writing, poems that I wanted him to praise.

He'd never tell me.

All of us in the workshop were learning a difficult lesson: we had to figure out our own poems on our own terms. We had to decide for ourselves what a poem was and what kind of poem we wanted to write.

Waterman Street

Graduation day: I was leaving Brown. With my boyfriend and my best friend, I was driving away in the U-Haul, heading to graduate school in creative writing, to my MFA degree, to what I believed would be the future that would teach me to write poems. The three of us stood outside the apartment on Waterman Street, truck packed and ready. And yet I was already ready to write my poems; I'd learned all my lessons about poetry at Brown.

The Day President John F. Kennedy Died

SUSAN CHEEVER

I t was one of those sunny autumn afternoons that smell of apples and falling leaves. Thanksgiving break was just a few days away. I checked the date as I walked out of Miller Hall and headed for the Thayer Street market. November 22, 1963.

I was happy at college, but I didn't know that then. Fear of what seemed like a hellish future eclipsed my good feelings. I knew I had to get married, but my attempts at dating were spectacularly unsuccessful. I was hoping to find a career, but the only things I liked doing were sleeping and reading. How would I manage? My delight in the campus—my friends, the solace of books, skating at Aldrich-Dexter, and exploring Fox Point—was dulled by anxiety.

My dread was part of a collective terror. Many of us thought the world would end soon in World War III. In grade school we had been taught to hide under our desks when the bombs dropped. As freshmen in college we toured a bomb shelter in downtown Providence with shelves of canned goods and a crank to filter radiation out of the air after the inevitable nuclear holocaust. When turned, the crank made a shrieking, metal-against-metal noise; I heard that noise in my dreams. When family neighbors in Westchester got drunk at cocktail parties, they confessed that they had armed themselves against others who might want to use their bomb shelters—sorry, but they wouldn't be able to share. As sophomores during the Cuban missile crisis we had listened to our young, handsome president telling about the risk he was taking by challenging Nikita Khrushchev. "Our goal is not the victory of might, but the vindication of right," he said as we listened to the scratchy radio in the lounge of Bates House. Would the Russians back down? Some classmates headed for home to be with their families at the end.

We stayed up late debating whether or not it was better to die in a fiery flash, be captured by the Russian soldiers who were waiting off the coast, or slowly starve the way characters did in *On the Beach* by Nevil Shute, which was set portentously in 1963. In late-night conversations we quoted the elegant despair of Edna St. Vincent Millay—*My candle burns at both ends / It will not last the night.* In class we studied the elegant despair of T. S. Eliot—*I had not thought death had undone so many.* The question was how we would survive. The answer, my friend, was blowin' in the wind. Would it all end with a bang, or with a whimper, as Eliot wrote? Fire or ice, as Robert Frost wrote? One thing we knew: it was going to end, and end soon.

So that sunny November afternoon when I saw a girl from my class sobbing as she stumbled down Thayer Street, I wasn't surprised to find the world indeed coming to an end. The president had been shot. The president had been shot in Dallas in a motorcade with the governor of Texas. The president was at Parkland Memorial Hospital in Dallas. Jackie's chic clothes—her pink suit and pillbox hat—were covered with blood. They were giving the president transfusions. By the time the afternoon sun sent its long shadows across the lawns in front of Sayles Hall, the president was dead.

In those days the only publicly available television on campus was a small black-and-white set in the Blue Room, where on that day it seemed the whole student body had crowded in, all of them standing or sitting on the floor and draping themselves over the few chairs to watch the long, sad four-day weekend of national mourning. The picture was grainy, the images tiny, but the little box seemed to hold the whole world. There was the young Walter Cronkite with his heavy black glasses and mustache, choking up as he announced that the president had been pronounced dead. There was CBS reporter Tom Pettit in the chaotic basement of the Dallas police station trying to keep up with the jumble of events. A pale Lee Harvey Oswald was saying he hadn't done anything as he was pushed toward a man named Jack Ruby. Then there was a popping sound, and the next minute Oswald was dead and the screen was filled with a shoving crowd of men.

Before that weekend, television was where we watched the Mouseketeers and *I Love Lucy*. Now our history was unfolding in miniature before us, in black and white, with the tinny sound turned up as high as it would go. There on-screen was little John-John saluting his father's coffin, and there was the weeping widow, with her sad face and lovely clothes, standing entirely alone with her two children. There was the riderless horse, bucking in the autumn sun. I watched. I went for walks. I came back to listen. The clatter of hooves drowned out the guns of the funeral salute.

As terrible as that November day fifty years ago may have been, its memories have not entirely overwhelmed those of my days and nights at Brown. My first days as a college freshman were passed in a haze of anxiety. My roommate was a beautiful blue-eyed princess from the Midwest who had special study clothes, date clothes, and classroom clothes—all pink or baby blue—and who read sitting up straight at the desk on her side of the room. The desk on my side was piled with papers, books, coffee cups. I read in bed, often under the covers, and I tried never to change my clothes. Trapped together on an upper hall of Andrews facing the back, we seemed helpless in our opposite ways. Soon we had gathered a few more helpless freshmen who huddled with us under the high ceilings of the cafeteria and made tea on hot plates brought from home. To get to class I would wander down the steps of Andrews and out past the Pembroke Library and down Brown Street.

In the fall of 2012 I returned as a visiting lecturer. I hadn't been back for more than an evening or an afternoon since graduation. As a teacher walking that same sidewalk down Brown Street last fall, I had vivid, nostalgic flashbacks: of sitting on the grass with friends;

of watching from the high windows of the Pembroke Library as a boy I had a crush on walked up Meeting Street (did he know he carried my heart in his pocket?); of buying my first yogurt (then a new, strange thing) at the Thayer market; of splitting a piece of cherry cheesecake at Gregg's (now Au Bon Pain); of spending that weekend in the Blue Room watching television. Nostalgia! Gone is the anxiety that killed my ability to appreciate the beauty of the place and the luxury of having nothing to do except learn. These shimmering images of the past seemed more alive than memories—I was reliving my experience at Brown, only this time I was reliving it joyfully.

Nostalgia is the bittersweet memory of the past, literally an ache for homecoming—the bitterness is the passing of time, the sweetness is our survival. The Brown campus, it turns out, is nostalgia central for me. Returning to it was like having a romance with an old friend. I reveled in the past that I can enjoy now. I did get married; I did find a career. Recently, dozens of academic papers on nostalgia have been published at universities from the Netherlands to South Africa and the United States. Nostalgia is a good thing, the psychologists all agree. We use our longing for the past to give our lives meaning. Nostalgia makes us feel more important and more generous: "It serves a crucial existential function," says researcher Clay Routledge of Britain's University of Southampton. British researchers have developed the Southampton Nostalgia Scale. (How often do you experience nostalgia? How significant is it for you to feel nostalgic?) I scored a seven out of seven. We'll always have Paris!

What do I remember learning at Brown? How to survive a broken heart. How to cook an elaborate stew on a hot plate. That my worst fears rarely come true. How to read a book a week. When Professor David Hirsch talked to me about Henry James and Edgar Allan Poe, the ghosts in their stories jumped out at me. I read F. O. Matthiessen's *American Renaissance* with Professor Barry Marks, and I have since written my own books about those Concord writers— Emerson, Thoreau, and their neighbors the loony, impoverished

Alcotts. I thought personal style was everything in those days—how could I be friends with a girl who wore pink? I got a little smarter. My first roommate and I became good friends after all. I loved her.

Now I'm smart enough to see that I was with my people at college, a generation of confused and frightened kids looking for and finding our answers in books. As it turned out, in spite of the death of a president on an autumn day, we didn't die at college, and we didn't die soon afterward. World War III was a fearful, exaggerated chimera. We didn't die, and instead we did something much more difficult than dying: we learned how to live.

You

AMITY GAIGE

I met B on my first day at Brown. He was my next-door neighbor in the newly renovated New Pembroke dormitories, the beautifully isolated dorms in the northernmost corner of campus, there at the threshold of College Hill, where all the cars decelerated to cruising speed. Just out my dormitory door were the bars and boutiques of Thayer Street, the café tables sitting in the cold sun late into October. One of the first things I did upon my arrival at Brown was to take up coffee and cigarettes. These, plus Anne Sexton's *Complete Poems*, were my accoutrements as I ploddingly set about becoming the woman I'd always known I was. My freshman roommate, I'll call her Lee, gamely rid herself of her neon T-shirts and leggings and she and I began to function as a mutual admiration society, a very small but sufficient consensus. We had both felt socially marooned for as long as we could remember—we felt *apart*, as poets do—and although I cannot speak for Lee, this apartness was always matched with the desire to close the gap. And this longing—romantic, mostly—felt like, to borrow from one of Sexton's more splendid metaphors, a *small coal I kept swallowing* ("Courage," 1972).

Longing. Some folks are just born with it. Men and women both. Saddled with it. Laden with it. It's a kind of spiritual handicap. It has to be dragged along via a complicated series of pulleys, belts, and cables. I remember the sensation of longing from earliest childhood, and I shiver to think how my life's escapades have been ruled by the attempt to avoid feeling quite so helpless against it. As I grew up and developed romantic longings, I found that poetry was the best receptacle of this newfound variation. The reading and the writing of it. So, apart from a brief phase of writing liberal-leaning poetry about homelessness and homophobia and other things I knew nothing about, I wrote love poems—overheated, technically uninteresting love poems written, of course, to the elusive, cruel "you." Despite the fact that "you" hurt me really bad, in numerous and specific ways detailed in these poems, I am embarrassed to admit I don't remember who "you" was. Thinking back on the boys I knew in high school, their fumbling advances and their food allergies, not a one seems heroic enough to be my poetic addressee, nor to elicit the emotions that "I" describe in my poetry. In fact, "I" have no clue what "you" did to "me." It's all lost to bad free verse.

B was a blond—I mean a real blond—I mean fundamentally, Teutonically blond, like gold ore; he would have looked good in a breastplate. He was tall, bug-eyed, intelligent, and dangerous. He was funny, very funny. When every other freshman in Pembroke 3 was out at a mixer or a sexual assault awareness talk, B would spend nights sketching caricatures of me and Lee with surreal words coming out of our mouths, while U2's "Zoo Station" blared out of his enormous stereo speakers and I lay belly-down on his bed, cheek smushed to hand, dreaming about all the truths I was about to tell him. Eventually, he would suggest that we do something spontaneous, like take a trip to Prospect Terrace Park in the middle of the night, for example, a night picnic, some night music—I mean, did we ever sleep? B played the requisite guitar, but unlike other boys, his music erred on the side of performance art. He sang long, whimsical songs resembling macabre children's stories featuring me and Lee, or elephants or death or the stars. He was just *different*, even within the sphere of captivating Brownies. He behaved with no inhibition. I often wished he weren't so beautiful. His beauty began to wear on me. He was a small coal I kept swallowing. Because as obvious as my love was, it never went anywhere. *Anywhere.* All day long I cavorted with B; I dined, studied, and argued with B, but inevitably, at some middle hour of the evening, the time would come when B would drag his phone into his dorm room closet to call his girlfriend back in New Paltz.

This time was my writing time. *I am in my own closet!* I would think, in a sweat. As in high school, the perceived rejection was a verbal diarrhetic. In my journal, I wrote reams of poems about B and about the ephemerality of love and youth and the gulf between us and our ideals and how we would surely both grow up to be miserable. At last, I had found my You.

An awful lot of time went by like this. An October Parents' Weekend left me weeping on a rock somewhere in Newport while Mom and Dad nattered on about the ocean. My wild, redheaded Theatre Arts 3 prof told us to bring our journals to class, and I was relieved to finally share my poems with somebody, anybody. Otherwise, I kept swallowing my coal. B and Lee and I went to Spats, and sat drinking Newcastle on tables that tottered over the old black and white parquet floor while B tried to shock us or make us laugh and we laughed and imagined and were good to one another, and the memory still floods me with love. Of course, one night, exhausted by the redundancy of his chaste rejection of me, I drank too much 'Castle and forced B to sit on my dorm room bed and listen to one of the angrier poems I had written about him. Afterward, he patted my head and drew up the covers and pretended that he wasn't You.

There was a smoke shop down on Waterman. Red Carpet Smoke Shop. The cartoonish lacquered statue still stands, though I hear he's been given a turban. I remember going into Red Carpet once to look for a billfold or penknife or some other useless male contrivance for my father's birthday. I stood inhaling the clove and honey and mulch of the tobacco, looking at the beautiful boxes of Nat Shermans, the pastels of the American Spirits that everyone was carrying around those days, and finally the trademark robin's-egg blue of French Gauloises. I thought, *A man who shops here must be very much a man.* Later, I met a graduate student with a broad, tanned brow who took me to Dunkin' Donuts and asked me to tell him why I loved Anne Sexton so much, and it occurred to me that B had never asked me this—that in fact no one had ever asked me this. And inwardly I understood that whomever I married would have to also marry my imagination, my creative mind, accepting all of the sunshine and shadow of such a commitment, and when we parted, the graduate student slid his hand inside a pocket of his blazer and withdrew, like a literary symbol, a robin's-egg-blue package of Gauloises.

Every writer needs an addressee. The addressee is, on the surface, the writer's listener, often the beloved—known or unknown to her. Of course, we could think of the writer's addressee as another version of herself. Her best self, awaiting her across the river, the end result of her slowly unfolding, timebound transfiguration. And all love poems are about the other and they are also about the self. When B was my muse, I was prolific. But my muse was also 1991 and "Zoo Station" and the fall of the Berlin Wall and how the dark tunnel of Faunce framed the quad in the sunny distance like a dream I kept having, and my muse was also myself, a self that was turning into a writer.

I don't know where B is now. I could argue that he is right here, in these words. And the other one, the man with the Gauloises? I know exactly where he is. He jettisoned the cigarettes circa 2004, before the first of our children was born.

BDH Editor Soars,
Stumbles, Snags a Wife

M. CHARLES BAKST

O n the morning of September 28, 1965, I walked into the Blue
Room in Faunce House, badly in need of coffee after spending
most of the night overseeing publication of a *Brown Daily Herald*
issue that would become a national media sensation.

The headline over the news story said, "For Women at Pembroke
College: Brown Health Center Prescribes Birth Control Pills."

As *BDH* editor in chief, I had penned a blistering editorial backing the policy but labeling the Pembroke administration—headed
by Dean Rosemary Pierrel—as hypocritical or blind for presiding
over a Victorian social system that obsessed over curfews and barred
women from living in off-campus apartments.

I bought my coffee at the counter, turned, and was accosted by a
Pembroke junior. Something about the issue had offended her. Amid
the torrent of her words, I asked contemptuously, *"Who* are *you?"*

She replied, "I'm Liz Feroe, and if you're going to write about
Pembroke, you better know who I am."

This would prove to be a key conversation in my life, but at the
time it meant nothing. After all, I was M. Charles Bakst, a senior, in
a hurry to be great—in my own mind, I already was—and I presided
over a mighty publication that routinely battled Brown and Pembroke administrators over long-running issues like women's visiting
hours in men's dormitories, or really, it could be anything, such as
the university's drinking policies or its handling of the Bicentennial

celebration. When student organizations disappointed us, we'd whack them too.

No topic was too large for our stories and editorials. We chronicled the national civil rights movement and the dawning opposition to the Vietnam War. And no topic was too small, not even the cranberry sauce in the Sharpe Refectory's Ivy Room. They served the whole-berry variety; we preferred jellied.

And now we had the attention of the national press, which was intrigued by the avant-garde story of a doctor for a women's college willing to prescribe birth control pills. So far only two students had taken advantage of this opportunity, but the precedent was set.

Of course, calling Pembroke a "college" was somewhat amiss. The university's classrooms were coed, student activities were increasingly coed, and, indeed, that very autumn would see the launch of coed dining at lunch, one of the paper's mini-crusades.

Still, Pembrokers had their own deans, dormitories, and social system, with sign-out times and curfews a constant issue for debate. Men had no curfews and, unlike the women, could live off campus.

It is startling to look back to those years, when tuition, room, and board came to well under $3,000. Each spring, three sign-up sheets would sprout on a bulletin board in Pembroke Hall. They were for Pembroke seniors heading for graduate school, or business careers, or marriage. Yes, you read that right. If a young lady became engaged, she would sign the engaged list so the whole school would know.

Other customs of the times? Well, if a guy was taking a girl to a football game, they would both dress up. If a girl didn't have a date, she wouldn't go. And speaking of dates, when a guy walked into Andrews Hall to call on a girl, he'd say whom he was there to see, and the receptionist would summon her. If you kept showing up for the same girl, the receptionist would summon her as soon as you entered the lobby. God forbid you were there to see a different girl.

I was often at the Pembroke dorms, but sometimes I was there on an academic mission, not a social one. Because my *BDH* duties often made me miss class, and because I was such an indifferent note-taker anyway, especially compared with my bright, industrious female course mates, I'd show up at Pembroke the night before an exam and ask someone to let me see her notes to bring myself up to speed. Which is more incredible: that I sought such favors or that I found students willing to oblige?

BDH editors served the second semester of junior year through the first semester of senior year. I was an American Civilization major, but, to me, studies ranked second to the newspaper. When production of a March 1965 issue reporting on the dismissal of eight students for smoking marijuana kept me up all night, I showed up at a political science quiz and announced to the professor that I had not had time to study and would have to take a makeup. I was frequently tardy on term papers.

It may sound like I waltzed through life at Brown. It certainly was rarefied. I hobnobbed with student bigwigs and with Bob Schulze, the dean of the college and a prince of a guy. He was a buffer for President Barnaby Keeney, who was somewhat remote and at times imperious. I talked big and wrote big, with thunderous, overwrought prose. (For example, here's what I wrote about the crush of students lining up for hockey games: "One of these nights there is going to be a riot outside of Meehan Auditorium and the Administration of this University will have no one to blame but itself.")

But, in fact, much of the time I was a bundle of nerves, worrying about how much trouble the next editorial would cause and chewing my way through rolls of peppermint Life Savers to calm my stomach.

We were often impatient with our fellow undergrads, such as the Pembroke leaders of whom we wrote, "Any governmental organization that allows its members to come to meetings in bermuda shorts and pass the time doing their knitting has something very wrong with it."

The larger battle, though, was with top university officials and trustees. When words alone weren't enough, we'd resort to italics or larger type, such as in this October 1965 editorial:

"STUDENTS WANT THE OPPORTUNITY TO BE RESPONSIBLE. THEY WANT IT AND THEY WANT IT BADLY . . . STUDENTS ARE TIRED OF HEARING THE ADMINISTRATION TELL THEM THEY ARE 'JUNIOR PARTNERS.' THEY WANT DEEDS, NOT WORDS."

Whatever my inner turmoil, I loved what I was doing. I had summer internships at the *Providence Journal*. With the *BDH* we had a newspaper all to ourselves. Articles written on manual typewriters in our Faunce House offices were shuttled by cab or messenger to a shop near the state house where a linotypist banged them out again in lead type and another man took the type and created the pages. My managing editors—Steve Veiner and David Gilbert—and I would often be down there into the wee hours supervising the process and making regular runs for hot dogs. Life was heady.

And then, in December 1965, our tenure nearing an end, our world crashed. Faced one night with a shortage of staff and of copy, Gilbert, Veiner, and I crafted a hoax issue announcing that, at last, up to one hundred Pembrokers would be allowed to have off-campus apartments; applications for permission would be taken immediately. Yes, we were looking for a short-term chuckle or gotcha. But there was a serious purpose behind this glitzy "news." It was something people would want to believe, something that would seem logical and desirable, and it had the potential to stimulate real debate.

It would not have embarrassed the university if it were true. But it wasn't. Many students were angry; we had violated their trust. The university administration was furious with us. Our credibility was shot. The three of us resigned.

Though shaken, I emerged a better person, less arrogant, more appreciative of the seriousness and consequences of journalism, a field that would be my lifelong career.

Interestingly, our bogus claim indeed presaged reality. That April, Dean Pierrel, so long a holdout, made the breathtaking announcement that university trustees had approved a plan for up to thirty Pembrokers to move off campus the following year. The new *Herald* editors reported the news with the very same page layout we'd used in the hoax issue.

I knew one of the Pembrokers who got an apartment. In a way, you do too. Remember Elizabeth Feroe, who scolded me in Faunce House on the day of the birth control issue? Well, in second semester, we found ourselves sharing a class, Professor Bill McLoughlin's "Social and Intellectual History of the United States." We began sitting together, and shooting the breeze, and dating.

In her senior year, she proceeded to live off campus. I was at Columbia Journalism School, but our romance endured. On June 6, 1967, we were married. And we still are.

Number One Tofu Scramble
with Johnny Toast

ROBERT ARELLANO

Under College Hill there are tunnels for discontinued trains.
There, in the dark, derelicts sleep along the ties, their heads on
rusty rails. And lower forms live there—rats, reptiles—and,
according to Lovecraft, something in between: creatures erect
once, beasts again.

> —Keith Waldrop, "Characteristic Pieces"

Matt Obert, a server at Louis Family Restaurant on Brook Street, is on his way out of the kitchen with a Cheeseburger Special, LTO on the side, when he's collared by owner Louis Gianfrancesco. "What do you think you doing! Onion's not a vegetable, it's a spice!" Louis makes Matt take some back. This moment, this withheld slice of onion, serendipitously sparks the insight of four diners and the plans for Brown's first Multimedia Lab, a state-of-the-art computer classroom on the ground floor of the Grad Center, get sketched out on a napkin over a tippy tabletop.

Since 1946, Louis has opened at five o'clock every morning, 362 days a year. In the 1960s, a young folksinger named Robert Zimmerman bounced Louis's son Johnny on his knee before playing to the packed diner. In 1994, it's Johnny and brother Albert who arrive at four thirty every morning to make sure the grills are hot for scholars pulling all-nighters and Providence cops coming off the graveyard shift. These days, everyone's talking about how a lawyer representing Brown showed up telling Johnny they wanted to buy him out. Johnny says, "Let's just say I told him he didn't have our kind of money."

I arrived in Providence in 1987 and have enjoyed several roles in seven years at Brown, from undergraduate, to faculty in English and Creative Writing, to teaching the hypertext fiction workshops I designed with Robert Coover as a grad student. My days are spent in an interdisciplinary orbit of Modern Culture and Media, the Center for Information Technology, and Louis, where Johnny and Albert know my usual. They know all the regulars, including faculty and staff from Creative Writing, Music, MCM, Art, and the Scholarly Technology Group, who, beneath Louis's lighted menu, are creating a vision for Brown's future as a digital-media leader. The Multimedia Lab is nourished on the blood of spinach pies with extra sauce.

I should be happy, and I am. I'm a happy guy. But in the summer of 1994 I go into a tailspin, precipitated by a breakup with a girlfriend. From the moment I wake to the time I finally get wearily back to sleep, I can think of nothing but the ex, the ruined relationship, and how badly I fucked up. I can barely manage to make a sandwich, much less cook a decent meal. Food has lost its flavor. I might stop eating altogether if not for Louis.

I check every book on mood disorders out of the SciLi and begin to accept that I have caught the family curse: depression. My mind roils with toxic thought. Some nights it's palpable in the brainpan, a physical sizzle, and the anxiety becomes so intolerable that I have to go on long walks to be able to breathe: past the baseball fields on Gano to the deserted tracks and the trestle jutting out over the Seekonk River, where an abandoned drawbridge rises two hundred feet above the water in an enormous underscore-slash.

My Providence is a hilly behemoth bound by the Seekonk and the Woonasquatucket, and by the hurricane barrier and Swan Point Cemetery. At the top of Hope Street, the Ladd Observatory is a cycloptic eye; running under Waterman from Thayer to South Main, the bus tunnel is a huffing snout; and at the end of the abandoned train tunnel, mouth gaping beneath Benefit and running for two miles under College Hill to the old drawbridge rising two hundred feet above the Seekonk, I scale the Beast's rigid tail. It is the summer of 1994, I have been in Providence for seven years, I am twenty-four years old, and I believe I may be capable of hurting myself.

My psychotherapist gets me to admit my potential. The question is couched just carefully enough to make me lower my guard: "Have you ever thought about causing yourself harm in any way?" No. But the question echoes in my head: In *any* way? When the brainstorm becomes unmanageable, no remedy is off the table. There is no way to stop this thought. And so I walk, ruminate, contemplate, until I can get back to my apartment too exhausted not to sleep. For weeks on end, the vicious cycle doesn't let up. How many months does it take to get to the bottom of a tailspin?

On a hot September afternoon on Benefit Street, I am biking over to teach at the MML when I stop to quench my thirst at the fountain in front of the Athenaeum. Carved in granite: COME HERE EVERYONE THAT THIRSTETH. When I get to the Grad Center a student from my hypertext workshop tells me, "You know the supposed curse about that fountain? They say you drink from it, you'll never leave Providence." I ask poet and Brown professor Keith Waldrop about it, and he's heard that in the 1800s Sarah Helen Whitman, a lifelong Providence resident, dumped Edgar Allan Poe at the Athenaeum, and he is rumored to have made this pronouncement. At least, the legend goes, you'll never leave alive.

Finally, one fall morning my therapist asks me whether I remember the last time I tried looking *up*, and I am surprised to hear myself say no. For months I've been looking down. "Try keeping your eyes at eye level or higher for the rest of the day," she tells me.

I am sitting in front of the Burnside statue in Kennedy Plaza when the light makes it through. The sun shines in my eyes and I cry. After months of steady depression, I begin to pull out of the tailspin.

By the spring of 1997, students in my hypertext fiction work-shops are pioneering the emerging field of electronic literature, and over the years I have worked with my colleagues in Creative Writing to organize several prominent literary events, including major African, Cuban, and vanguard writers' conferences. Since I climbed out of the last tailspin in '94, things have gone all right. I now have a gorgeous girlfriend on Governor, a new relationship I can't live without. My place on Ives and Williams is on the fourth floor above Fox Point Video. A block north at Power, it's left to Brown or right to the Seekonk. On good nights I write until two or three o'clock in the morning, my Mac set up at a window with an unobstructed view of the drawbridge.

One night I am looking forward to getting together with my girl-friend when she calls and breaks the date. She tells me she has to stay on at work, a fancy restaurant downtown. "One of the other servers canceled and I have to pull a double."

I say, "Can we get together after?"

"I'm pretty beat already, and by the time I finish the dinner shift I'm just going to want to go to bed."

"I could come over and we could just sleep."

"Why don't we just get together tomorrow, okay?"

"Okay, I love you."

"Love you too."

Before the phone is back in the cradle, the bleak ruminations begin. I try to tell myself this is just a bad day, not a new tailspin. She only asked for a night alone. It's not like she's cheating on me. She said she loves me. I'll see her tomorrow. I can make it through the night. I write in all caps in my journal: "STOP THIS THOUGHT."

Is it coincidence that my walk this night takes me by Governor? Down on the street, I see a light flickering in her upstairs window. Candlelight. It's still early. There's no way the restaurant could already be closed. She must have forgotten to put it out when she left for work. I don't have a key to her place, but ah! Providence, with your fire escape ladders so close to the sidewalks! Maybe she left the window open or at least unlocked. It will make my night go easier to know there's nothing to worry about. I jump and catch the lowest rung, pushing my sneakers against the side of the apartment building to get myself onto the ladder and up the fire escape.

If you've ever caught a lover with another, you know how good it feels that second, perched on the fire escape, peering at them seated beside the open window at a table for two, to shout, "You *lied* to me!"

They jump out of their chairs, freaking out, and she lamely rejoinders: "You don't *listen*!" The guy says, "Maybe I should go."

The rush is once-in-a-lifetime. I climb down the fire escape, high on righteous indignation. He'll leave and she'll try to call me at home. Let her fret. There will be messages when I get back. Good friends Rich Schuler and Chris Dunn live around the corner on Williams. I'm not going home right away.

I tell them the story and Rich opens me a beer. And another. And another. Chris cranks up the Tropicalia music, cheerfully shouting to keep me from spiraling, "Bob! You pooped in the punch bowl!" They stay up with me for hours. They don't let me leave. Toward dawn they tell me I can crash on the couch. But I live just around the corner. I want to go home.

It's four thirty in the cold twilight when I climb the stairs and open the door to my apartment. In the dark kitchen, the little red light on the answering machine is not blinking. There are no new messages. I look out my window to the drawbridge.

The guy didn't leave. She prepared him a candlelight dinner, and he stayed all night, and not even my yelling a few feet from them in the window could stop her.

Power: left or right? All my friends are sleeping. And she's sleeping with him. I feel the sizzling in my brain and I know what it is: another tailspin coming on. It is the summer of 1997 and I have been in Providence for ten years. I am twenty-seven years old.

When I walk into Louis at five a.m., I think I am doing a pretty good job of hiding it. Growing up in a house full of crazy people has made me a very secretive person. I might just have been writing all night, right? But Johnny barely has to turn from the pile of home fries on the grill to understand that something is wrong. "Albert, I think Bob needs to peel some potatoes."

What? What's happening? I'm a customer, not a cook. I just want a cup of coffee, regular. Wordlessly Albert comes out from behind the counter, taking me, a sightless man, by the elbow. He leads me back through the kitchen down the cramped staircase to Louis's fluorescent-lit basement, where fifty-pound bags of flour and five-gallon cans of tomato puree vie for shelf space with the gleaming machines of commercial food prep.

Albert sits me at a bench in front of a contraption with an intake that looks like an old gramophone horn. The chrome lettering reads HOBART. He sets me up with a seventy-five-pound sack of potatoes and an empty plastic barrel. Albert flips on the machine, conjuring a terrible noise. He shows me how to use it. Put a potato in the top, clear away the peeled skin, put the clean potato in the bucket, repeat. There are two manifolds on the side: one pops out the shaved potato; the other discharges the ribbons of peelings. "Don't put your fingers in the top," Albert says. "It will make a big mess." He leaves me to my work.

I put a potato in the top and bits of peel and water droplets spray my face. The potato comes out so clean! I feed the machine potatoes. I drop in another, and another.

Alone in Louis's basement, I am aware of my regret, of all that I've done wrong. I know that I have to stop using girlfriends as Band-Aids. The gash goes down too deep. Down to the kitchen where my father, a refugee from Cuba who "lost everything" when the family left Havana, stumbled in drunk too many times to count. Down to the nursery where I cried for hours while in the next room, drapes shut against the midday sun, my mother could not be roused from bed.

Albert returns in half an hour. My hands are wet and pruny from the work, and I am proud of my barrel full of bare potatoes. Albert does not conceal his irritation when he says, "Jeez, Bob, I didn't say peel the whole bag."

Back up in the restaurant, there at my place on the counter, is the coffee: cold. Swiftly Johnny serves my regular, piping hot. Two topographies are my Providence: the jagged scar of the distended train bridge silhouetted against the East Providence skyline, and the rolling hills of a Louis Number One. Those home fries taste better than anything I've ever eaten in my life.

That October

CHRISTINA HAAG

That October there was a spike of heat in the Northeast, a brilliant backlash of summer. Providence, a city that would soon be bundled and galoshed—held captive by snow and rain for the next five months—was drinking in whatever warmth it could get. At Brown, on one of the highest of the seven hills that overlook the city, coats and sweaters were abandoned, classes were cut, and stereo speakers, perched high in open windows, blared the Allman Brothers and Grateful Dead, the drum solos drifting down through the air like a wild pagan call. Banners—sheets spray-painted NO NUKES/END APARTHEID NOW in black and red—were draped over dorm walls of brick and limestone.

On the Green, the patch of calm surrounded by the oldest buildings on campus, dogs chased after tennis balls and Frisbees or lounged in the still-bright grass. On the Faunce House steps, theater majors bummed cigarettes, and aspiring novelists and semioticians sparred over Derrida. Rich foreign students congregated in the middle of the terrace: the men, with Lacostes tucked tight into jeans and collars flipped high, the women, impossibly sleek, their tousled heads thrown back in charmed laughter.

I was a junior in the fall of 1980. I had just gotten back from a trip to Ireland, but for most of the summer I'd stayed in Providence to act in three plays. In New York, I'd done commercials, but this was the first time in my life I'd cashed a paycheck for a play. And Oscar Wilde, no less. I was incredibly proud.

Sophomore year, I'd moved out of the dorms to a rambling house on Waterman Street, five blocks east of campus, one of three student-run co-ops. There was a couch on the porch, a caricature of Nixon in one of the windows, and a king-size water bed with a sign-up sheet in the living room. My parents refused to set foot inside, proclaiming it "filthy," but I loved it. It had a measure of expressiveness and rebellion that I craved. In the basement, a mute computer science major slept, worked, and tended to large vats of sprouts, his sole source of nutrition. For the rest of us, jobs rotated and dinners were a festive event. That night, I was in charge of cooking a vegetarian casserole for twenty.

As I crossed the Green, a knapsack slung over one shoulder, my mind was racing. The coffee from the Blue Room hadn't helped. A paper due. Lines to learn. Cooking at the co-op that night. And the dark-haired French Canadian hockey player I'd met, who took art classes at RISD and spoke of training as if it were poetry. He slipped notes under my door that read like haiku. I, who had previously had zero interest in collegiate sports, now shivered in the stands of Meehan Auditorium and watched as he, outfitted like a gladiator, knocked equally well-padded men into the walls of the rink. Terrified and thrilled, I looked up at the bright banners and the fans cheering and the clean white ice below and thought, *this* is performance. On a cool night, when the embers were dying in his fireplace and there was no more wood to burn, he broke a table apart—wrenched the legs off, then the top, plank by plank—to please me, to keep the flames going. But the beginnings of love were distracting, and I kept forgetting things.

I couldn't find my bike for days, then realized I'd left it outside the Rock, the main library on campus. Hoping it would still be there, I walked quickly down the corridor between two of the buildings that bordered the Green. Light and noise began to fade. I kicked the heels of my new cowboy boots along the walkway, and the wine-colored gauze skirt I wore fluttered over the cement. When the path dipped down to the more shaded Quiet Green, I saw the Carrie Tower. Red-brick and granite, it reached high into the bright sky. I loved the tower, loved walking by it, and always went out of my way to do so. The four green-faced clocks, one on each side, were worn by weather. They no longer kept time; the bell had been removed. But the tower had a story. At its chipped base, above an iron door, the words LOVE IS STRONG AS DEATH were carved into the stone, a memorial to a woman from her Italian husband after her untimely passing almost a century before. I stopped for a moment and looked up. I wanted to be loved like that.

When I passed through the main gates onto Prospect Street, I spotted my bike, an old Peugeot that took me everywhere. Relieved, I bent over the wheel and tugged at the lock. Then I heard my name. A voice I knew. I looked up, squinted.

"Hey, stranger." Someone wearing white was smiling at me.

I raised the back of my hand to shade my eyes. The sun glinted off a railing.

"I was wondering when I'd run into you," he said.

John was sitting on the bottom set of steps outside the Rockefeller Library talking with a large, preppy blond guy. "Catch you later," the blond guy said when he saw me, and took off in the direction of George Street.

I sat down on the step next to him, tucking the filmy skirt under my knees. I was happy to see him. He was now in his sophomore year, one behind me. He leaned in to hug me. His shoulders were broader. Around his neck, a shark's tooth on a string.

"It's been a while," I said, and we began to try and place when we'd last seen each other—a Little Feat concert where he'd teased me mercilessly about the Harvard guy I was with, a party in New York, his performance in *Volpone* on the Faunce House Stage the previous spring.

What had I done over the summer, he wanted to know. I didn't mention the French Canadian. I told him about Ireland, the double rainbow in Donegal, the pubs in Dublin, and a castle I stumbled upon near Galway Bay that turned out to have belonged to my clan hundreds of years back. Before that, six weeks of summer theater at

Brown. His face lit up, and he wanted to know more. "That's cool. You seem into it," he said, adding that he wouldn't be doing any plays for a while. Something cryptic about needing to stay focused, as if the words of Shakespeare and Shaw were a sweet drug that he needed to pace himself around. He'd been in Ireland, too. Also Africa, and helping out on his uncle Teddy's presidential campaign. And Martha's Vineyard. "My mother's building a house there. You should come up sometime."

As we spoke, I searched his face. Something about him was different. In a summer, he had changed. Taller, more handsome; I couldn't put a finger on it. Maybe he was in love. Maybe it was the white garb. But he seemed at ease with himself in a way he hadn't before.

"I can't bear to be inside on a day like this." He exhaled deeply and cocked his head toward the library, a rectangle of cement and glass whose revolving doors whirred behind us. He leaned back, propping his elbows against a step, and stretched his legs. His linen pants were rumpled. I saw that he was wearing sandals, the woven kind, and that his feet were still brown.

"Where are you living?" I asked.

"Phi Psi. I pledged."

"Oh." I tried not to wrinkle my nose.

"And you?"

"Waterman Co-op."

"Huh. Tofu."

The first bell rang, and I moved toward my bike. The lock came off easily.

"I'll walk you," he said, following. "I've got time."

I crouched down and slipped the U-shaped metal bar neatly in its holder on the bottom bar of the bike. His feet. I've never seen them before, I thought, and threw my knapsack in the front basket. They were elegant, and that surprised me.

I steadied the bike, and we began to walk up the uneven street, past the Van Wickle Gates, past the Carrie Tower, to the rise at the top of Prospect and Waterman.

The second bell rang, and people began darting around us.

"Well, stranger, this is where I get off. Thanks for the chivalry."

"My pleasure," he said, and with that, he slid his foot between mine, tapping lightly against the inside edge of my boot. "Nice."

As I ran up the steps of the Am Civ building late for class, I felt a lightness and a bitter/sad tug deep in my chest. I may have chalked it up to the splendor of the day. If I'd been wiser, I would have guessed that I was a little in love with him even then. But I was twenty, and whatever I knew on that autumn-summer day was a secret to myself. And when a friend who had also known him in high school and noticed his metamorphosis from cute to Adonis later whispered, "God, he's gorgeous," I agreed. "Yes," I said, "but I wouldn't want to be his girlfriend." I had seen the way some women looked at him, sharp sideways glances my way simply because he was talking to me. I'd heard about the campus groupies. Besides, I was with the French Canadian, and I thought it would be forever.

How Brown's Food Changed My Life

DANA COWIN

The food served at Brown University in the late seventies and early eighties was not memorable. Pizza at the Gate. Falafel at the Ivy. Scrod at the Ratty. Because that food was so distinctly unremarkable, so broadly unappealing, I ate out frequently, energetically, and curiously for the first time ever.

I wasn't on the lookout for amazing meals; I was unconsciously hunting out exciting experiences. As the editor in chief of *Food & Wine*, that turned out to have been an important lesson. It's so easy for me to get caught up trying to identify the most original eighteen-course tasting menu in the world or obsessing over where my dinner grazed and died that I can lose sight of some of the reasons that people want to go out in the first place—to have fun, to be part of a scene, to feel included, to go on an adventure. I learned the value of all this when I was in college.

At Brown, I'd often start my day with breakfast at a diner. I'd head to Louis's on Brook Street for perfectly ordinary, somewhat greasy scrambled eggs and buttered toast. And I loved it! With heavy plates and paper napkins, it was such a real diner that it almost felt ersatz, like a movie set. There were students, professors, locals all around me ordering "the usual." My friend Barbara achieved that vaunted "regular" status and was rewarded by having her photo pinned on the wall.

Lessons: The atmosphere of a place can be more important than the food. And becoming an insider has its privileges!

After some classes, like new journalism with Roger Henkle or twentieth-century architecture with William Jordy, I'd drop into one of the student lounges, get a tea, and sink into a seat and watch the people slink past. I was also well trained in eavesdropping by my mother, who was a pro (often to the detriment of dinner table conversation), so I listened in, catching the drift of intense conversations. I went to the lounges where the people were way cooler than I was: Big Mother, the subterranean spot near the mailroom. Or the Blue Room. Or, my favorite, Carr House. Carr House was (and still is) on the RISD campus in an imposing Queen Anne–style building with two wonderful, bowed bay windows overlooking Waterman Street. My friend Bob described it as his Café de Flor, a place "to watch the artsy poseur world go by." Clearly my affection for this place had nothing to do with the tea. All the lounges essentially had the same tea bags, but they each had a different clique or culture. Though today I will often search out spots with ultrapremium artisanal ingredients (if it's tea it has to be the first flush picked by the nimblest fingers on the highest mountains to be interesting), it's important to remember, sometimes going to a restaurant is great just for the scene.

In search of lunch, I came across the unfamiliar world of the *really* big sandwich. Growing up, I had come to know the holy trinity of classic little paper-bag sandwiches—PB & J, tuna, and egg salad—but during college I was dazzled by the far more exotic possibilities of what could be put between two pieces of bread. And the sex appeal that could be brought to a dish simply by giving it a person's name. At Geoff's on Benefit Street, I had gigantic sandwiches named for politicians, actors, locals. Geoff's continues the tradition today. You can order a Judy Garland (roast beef and coleslaw) or a Groucho (hot corned beef, melted cheddar, Shedd's sauce, lettuce, and tomato) or the Will Rogers (hot kosher salami, melted Muenster). There's an unprecedented trend in high-quality, huge sandwiches today, and I guess Providence was thirty years ahead of the curve!

At Penguin's on Thayer Street, I discovered the hippie combo of sprouts and Muenster poked into a mustard-slathered pita, then microwaved to gooey perfection. Even now, on the odd winter night,

I still crave that salty, stretchy, chewy sandwich. For most people, food nostalgia is rooted in childhood. For me, it all started in college.

In the afternoon, if I didn't have classes, I'd set out for an adventure, with food as the final destination. My first discovery was Faria's Bakery on Wickenden Street. Inside the dimly lit, spare shop, they sold a couple of different kinds of Portuguese sweet bread with smooth, rounded tops. If cotton candy were a bread, it would be Faria's sweet breads. Light, sweet, delicious. I'd eat the loaf as I walked around the nearby vintage clothing and antiques shops, before getting back to my dorm room almost empty-handed. The bread came with a history lesson: I learned that the store thrived because of the large Portuguese population that had landed in Fox Point in the early twentieth century and had stayed on.

An even bigger adventure was going to the Italian enclave on Federal Hill. It wasn't the restaurants I fell in love with there (I'm not sure the pasta with red sauce was much better than that offered by the Ratty) but the poultry shop off Atwells Avenue called Antonelli's. You'd walk through the shop into a back room and choose a live bird, and they'd kill it on the spot, so you could bring it home still warm. Admittedly, this is something I never did, but it was a spectacle: it felt tinglingly exotic and foreign even though it was just twenty minutes from campus.

Going on food adventures is one of the most exciting things I do for my job, looking for trends or new talent. Now, though, it isn't always by foot. A couple of years ago, I flew to Copenhagen just to try the number one restaurant in the world, the fanatically naturalistic Noma. Or just this past winter, I went to India on a food safari. I ate in a palace restaurant that celebrated maharaja cuisine, but also took crazy rickshaw rides to street-food vendors—the most memorable of which was the fried chicken stall where the coated chicken was hacked with a machete and then tossed in a huge vat of boiling oil.

Dinner out during my Brown years was a big treat, sometimes requiring someone else's car and checkbook. Each semester my dry-witted, indulgent grandmother would send me a check with a simple note: "Please go get yourself a decent meal." I'd find a friend with a car and a big appetite and head to the Old Grist Mill Tavern in Seekonk, Massachusetts, for a juicy, medium-rare prime rib, queen's cut, a meal reminiscent of those I would have had with my grandmother back home. It was a primal experience at the Mill—a Paleolithic feast before the Paleolithic diet was born. Other dinners introduced me to entirely new foods that are now as common as the pizza slice was back then, such as the oysters at Blue Point and cheesy French onion soup at Rue de l'Espoir.

My eating experiences never went much past midnight. I was (and still am) an early-to-bed person. But I always had a huge amount of curiosity about late-night expeditions. The place I longed to go was the Silver Top Diner. I'd heard about the huge bran muffins, split, slathered with butter, then griddled. I wanted a taste of the muffin, sure, but what I really wanted was the experience of being there late, under the moon, near the shiny diner, with a group of friends, cool.

If I ever get too pretentious about food, I can look back to my time at Brown, the time before I became a judge on *Top Chef,* before I began eating out for a living, before I began choosing the best new chefs in the country, and remember that, at the end of the day, sometimes all you want from food is an amazing experience.

The Net

DAVID LEVITHAN

We were pioneers, but we had no idea what we were exploring. We were venturing into new territory, but we didn't realize how soon the entire topography would change.

There were fewer than seventy of us in Littlefield in 1991 when we were chosen to be a pilot dorm for what we didn't know to call the Internet. We were given special jacks to hook up to our Mac SEs. I doubt everyone installed them, so we're probably talking fifty people here at the most. The appeal—the way they hooked us in—was email.

We were given identity numbers; I think mine, drawn from the recesses of my memory, was something like ST101540. We were given rudimentary instructions to get to an even more rudimentary interface. It took a few minutes to dial up. It was called Ethernet.

Ethernet. In the beginning, emphasis was on the *ether*, because it was like the words would condense out of the air, the ever-instant telegraph delivered to the Apple screen. It was only later—much later—that we would start to feel the *net*.

Since we were the only ones with a connection in our rooms, the only people we could reach were . . . each other. We would spend the five minutes it took to log on and compose and send, just to contact someone two floors down to see if he was ready to go to dinner. And then we'd wait five minutes—at least—for the reply. It didn't matter that it would only take a minute to walk to his door or five seconds to call him on the phone. We preferred—instinctively, tellingly—the less vulnerable remove of sending typed-out words as our emissaries. Efficiency was secondary to novelty and avoidance.

Certainly there were other people on campus with email accounts, but they had to log on at a computer center. And maybe there was a computer science concentrator among us who knew the tricks of this trade, who understood that the connection we were establishing could lead to places beyond our dorm, beyond mail. But mostly, when we used it at all, we kept it within the closed circuit of our already close quarters.

It was the year I got my first CD player. (I was a late adopter.) It was the year a friend would come over every Thursday to watch *L.A. Law*, each of us talking about everything besides the fact that we might want to kiss boys more than we wanted to kiss girls. Whenever someone I didn't know was mentioned to me, I would pull out my well-worn copy of the facebook from last year, to see who they were. When the girl across the hall from me wanted to share her music, she left her door open. I was always forgetting to turn my answering machine on.

It did not occur to me, on any level, that things would change.

It was only the next year that things got serious. Because when we arrived at the dorms in the fall of 1992, everybody had access to email. Or at least everybody who had a computer that had a modem—a somewhat small percentage—had access to email. The transformation hadn't completely taken hold; I remember having one high school friend at Stanford who also had an email address and exchanging a few messages with him, but mostly my words remained postal when they left Brown. And for the most part, people still stopped by the doorway when it was time for dinner.

At the same time, though, we were acclimating. By the time the fall of 1993 hit, we were more and more used to being wired. There were still the haves and the have-nots—but as a result, the have-nots leaned on the haves. My SE didn't have a modem, so I relied on the kindness of my dormmates. (I was a dorm counselor, so I was relying on the kindness of my freshmen, for the most part.) It was almost old-school of us—we were like a dorm with only three or four pay phones, and lines would form to use them. Only they weren't pay phones, but computers in other people's rooms. In Perkins, I think the most gracious among us was a girl named Phil, who never seemed to begrudge our constant presence in her room, on her computer. If anything, the room became a social hub, as we would congregate to talk while we waited to use her modem-enabled device.

If 1991 showed us email's potential for communication, by 1993 we had a deep awareness of its capacity for drama. We became essayistic in our diatribes and perpetual in our expectation that there would be a reply waiting for us whenever we logged in. Life histories would be divulged not in a late-night, common-room, too-giddy-drunk-to-sleep conversation, but in long emails sent while sitting solo. There were not yet things to forward; there were not yet sites to link to. We were our own sole content providers, and more often than not, the content came from our more discontented emotions. Email became not only the place to ask someone if they wanted to go to dinner, but also the place to examine why dinner had gone so wrong.

We walked through the door before we knew what it led to. We thought we were rewiring our computers but we were really rewiring ourselves. When I was a kid, I thought the most mind-blowing science fiction concept in the world was a video phone. Now I have one in my pocket. And this first wiring—this first step into the Internet—was the hinge between the science fiction and the reality. More than anything else that happened to me in college, or happened to the world while I was at college, this was the biggest change. This was the generation-defining transition.

Soon all of the possibilities, good and bad, would come flooding in. In college, I never felt like I was broadcasting myself farther than the other side of the room. There were hours at a time when no one could find me. I wrote letters. Many, many letters. And at the same time, I remained oblivious to so much about myself, so much about the world. The only voices I heard were the ones immediately around me and the ones I found in books.

I think a lot about Littlefield when I think about what the connectivity of technology is doing to my life and my mind. I think about the fifty or so of us, dipping our toes into the tub that would turn out to be an ocean. There we were in the middle of campus, at the height of our youth, and when given the right tools, we would use our time to send brief messages to the people in the room next to ours, or down the hall, or two floors down. To someone my age or older, it's comical to think of the slow dial-up connections and the primitive screens and the way we would hang on every electronic word. To someone younger than me, what was once comical is now commonplace and instantaneous. I have to imagine that the residents of Littlefield now spend a lot more time on their devices, communicating with each other. It's just a question of what else has fallen away, what we knew that they no longer know.

When I think about college, I picture myself walking to class from Pembroke, cutting through parking lots to get to the Green. I have my headphones on—my black, fuzzy headphones, plugged into my Walkman, playing 10,000 Maniacs, or REM, or Suzanne Vega. I am in my own world, but every now and then I step out of it as I bump into friends. To find out what's going on with them, I have to talk to them. And when I'm done talking to them, I can return to my own world.

I have to imagine it's different now.

Love is a long, close scrutiny

DAVID SHIELDS

From the sound of things, the girl who lived next door to me my sophomore year of college was having problems with her boyfriend. One night Rebecca invited me into her room to share a joint and told me she kept a journal, which one day she hoped to turn into a novel. I said Kafka believed that writing in a journal prevented reality from being turned into fiction, but as she pointed out, Kafka did nothing if not write in a journal. I liked the way she threw her head back when she laughed.

The next day I knocked on her door to ask her to join me for lunch. Her door was unlocked; she assumed no one would break into her room, and in any case the door to the dormitory was always locked. Rebecca wasn't in and neither was her roommate, who had all but moved into her boyfriend's apartment off campus. Rebecca's classes weren't over until late afternoon, I remembered, and I walked in and looked at her clothes and books and notebooks. Sitting down at her desk, I opened the bottom right drawer and came across a photo album, which I paged through only briefly, because underneath the album was a stack of Rebecca's journals. The one on top seemed pretty current and I started reading: the previous summer, she'd missed Gordon terribly and let herself be used on lonely nights by a Chapel Hill boy whom she had always fantasized about and who stroked her hair in the moonlight and wiped himself off with leaves. When Rebecca returned to Providence in the fall, she knew she wanted romance, and after weeks of fights that went all night and into the morning, she told Gordon she didn't want to see him anymore.

Me, on the other hand, she wanted to see every waking moment of the day and night. As a stutterer, I was even more ferociously dedicated to literature (the glory of language that was beautiful and written) than other English majors at Brown were, and I could turn up the lit-crit rhetoric pretty damn high. She loved the way I talked (my stutter was endearing); her favorite thing in the world was to listen to me rhapsodize about John Donne. She often played scratchy records on her little turntable (this was 1975), and when I said, "The *Jupiter Symphony* might be the happiest moment in human history," her heart skipped a beat. Toward my body she was ambivalent: she was simultaneously attracted and repelled by my strength. She was afraid I might crush her. These are near-verbatim quotes.

I finished reading the journal and put it away, then went back to my room and waited for Rebecca to return from her classes. That night we drove out to Newport, where we walked barefoot in the clammy sand and looked up at the lighted mansions that lined the shore in the distance. "The rich, too, must go to sleep at night," I said, offering Solomonic wisdom. We stood atop a ragged rock that sat on the shoreline; the full tide splashed at our feet. The moon made halos of our heads. I put my hands through her hair and kissed her lightly on the lips. "Don't kiss hard," she said. "I'm afraid I'll fall."

Tuesday and Thursday afternoons—when she worked in the development office—I'd go into her room, shut the door, lock it, and sit back in the swivel chair at her desk. She always left a window open. The late fall wind would be blowing the curtains around, and the *Jupiter Symphony* would always be on the little red record player on the floor. She often left wet shirts hanging all over the room; they'd ripple eerily in the wind. On the wall were a few calligraphic renderings of her own poetry. Her desk was always a mess, but her journal—a thick, black book—was never very difficult to find.

I was nineteen years old and a virgin, and at first I read Rebecca's journal because I needed to know what to do next and what she liked to hear. Every little gesture, every minor movement I made she passionately described and wholeheartedly admired. When we were kissing or swimming or walking down the street, I could hardly wait to rush back to her room to find out what phrase or what twist of my body had been lauded in her journal. I loved her impatient handwriting, her purple ink, the melodrama of the whole thing. It was such a surprising and addictive respite, seeing every aspect of my being celebrated by someone else rather than excoriated by myself. She wrote, "I've never truly loved anyone the way I love D. and it's never been so total and complete, yet so unpossessing and pure, and sometimes I want to drink him in like golden water." *You* try to concentrate on your Milton midterm after reading that about yourself.

Sometimes, wearing her bathrobe, she'd knock on my door in order to return a book or get my reaction to a paragraph she'd written or read. She'd wish me good night, turn away, and begin walking back to her room. I'd call to her, and we'd embrace—first in the hallway outside our doors, then soon enough in my room, her room, on our beds. I hadn't kissed anyone since I was twelve (horrific acne throughout high school), so I tried to make up for lost time by swallowing Rebecca alive: biting her lips until they bled, licking her face, chewing on her ears, holding her up in the air and squeezing her until she screamed.

In her journal, she wrote that she'd never been kissed like this in her life and that she inevitably had trouble going to sleep after seeing me. I'd yank the belt to her bathrobe and urge her under the covers, but she refused. She actually said she was afraid she'd go blind when I entered her. Where did she learn these lines, anyway?

Shortly before the weather turned permanently cold, we went hiking in the mountains. The first night, she put her backpack at the foot of her sleeping bag—we kissed softly for a few minutes, then she fell asleep—but on the second night she put her backpack under her head as a pillow. Staring into the blankly black sky, I dug my fingers into the dirt behind Rebecca's head and, the first time and the second time and the third time and the fourth time and probably the fourteenth time, came nearly immediately.

From then on, I couldn't bring myself to read what she'd written. I'd read the results of a survey in which 40 percent of Italian women acknowledged that they usually faked orgasms. Rebecca wasn't Italian—she was that interesting anomaly, a Southern Jew—but she thrashed around a lot and moaned and screamed, and if she was pretending I didn't want to know about it. She often said it had never been like this before.

Every night she'd wrap her legs around me and scream something that I thought was German until I realized she was saying, "Oh, my son." *My son?* She had her own issues, too, I suppose. We turned up the *Jupiter Symphony* all the way and attempted to pace ourselves so we'd correspond to the crashing crescendo. I was sitting on top of her and in her mouth, staring at her blue wall, and I thought, *My whole body is turning electric blue.* She was on top of me, rotating her hips and crying, and she said, "Stop." I said, "Stop?" and stopped. She grabbed the back of my hair and said, "Stop? Are you kidding? Don't stop."

At the end of the semester, packing to fly home to San Francisco to spend the Christmas vacation with my family, I suddenly started to feel guilty about having read Rebecca's journal. Every time I kissed her, I closed my eyes and saw myself sitting at her desk, turning pages. I regretted having done it and yet I couldn't tell her about it.

"What's wrong?" she asked.

"I'll miss you," I said. "I don't want to leave."

On the plane I wrote her a long letter in which I told her everything I couldn't bring myself to tell her in person: I'd read her journal; I was very sorry; I thought our love was still pure and we could still be together, but I'd understand if she went back to Gordon and never spoke to me again.

She wrote back that I should never have depended on her journal to give me strength, she'd throw it away and never write in it again, and she wanted to absolve me, but she wasn't God, although she loved me better than God could. Anything I said she would believe because she knew I'd never lie to her again. Our love, in her view, transcended time and place.

Well, sad to say, it didn't. The night I returned from San Francisco, she left a note on my door that said only, "Come to me," and we tried to imitate the wild abandon of the fall semester, but what a couple of weeks before had been utterly instinctive was now excruciatingly self-conscious, and the relationship quickly cooled. She even went back to Gordon for a while, though that second act didn't last very long, either.

It was, I see now, exceedingly odd behavior on my part. After ruining things for myself by reading her journal, I made sure I ruined things for both of us by telling her that I had read her journal. Why couldn't I just live with the knowledge and let the shame dissipate over time? What was—what is—the matter with me? Do I just have a bigger self-destruct button, and like to push it harder and more incessantly, than everyone else? Perhaps, but also the language of the events was at least as erotic to me as the events themselves, and when I was no longer reading her words, I was no longer very adamantly in love with Rebecca. This is what is known as a tragic flaw.

ACADEMIC LIFE

As much as we sometimes roll our eyes at the ivory-tower isolation of universities, they continue to serve as remarkable engines of innovation.

—**Steven Johnson** ('90)

The semiotics program articulated instincts I already had, that film was not some unencumbered mode of expression, but has a direct relationship to social ideas and meanings and institutions.

—**Todd Haynes** ('85)

No matter what I study, I can see patterns. I see the gestalt, the melody within the notes, in everything: mathematics and science, art and music, psychology and sociology. . . . As glorious as these patterns are, they also whet my appetite for more. There are other patterns waiting to be discovered . . . I want to find them, and comprehend them. I want this more than anything I've ever wanted before.

—Leon in *Understand* by **Ted Chiang** ('89)

Higher Learning

MARILYNNE ROBINSON

I was not very good at youth, as that word is generally understood. I came to college rather grudgingly aware that I might encounter high-spirited pranks and bonhomie, that I would witness the formation of lifelong friendships, and stand at the margins, at least, of moments that would stir nostalgia for decades to come. No doubt these things did go on around me. I found shelter from them all in the cocoon of mild anxiety better called my studies.

Two things are true simultaneously—that my years at Brown provided me with a core of learning and a model for thought that have been endlessly fruitful for me, and that those years seemed at the time to have been an unbroken trance of undifferentiated receptivity. To pass is better than to fail: therefore the requirements of a course are to be satisfied. This may not sound especially lofty or aspiring, but it reflected in part a great trust in the institution, in Brown itself. I thought its expectations must be wise and worthy. In retrospect, it seems to me that my youthful credulity on this point was itself a kind of wisdom. It has taken years for my education to fall into place, for me to realize what part of it is still full of value and suggestion and what part is to be criticized and rejected. The interior conversations that have come from this need to appraise have also had great value for me.

The winnowing really began when I was an undergraduate, obliged by my American philosophy professor to read, of all things, Jonathan Edwards's essay "The Great Christian Doctrine of Original Sin Defended." As it happened, I was then and had been for some time silently and deeply morose on account of the determinism I was absorbing in my psychology class. In those days, still early in what was called the paperback revolution, a nineteenth-century edition of Edwards's works was on reserve for the course in the John Hay Library. I went off dutifully to what I expected to be a truly crepuscular reading experience. I found, in a long footnote on moonlight, a conception of being that implied a free play of possibility. For Edwards the freedom is God's altogether, of course. But to find this leavening of being with what in effect is indeterminacy was an immediate and memorable relief. It was no doubt very young of me to stagger under the burden of one idea and to feel truly rescued by another, but it was a lesson in the importance of ideas that I have never forgotten. It was also a lesson in the potency of metaphor and in the endless contemporaneity of good thought.

My brother David was a senior at Brown during my first year. He was writing an honors thesis with weighty philosophic themes, and he and I walked and walked through the Providence rain and the Providence snow while he thought through his thesis out loud. I had no way in the world to understand anything about its content, but I certainly admired its scale. I had applied to Brown because my brother liked it there. He had been bookish from childhood, and he led me along from a very early age into what might be called the life of the mind. If I had any aspiration, it was to be as smart as he was. I can explain my own course of life in terms of his influence. He, however, eludes explanation. Be that as it may, there he was to continue my initiation into the high seriousness of the world of ideas. Again, it was all very young, quite naïve. On my part, it was another feat of indiscriminate receptivity. But it evoked a very grand cosmos for me to furnish and populate at my leisure.

David had decided years before that I should be a poet. I put some effort into living up to his hopes, then recognized, thank goodness, that my poetry was thoroughly mediocre. My attempts at fiction were also mediocre, and I might have been stalemated altogether if my freshman roommate had not told me that I somehow managed to consider myself a writer though I lacked the courage even to take John Hawkes's fiction workshop. This was true, I did lack the courage, and if she had put the matter another way I might have excused myself from this experience. She was quite right to point out that I would have to justify my claims or else drop them. She was clearly prepared to consider me ridiculous otherwise. So I signed up for the workshop, which is among the best decisions I have ever made, even if the decision was not quite mine. John Hawkes was a wonderful teacher, contemptuous of chaff and deeply pleased by anything he found in the way of wheat. He directed me firmly toward what was best in my own writing. I have tried over the years to do as much for my students. Questions are mooted often about the effectiveness of writing workshops, which I have taught for many years. No doubt they vary in their usefulness, but I can certainly testify to the importance to me of the criticism and encouragement I received from him.

The moral of my life is that there is no way of anticipating the importance any learning might assume. The same philosophy course that brought me to Jonathan Edwards also introduced me, passingly, to Charles Sanders Peirce. On the basis of this very slight acquaintance I found myself sitting on the bank of the Iowa River reading his *Monist* essays while I was writing my novel *Gilead*. I had not thought about Peirce in decades, but I remembered a quality in his voice that seemed to me to refine the voice of my narrator, John Ames. Brown did well by me in giving me this resource to exploit under circumstances that were, at the time I received it, hardly to be imagined. I would never have thought I could be taking away from the usual small emergencies of assignments, papers, and exams a particular affable and gentlemanly voice—not Josiah Royce, not William James, but exactly C. S. Peirce.

This is a rather odd instance of an ongoing phenomenon, the emergence of some seemingly forgotten detail of my education that becomes a nucleus of associations, precipitating other thinking. I am persuaded that the institutions of learning arose out of profound intuitions about the nature of the mind, specifically that the mind creates relevance out of whatever stores of learning are available to it, if they are generous and of good quality. There is, or was, a particular romance in the encounter between the young and the venerable. For a long time the colleges all seemed to try to look older than they were, Gothic, if possible. Their bell towers and gates and quadrangles were the monuments of unaging intellect, even though these enclaves were meant to be the country of the young par excellence. That they were indeed for the young seems to me to have been truer when they were slightly anomalous survivals of Renaissance civilization than now, when they are coerced into responding to the hypothetical or momentary demands of our seismic global economy.

More to the point, the generations that created them seem to have understood how powerfully an idea can live in a young mind, a perfect analogy being the special intensity with which such a mind might encounter a poem or a novel. I have come more and more to realize that the trust I placed in Brown was very graciously answered by the trust Brown placed in me. Learn so that you may continue learning, think until you are at home with thought.

Syllabus (Annotated)

RICK MOODY

The following motifs may be used as a syllabus for any such course offering as may be useful, or may be considered a record of classes past,[1] or these motifs may serve as topics of conversation to be held with tax collectors or persons embarked on reconnaissance of haunted locations, or as conversation starters for shy persons required to give public lectures. Additionally, instructors into the arcane arts of mummery[2] may apply here, only to retreat for further divinations into *a cave.*

Week One: Enmity of Bear and Ant[3]

Per the course description, during the first week of class, students will memorize constitutive literatures of cultures past, such as those of the

---

[1] Adapted from an encomium I wrote on the occasion of Robert Coover's retirement from Brown University, this piece is probably more precisely a recollection of *all* my classes in the creative writing program there, between 1979 and 1983.

[2] With *mummery,* I allude to Coover's great novel *Gerald's Party,* among my very favorite works by him. *Gerald's Party* has lots to say about the relationship between theater and literature.

[3] When I took Coover's class "Exemplary Ancient Fictions," in 1982, we read from Stith Thompson's *Motif-Index of Folk-Literature,* and all the titles of the various weeks in this piece are appropriated from Thompson.

Khazars, the Hottentots, the Anasazi. Students will wear bear pelts. The design specifications of pelts will be left to individual choice—this is a course of higher learning, not a babysitting agency! There are many things to say about *Ursidae*, besides simply dwelling upon the traditional enmity between these animals and ants. The tendency of bears to write upon the carcasses of their prey, the tendency of bears to be quarrelsome about phases of the moon, the tendency of bears to find other bears irritating, the tendency of bears to be humorous in an obscene way, even when to do so will be embarrassing and damaging to reputation. The instructor's job is to efface the role of the instructor, to eliminate his role in the classroom dynamic; fighting among bear-pelted cubs in the classroom setting is encouraged, even rewarded.[4]

Week Two: Creature Changes Size at Will

Add to the following catalog: She had a female body . . . like an act of desperation. She had a female body . . . like the translation of a Russian novel. She had a female body . . . like the Sargasso Sea. She had a female body . . . like Icelandic volcanic eruption. She had a female body . . . like an egregious grammatical error. She had a female body . . .

---

[4] The undergraduate creative writers were somewhat competitive. It made the classes go. One of my classes with John Hawkes, who had a very significant impact on me, also contained Jeffrey Eugenides, Cary Twichell, and Melora Wolff, all of whom were working at a very high level. The competition to produce more original writing, better work, was probably good for all of us. But it made the classes very demanding.

Week Three: Devil Plays Fiddle at Wedding[5]

Since I was unable to procure the incendiary materials I wanted to use this week from the *anarchist bookstore,*[6] owing to the fact that I was badly injured there when my pyrotechnical device was detonated by the triggering mechanism of *another* anarchist, a rather wealthy girl from a yachting family down the coast, we will have a makeup assignment. My fellow anarchist had been to hear some Portuguese music, she told me, in particular, the form called *fado,*[7] mostly about lovers dying unfortunate deaths while narrators pine ceaselessly. Also present at the venue was a certain wedding party. The wedding party was intoxicated and rowdy and baiting the newlyweds into displays of amorous behavior, even erogenous display, and this young anarchist watched with horror as a certain accompanist of the *fado* singer, the musician playing the congas, was, while observing the proceedings, *transformed into a peccary.* What, the young woman wanted to know, as we stood chatting amiably on the step of the anarchist bookstore, were the internal conditions inhering in the life of a conga player that would make it not only possible but *likely* that he would suddenly be transformed into a peccary?[8] Was his character, at that moment, like the alleged character of the peccary? Was he aggressive

---

[5] This version of "Syllabus" is heavily redacted (see below) in order to justify the liberal inclusion of footnotes in the text. There are entire weeks from the semester missing.

[6] Can't remember the name of that indie bookstore on the East Side that people used for the arty courses—instead of the Brown Bookstore. But I sure loved it in there. Some bookstores *smell* like books, and that is a powerful and evocative smell. E-books do not have the same quality.

[7] Robert Coover once threw a dinner for hundreds at a restaurant in Fox Point that specialized in *fado.* The food was really slow, but the music was fabulous.

[8] By which I mean: how do we interpret Ovid? A question we asked in Bob Coover's "Exemplary Ancient Fictions."

when cornered, homely, truculent? *Funny you should ask*, said I. And then the deafening crash as the window of the bookstore was reduced to shards, the stock of hardcovers and paperbacks incinerated, passersby thrown from their feet. What I ought to have said was: *Is this a trick question?*

Week Five: Heroes Dislike to Kill Sleeping Persons

A sleeping preparation has been administered. After last week's quiz, some of you came to office hours complaining about your grades.[9] I've never heard such a collection of whiners in all my years. I had just closed the door in order to have some few moments to myself, whereupon this malcontent burst through the door waving around a small-caliber handgun. The muzzle was short, and I instantly surmised that there would scarcely be audible report or muzzle flare. In short, it was a weapon made specifically for *knocking off a professor* who had perhaps given a pop quiz on the subject of the conquest of Troy. I did manage to distract this kid by droning on about a certain Persian kingdom, and the soothing qualities of my voice rendered him inert enough, in due course, for a *struggle to ensue*. I prevailed, made a timely citizen's arrest, and upon causing the student to be incarcerated, I went to the pharmacy to procure, in bulk, a sleeping potion.

---

[9] I was always sort of terrified of office hours. But Angela Carter insisted that all students come to her office once or twice a semester. She would then suggest reading, among other things. Once I happened by Bob Coover's office while he was there, even though it wasn't a day for office hours, and I remember overhearing him say, firmly, into a phone: "No more magazine articles!" I think of this moment a lot these days.

Week Seven: Dwarf Turns Gold into Lead[10]

Commonly, the dwarf turns the *lead* into the *gold*, not vice versa, and that is where the power in this week's assignment comes from. The power comes from the inert qualities of lead, and from the refusal of the dwarf to behave as dwarves commonly do. In the traditional stories, the dwarf battles giants, or magically keeps ghosts from rising, or the dwarf is a cannibal, or appears in the form of vermin, or serves as a midwife, or the dwarf pastes animals' eyes shut and pretends that hunters are at hand. There are a lot of dwarf stories, it's true,[11] but this is a completely different sort of dwarf story. Your assignment is to seek out stories with dwarves in them, and to find a way to repurpose these dwarves, by adding other elements, a faun, for example, or some poisonous flowers, or a magic net, or a seafaring marauder who kills and eats young girls. A couple of small children lost in the forest leaving a trail of bread crumbs could instead become a blind penitent whose fortunes are changed once and for all by a dwarf. With gold ingots.

---

[10] In "Exemplary Ancient Fictions," our assignment, one week, was to take the aforementioned Stith Thompson's *Motif-Index*, find a few beguiling entries, and then make stories out of them. This one is incredibly tempting, because of its reverse-alchemical shape. Often the rules of a form get their value from those who fail to respect them.

[11] Obviously, there are a lot of dwarves in folk literature, but the question would be: why was a writing program self-evidently indebted to what was most modern at the time, or even most "postmodern," so interested in old forms? Hawkes was known to say in class that "what was most old was most new," and this is exactly the kind of utterance he favored: the paradoxical utterance, at least in my understanding of him. So dwarves, because they were important in fairy tales, to describe that time, that instant of the "modern" and "postmodern."

Week Eight: Man Threatens to Cleave Bear's Skull with Penis

The theory of V. Hornblower concerning the nature of entertainment is: all things entertaining derive amusement from proximity to the penis. You will find a variety of writings by Hornblower on reserve. The reserve room is next to the room displaying a treasury of decorative daggers.

Week Ten: Repartee Between Shoemaker and Ruling Lord

The heroes are twins,[12] as in all the best hero narratives, twin wolves suckling at their mother, separated after a dark prophecy about their potential to rule. This is all written down in a heroic narrative transmitted to a benevolent priest in the seventeenth century. This priest is lucky enough to have a few words in the native dialect, noteworthy for the abundant use of the letter *X.* The priest inscribes a manuscript in this dialect, dictating, translating, expending his poor eyesight and many thousands of candles in the process. The manuscript is in Spanish, it is in English, and it is in the local dialect with the *X*s. Just like the Rosetta stone. He puts the manuscript in a neglected cave near his priestly dwelling, just before he is set upon by bandits. His head is mounted on a pike. Let this be a lesson to you, etc. After the priest is murdered, the rain forest falls into the hands of indigenous tribes, and those panning for gold give the rain forest a wide berth. And yet, in the nineteenth century, a pair of British adventurers of the intrepid sort, armed with machetes and a battalion of yage-chewing mercenaries,[13] venture in. Many die of Chagas' disease,

---

[12] See, e.g., the *Popol Vuh,* which I read first in Coover's class.

[13] Angela Carter, during her time at Brown, gave me a list of things to read (scrawled in her beautifully ornate hand, on a scrap of notebook paper) and it said: *"Our Lady of Flowers, The Wild Boys, Naked Lunch."* I knew nothing of William S. Burroughs, author of the latter two, and I was astounded by his work. WSB, of course, was afflicted with the legend of yage.

leprosy, malaria, and dengue fever. And yet the British explorers will not give up, ever pressing on, if only for the crown, until at last they find themselves in the deepest part of the forest, with only the one last canteen. *Alone.*

These explorers are then surrounded by a crew of highly decorated cannibals, many wearing those little earlobe-stretching decorations that would make them unsuitable for any public relations position. A long and unsettling dialogue takes place between the cannibals and the explorers. Gesturing is the common vocabulary. The explorers realize the terrifying bargain that is now theirs to contemplate. Either they can join the cannibals, who that very night intend to ambush a nearby tribe, from whom they will select and eat a few enemies. Or the explorers can themselves be served as the meal. *The outcome is this*: one of the explorers stays, joins the band of indigenous brigands, and is never again heard from. The other escapes. And in the midst of his escape, the second adventurer stumbles into a certain cave, and in this cave is: *a manuscript.*

Week Twelve: Love Cured by Bath in Beloved's Blood

Compile a list of rules of contemporary romance[14] using primeval source material, e.g., 1) if a lover is not to be wooed, call in favors from elves; 2) do not love a giant, there will never be *compatibility*; 3) if your lover dies and you are unfaithful to her memory, she will come back from the grave; 4) it is fine to ask if you can kill your lover's parents; 5) before marrying a woman first see if you are able to lift her; 6) it is only prudent to trick a poet into writing your love letters;

---

[14] This list is a parody of a list of requirements for courtly love by Andreas Capellanus, author of *De amore*. The list, from the Coover syllabus, had such an impact on me (I thought it was so funny) that I wrote a song for the band I had at Brown in those days, "The Thirty-Nine Rules of Courtly Love." The song contained no suggestions about love at all.

7) elopements should always involve a forest and military engagement; 8) if you have seven lovers, see one each day of the week; 9) if your lover has no sense of touch, conduct assignations *symbolically*; 10) heroes often win the most attractive lovers but also perish first; 11) a fine aphrodisiac can be made from what is found in a lover's ear; 12) love is best explained by parable.

Week Fourteen: Priest's Concubine Cannot Rest in Grave

My hours are few, my time is nigh, my body has been much extended beyond its natural span. Now that my fingers are no longer able to use a quill, I have purchased a digital software program which allows me to pronounce magic spells in a voice-to-text interface. Among my spells is this one: I have turned you all into proper scholars. A scholar is a necromancer. The life of scholarship is exceedingly lonely. What matters are things that have lasted for a thousand years. Or more. The language can only be preserved in your *mouths*,[15] pronounce the

---

[15] In the end, the legacy of American experimental writing, which was what I believe I learned at Brown, is more about *the language* than it is about anything else. Or this was John Hawkes's position. I remember, in my last semester there, having a discussion with him about computers. A vanguard of students in those days were writing their papers at the computer lab, alleging that this made composition easier or more convenient somehow. Hawkes wanted to know, however, what the effect of this would be on language. He would have been shocked to see the results, to see the language crammed into the 140 characters of a Twitter post or into the status updates of Facebook. Robert Coover, on the other hand, has restlessly looked for the new in technological interfaces, and with a zeal that I find charming and persuasive. But in each case these writers were mainly interested in the words on the page. I understand my own job as a reflection of their tutelage. It's not about the theme of the work—all of the themes have been dealt with—it's not so much about the story, it's about the language deployed to do the job. I hope one day I can live up to this lesson, the lesson that I was lucky enough to get at Brown.

language, use divinations with the language, trample the language, call the language by name, deform the language, make sacrifices on behalf of the language, fashion an altar to the language, make the language profane, make the language sublime, make the language laughable, make the language deadly serious, hand the language out at a party, tear the undergarments off the language, where the language is concerned, employ *frottage*, cause the language to take to its bed, refuse to pity the language or pander to it, force the language outside and smack it around, give the language multiple orgasms, spirit the language away to an undisclosed location, go joyriding with the language, buy sled dogs with the language, get an artificial tan with the language, visit the language in prison, have a language uprising, depose a dictator with the language, write a prayer in the language, curse enthusiastically with the language, teach the language to a child.[16]

---

[16] And this is the last line, of course, because I had a two-year-old at home at the time I wrote the first draft. Who was just getting a grip on the language happening around her. And now she's four and every day asking me, again, to read to her about . . . Medusa.

My Own Core Curriculum

MARIE MYUNG-OK LEE

My parents warned me this would happen. I arrived at Brown in medias res, after spending two years at a college they had picked for me, and here I was, on an unfamiliar campus, friendless, clueless, confused, and filled with a shifting ratio of hope and terror. I was not supposed to be here.

A dutiful, tiger-parented child of Korean immigrants, I had never openly gone against their wishes and advice before. Despite my itchy unhappiness, my parents had advised me to stay at my current college and merely study harder. Rupturing a college experience, much less a transcript, is never a good idea. Also, why leave a perfectly good (i.e., prestigious) college? Some backstory: In order to give their children a better life, my parents immigrated to the US from Korea as war refugees, leaving behind family, and for my mother, her own college education that had been interrupted by the war. In return, my parents—reasonably, they thought—expected their American-born children, with much easier lives, to strive for conventional, secure careers. I was supposed to follow my father's footsteps into medicine.

Instead, I'd begun to realize medicine wasn't the right field for me. I actually already knew what I wanted to be: a writer. I'd written my first "novel" when I was nine and had an essay titled "Volunteer Work Does Pay Off!" published in *Seventeen* when I was sixteen. My parents, however, forbade writing as a career ("Too unstable!"). It became such a point of tension that the only solution in our confrontation-avoidant household was to ignore it.

There were no creative writing courses at my previous college, so I'd sought out the college literary journal, whose editor was excited and impressed that I'd already had something published. I agreed to submit, and departed from the perkiness of my *Seventeen* essay to write a much more emotionally risky piece describing my experience with racism growing up in a small, "Minnesota-nice" town. I never heard back from the editor, who did not return my calls and avoided me on campus. I can only presume the piece was met with quiet horror and quickly killed, in the way most things happened at my Seven Sisters school: with a clenched-teeth smile overlying an abject fear of things that were "not nice" or "vulgar"—and racism was both.

I informed my parents of my plans after I'd been admitted to Brown as a junior transfer student. Normally, they did not miss any opportunity to visit the schools my siblings and I attended; for my Seven Sisters school drop-off, they had taken a hotel room and spent five whole days there. For my entry to Brown, they stayed home and I drove my tiny Dodge Colt north from New York City, where I had been doing an internship.

Here I was, in nirvana, a university that had a creative writing *department*. Nevertheless, I was immediately, unceremoniously rejected by the competitive intermediate fiction writing workshop. At the very last minute, a professor, Meredith Steinbach (to whom I'll always be grateful), somehow having seen my sample, admitted me.

"Intermediate Fiction" was for serious writers; one classmate would later attend the prestigious Iowa Writers' Workshop. I, however, found myself strangely unenthusiastic to be living my dream; in my rush to write "big" and "universal" stories, I mostly aped my favorite writer, Flannery O'Connor, even though I wasn't a Southern Catholic white lady. While praised for their technical proficiency, my stories were blaring mediocrities, boring to read, and—I didn't want to admit to myself—boring to write, too.

Having already shattered my self-image as a broody Creative Writing (now Literary Arts) concentrator, I turned to writing for the *Brown Daily Herald*. My first story was an interview with Sasha Frere-

Jones, a first-year whose great-grandfather had written *King Kong*. The next, a piece about other published writers on campus. I didn't show much talent for journalism, either; the editors complained that I wrote too slowly, turned in items that were much too long, and always, always buried the lede. At the end of the day, this wasn't what I wanted to do, either.

Around this time, I came up with a new concentration: economics. My parents were unhappy with my fleeing the premed program, but they felt economics was an acceptable substitute—all signs pointed to a lucrative career in finance, perhaps with Harvard Business School as a future stepping stone. I had developed an interest in developmental economics, but another facet of my decision was the relatively low number of classes the econ concentration required. Beyond that, I had no grand plan.

All my life I'd reflexively excelled, or at least striven for extreme competence in anything I tried. Show me a structure and I'd work within it with utmost discipline and effort. I could easily have forced myself through premed or, say, an English major (professor being deemed another acceptable profession), but my odd, jerry-rigged academic experience, sorely lacking in specifics on how this was going to help me become a writer, was weirdly pleasing to me, perhaps because my life up until this point had been severely regimented. The range of available courses was intoxicating. Reading the course catalog was like opening a novel written in a strange new dialect: religious studies, Shakespeare, bio, Russian literature in translation, intellectual history, American civilization, economic history, semiotics. There was Engine 9, which wasn't really an engineering course, and one, I remember, named "Rock and Roll Will Never Die."

My friend Phi, who was a history concentrator, alerted me that the US history survey, History 52, was going to be taught by the eminent scholar Bill McLoughlin, who rarely taught these large lecture classes. Even though I didn't have any particular interest in history, I signed up. I was surprised and delighted to find that the class was taught using novels: *The Jungle*, *Babbitt*, *The Damnation of Theron Ware*, *The*

Man in the Gray Flannel Suit, The Milagro Beanfield War. Professor McLoughlin's lectures started at Reconstruction and went through the Gay Nineties, the Gilded Age, the Depression, World Wars I and II, and McCarthyism, and ended at the Nixon administration. I can't say exactly what constituted the alchemy of combining novels and history, but some kind of nuclear fusion occurred in my brain. When we covered anti-immigration sentiment in the 1920s and arrived at the racial unrest of the sixties, I knew I wanted to write about the ethnic and racial aspects of those moments in history.

The teaching assistant who taught my section noticed how hard I was working and correspondingly wrote me pages and pages of detailed critiques. I'd had no previous experience with historical analysis, but I was understanding that I could mine the vein of my personal experiences. Ideas from that essay about racism in my hometown that I'd written at my previous college could be thrown into a larger, historical context, and eventually achieve a lock-and-key melding of historical analysis with original writing. Similarly, reading these excellent novels helped me to understand how these writers had assimilated social issues into their work.

My final paper, an exploration of the changing tides of anti-immigrant sentiment and racial unrest in the twentieth century, was easily one of my proudest collegiate achievements. For a moment, I considered switching my concentration to history. But I understood that I didn't actually have the passion and aptitude that the concentration would require; instead, this class would somehow be important as a kind of undergirding, a bedrock of knowledge that I would work from in the future. Subsequent courses included a religious studies class that explored Christian themes in the work of authors such as my beloved Flannery O'Connor and Walker Percy. Classes in economic history and developmental economics let me follow an offbeat interest in capitalism. Basically, I was creating my own core curriculum for becoming a writer.

When I graduated, I had a manuscript: *Economic Development and Women's Labor Force Participation*, i.e., my honors thesis. Not what I'd expected when I'd first transferred to Brown, but in retrospect it was absolutely right. This background gave me the credentials to land a job on Wall Street, doing the kind of economic analysis I'd worked with for my thesis, but this, in turn, financed my writing *and* made my parents happy. Eventually, I'd publish enough to leave my day job. And the coup de grace? I eventually returned to Brown to teach writing.

This last election season, I was even called upon to do some political writing for *Salon*, and I wrote a *New York Times* op-ed, "My Asian Dad and Mitt Romney's Muffin Tops," a satire not at all out of step with *Babbitt*. For my fiction, my vestigial interest in medicine has been transformed into a novel about a doctor struggling to fit his practice within the capitalistic confines of consumer-based medicine. At one point, I even wore a white coat and was embedded with the Brown medical students on their ob-gyn rotation. I have an abiding regret that my father is no longer alive to see that I did, in my own way, finally make it to medical school. The novel has demanded years of immersing myself in subjects traversing literature, nanotechnology, biomedicine, history, and finance. This very much includes my economics study as well as being literarily indebted to a little-known Sinclair Lewis novel about medical education, *Arrowsmith*, that I probably would not have discovered if I hadn't encountered *Babbitt* in History 52.

I tracked down three additional alums who'd been in that singular class, and even though it was more than twenty years ago, they all remember that course we took in the spring of 1985—and have lively memories of the novels, the outstanding TAs, and how, on the first day, the dignified professor grabbed our attention by blasting Bruce Springsteen's "Born in the USA." He then asked us to take a moment to think about what the experience of being born in America meant to us personally and in the larger context of history.

Currently on leave from Brown, I am teaching at an institution that has a rigid core curriculum. I can appreciate the benefits of a shared body of knowledge, a personal intellectual toolkit, and many students desire and need that structure. But it also puts my Brown experience in context; my four History 52 classmates (an English professor, a lawyer for the Inter-American Foundation, the director of leadership programs in continuing education at Brown, and Phi, an elementary school teacher) and I have our own personal cores that seem to stay bright and polished with constant use—I wink at my Brown education every time I use a phrase like "the new Gilded Age."

We also all remember reading *The Man in the Gray Flannel Suit*. Anyone who makes it to Brown is already at home with questioning conformity, but my classmate Paul Zimmerman ('88) recalls that "reading the *Flannel Suit* triggered a strong feeling in me, and I think many others, of, 'Yeah, I am so *not* going to be him.' We wanted to find or create our own way to navigate the world."

My parents continued to be upset about my career choices, especially after I left my last financial position, at Goldman Sachs. They called weekly to lobby for graduate school (any graduate school, at that point), even after my first novel was published. However, some years before my father's death, on seeing how I was absolutely at the place I needed to be in my life, with my degree from a school they hadn't heard of in Korea (and assumed, wrongly, wasn't very good), he queried, "How did you *know*? How did you know not to listen to us?"

My father's question was a welcome validation of my scary, uncertain, but exhilarating decision to go to Brown, and my Ahab-like certainty that Brown would help me become the writer I wanted to be and that on the way, if there wasn't an established path to my dream career, Brown would give me the inner resources I'd need in order to create it.

This initially chaotic, mapless, planless journey has also led me to a most delightful and serendipitous twist: while I am still the slow, wordy writer I always was, the publisher of the house that is issuing my next novel, a doorstopper that was almost a decade in the making, is none other than Jonathan Karp, who was my editor at the *Brown Daily Herald*.

Your Dinner with Susan Sontag

JOANNA SCOTT

I t's a typical April day in Providence in the year 1984, and you're an eager, impatient first-year graduate student enrolled in the writing program at Brown University. You've been telling yourself that you must be a sponge and absorb whatever there is to learn, but so far you haven't been satisfied with anything you've written. Your wastebasket is overflowing with false starts. One moment you feel defeated, the next, exhilarated. Everything matters too much, or too little. You are in a hurry to get on with life. No, you want to slow it down. You want to make every moment count. You type too quickly and read too slowly. You tell yourself that for every window you've ever looked through, there's a story to tell.

You live off campus, in the third-floor apartment of a boxy, yellow, Federal-style home on Governor Street. Last night, you went with friends to a Violent Femmes concert at RISD; all agreed that it was a blast, though one of your friends got a bloody nose while slam-dancing in the aisle. Back in your bedroom, you fell asleep to the sound of rain against the window.

When you blink awake, the morning sunlight has turned the fog drifting through the Fox Point neighborhood to gold. You hear a robin in the garden. You hear your landlady in the driveway declare that Narragansett Bay is beautiful this time of year. You hear a man blow his nose—you look out the window and see him there, dressed in red jeans, holding his car keys as he listens to the landlady.

You get out of bed and shuffle between books scattered across the warped pinewood floor, navigating through Homer, Dante, Goethe,

Dickens, Fielding, Auerbach, Hardwick, Gadamer, Carter. There is a stack that includes Joseph Conrad's *Under Western Eyes*—the subject of an essay you're supposed to write for Professor Henkle; *The Phaedrus*—bookmarked at the passage when Socrates compares the soul to a chariot; and paperbacks by Handke, Chekhov, and Gass—recommended by your current writing instructor, Susan Sontag, or the Duchess, as she's known among you and your classmates.

What an honor it has been to study with the Duchess, one of the country's leading intellectuals. You've read every word she's published. You are starstruck. You hang on all her comments. She makes a point of having dinners with her students, and it's your turn tonight. You are praying you won't say something unbearably stupid.

You shower, brush your teeth, part your hair with a comb, then set out on your morning walk, ambling along Wickenden Street, inhaling the good smell of sweet bread wafting through the open doors of the Portuguese bakery. The breeze off the Seekonk River makes your face tingle. On the wall next to the restaurant Rue de l'Espoir you see a poster for Sam Shepard's *Fool for Love* opening at Trinity Repertory. You memorize the production dates.

Back in your kitchen, you have breakfast with your roommates. Jen, an applied mathematician in the PhD program at Brown, pours cereal. Sloan, studying graphic design at RISD, heats up milk. You prepare the coffee.

You pack your book bag and walk up George Street, stopping in the English department to check your mail. There is a note from your instructor from last semester, Robert Coover, who besides teaching you about writing also generously gave up several hours of his free time to teach you how to use that fancy new machine called a computer. His letter is an addendum to a conversation you had with him the day before about a word processing program: "If you type RECEIVE the next time you're logged on, you will have improved up-front material. Not a bad idea to type RECEIVE each time you log on, for that matter. Best, Bob."

You spend the morning in the basement of the Rock writing what looks like chicken scratch and supposedly is the beginning of a novel. A few minutes before eleven you head to your part-time job at the Hay, where you spend two hours making catalog notes about Bromo-Seltzer song pamphlets from the 1890s. After work you grab a quick onion bagel from the Blue Room, which you eat in your Romanticism class while a fellow student presents a paper called "The Quest for Forgetfulness in Byron's *Manfred*."

All day, you worry about what you will say during your dinner with Susan Sontag. She is a formidable woman, precise and passionate, never, like you, at a loss for words. You imagine her asking: *How can you aspire to be a novelist when you're always at a loss for words?*

The afternoon speeds on. As you are walking back down George Street, it starts to rain again. You feel defeated, useless, misled by your dreams. You rehearse what you're going to record in your journal: *I am a drive-in movie theater and the parking lot is empty because of the rain, but the film still flickers on the screen, like a school of silver barracuda in the gulf off Key West.* This is wretched writing, you have to admit. At least you haven't written it yet.

You change from your sweatshirt and jeans into a skirt and sweater. On your way out, you meet your landlady, who is repotting her night-blooming cereus. She promises that on the night the cereus blooms, she will have a party, and you and your roommates are invited.

You take it as a good omen that the unreliable alternator of your Volkswagen Rabbit is functioning properly, and you drive to an Armenian restaurant in East Providence. There is a neon Schaefer sign in the front window, and the restaurant is empty except for the waitress and the cook, who grills meats over open coals. You wait on a bench for the rest of your group. Laurie arrives first, then David pulls up in his Dodge coupe, with the Duchess in the passenger seat.

At the table, you and Susan Sontag share a bowl of pistachios. She tells the waitress, "We are going to be here a long while," and orders two carafes of Valpollicella wine. "I. Am. Having. A. Difficult. Time. Keeping. My. Wits," she announces once the wine has been poured.

Then she launches into a story about a thirty-odd-year-old friend of hers who recently confessed that she'd slept with her own thirty-odd-year-old brother. The friend made a plan with her brother to meet in a city far away from family and friends; they had dinner and went to a hotel.

Susan Sontag sips her wine and continues: "I asked her what she felt. She said, 'We just lay in bed and giggled. Thought—if our parents could only see us now.'"

You don't know whether to laugh or express horror. Luckily, your friend Laurie takes the risk and laughs first, then David laughs, and Susan Sontag laughs, so you are safe to join them.

Susan Sontag talks about many things. She talks about famous writers she has met over the years. She tells us about their secret scandals, their obsessions and peccadillos. About one she says, "I know someone who had an affair with her in the 1940s, but she doesn't know that I know." About another she says, "His wife is a slave, and he dictates all his books to her."

She talks about meeting Nadine Gordimer at a writers' conference. "Nadine approached me in the hotel lobby and said, 'Susan Sontag, I really admire your work.' And though I am usually irreproachably honest, I said, 'Nadine Gordimer, I admire your work so much,' though I had never read a word of it." She pauses, stabs at her food. "We became fast friends," she recalls. She explains that for a week she and Nadine shunned other conference delegates and ate breakfasts and dinners together and talked through the night. The whole time she was worried that when she finally had a chance to sit down and read Nadine Gordimer's work, she wouldn't like it. But she did like it, in fact was overwhelmed by it, and now Susan and Nadine are good friends.

You can't help but be enthralled. On she goes, talking about how she lived in China and Tucson and Southern California, how she married when she was seventeen and divorced when she was twenty-six. She loves New York, she says. She has a duplex on East Seventeenth Street, and the man at her local deli tells her, "Susan, I got a name for your next book—*The Life of a Deli Employee*. No, here's a better one. *The Death of a Deli Employee*."

She says it's easy to make friends in New York. She says that everyone in the Soviet Union hates the government there. She says that John Updike will never write a great book, but he has a great prose style. And after finally noticing the waitress dozing in a chair across the empty restaurant, she says, "They want to close up here," and puts on her coat.

Back in your own room, you call your boyfriend, who is studying in a graduate English program at another school, two hundred miles away. It's after eleven p.m. and the rates are low, so you talk for an hour. You talk about his paper on Wallace Stevens and your paper on Joseph Conrad. You discuss arrangements for the upcoming weekend. You tell him all about your dinner with Susan Sontag.

It is still raining when you climb into bed. You scribble something in the spiral notebook you use as your journal, but language strikes you as inefficient. You wish you could make your words sound like the rain. You consider all that you have learned since the morning. You can't include everything, so you try to anticipate what you will want to remember years from now, if you ever set out to tell a story about a typical day in the life of a Brown graduate writing student, circa 1984.

The Place of Lucky Accidents

DAWN RAFFEL

Late in the seventies, I became an accidental semiotics major—
I mean, concentrator. To be honest, I didn't know what semiotics was. I had transferred to Brown, sight unseen, after two years at a well-known journalism school. For a would-be writer, j-school appeared to be the practical path. Given that I had graduated from high school roughly five minutes post-Watergate, it was also a popular path. The school was hot; the city was freezing. Worse, the longer I stayed in journalism school, the more I wanted to write fiction, and the longer I stayed in the Midwest, where I'd been raised, the more I yearned to go someplace new. But where?

Several East Coast schools made it clear that to transfer would be to lose all of my journalism credits. "Trade school," sniffed one admissions officer. "Well, why don't you look at Brown?" said another. Brown! The creative writing faculty was—forgive me—storied, and the have-it-your-way curriculum meant that Brown would accept credits from classes like Reporting 101 and "Introduction to Advertising." "We'll call those semiotics," said an angel of mercy in the admissions office. Journalism was connected, sort of, to the classes I'd be taking in creative writing, linguistics, theory, and comp lit. I could even toss theater into that happy basket. *If.* The *if* was: Brown didn't take many transfers, and the odds against me that year, I later learned, were worse than one hundred to one. At the welcome reception for the tiny handful of newbies, an admissions officer told me that what put my application over the top was the "hilarious" writing sample. Alas, it wasn't intended to be funny.

Feeling like I was pulling a fast one and wanting to meet people, I signed up for a yearlong, five-day-a-week acting class. It was fun; it was pass/fail; and since I had no illusions about ever acting professionally, it was as stress-free as a college class could be. "Don't be afraid to fall on your keister," our professor, James O. Barnhill, said to us.

So I wasted no time in bruising my metaphorical backside, in acting class, in Production Workshop, in my writing classes. I learned to peel my keister and my ego off the floor and have another go. While hanging out in the theater department, I read—and memorized—Chekhov and Pinter and Ibsen and Beckett and Shepard and Stoppard, in no particular order. Without realizing it, I learned to write dialogue. Absorbed how actors use space and applied it to the page. Studied timing. Picked up the ability to stand in front of people and not visibly freak out. Ditched a thick midwestern accent, at Professor Barnhill's insistence—an insistence that initially offended me and that I soon realized might have been the best advice I'd ever gotten. I learned how not to sound hilarious when I meant to be serious. And I learned how not to be so serious.

Decades later, Brown's loosey-goosey, roll-with-it curriculum—that Escher-like jungle-gym structure—has proven to be the most practical education I could have possibly gotten.

I'll still thank you for not asking me to explain semiotics.

A Doctor Poet?

CHRISTINE MONTROSS

I would not be a doctor were it not for Brown. I don't mean that with hyperbolic nostalgia, as in: *Brown made me what I am today.* Nor do I mean it concretely, as in: *I went to medical school at Brown, ergo Brown transformed me into a doctor.* What I mean is that I can't imagine I would ever have gotten into medical school were it not for Brown.

After majoring in French in college I went to graduate school for creative writing and then took a job teaching high school English to support my entirely nonlucrative life as a poet. I was one of four faculty members in the first year of a new charter school in California. Which is also to say that at twenty-four years old, I was a high school's entire English department. To fill the student body, the school's founders had accepted a large number of students who had been expelled from other public schools. Many had spent time in juvenile detention centers. Many were on legal probation. I had never taught high schoolers before. It was, perhaps, not the arrangement most likely to foster a love of teaching.

Nonetheless, it did give me insight into the weighty and numerous issues that the fourteen- and fifteen-year-olds in my classroom were juggling as they tried to read the books I had assigned them.

"Ms. Machine," they would call out to me, because my last name reminded them of the Spanish word *motor*, "if Holden Caulfield has two parents and a fancy school and all this money, then why does he spend so much time bitching about his life?"

"Yeah, or at least why do we have to *read* all his snively, pansy-ass bitching?" another would chime in.

"If I met him near my *casa* I'd give his spoiled white ass something to bitch about!" a third would shout out, at which point the class devolved into laughter, clapping, and congratulatory fist bumps.

"Let's watch the language," I'd say, reflexively, as I did a hundred times a day. But all the while I'd be thinking how perfectly right it was for them to be impatient with Holden Caulfield. How little I'd understood about the students I would have, and their lives, when I had taken the job. How irrelevant my reading list had turned out to be, carefully culled from the books I had taught to the eager students of a prestigious university just the year before. How inaccurately I had imagined these children, who turned out to be all full of bravado and street smarts and dressed in rival gang colors, but who were inarguably *children* all the same.

The stresses of my students' lives sometimes seeped into school time and sometimes poured in. Our school had no money for a guidance counselor. We four teachers filled in where we could. That meant that I went to the hospital with a fourteen-year-old freshman who needed a rape kit done after a friend of her father's had gotten drunk and come into her room the night before. It meant I took assignments to the juvenile detention facility where my fifteen-year-old student was held after she beat a neighbor girl so badly that the girl fell into a coma. It meant that I talked with the psychiatrists who had questions about my students' school performance, and who prescribed them medication upon medication upon medication.

One of my students was so sedated by antipsychotics prescribed for aggression that his words slurred, and he fell asleep in class. Another began an antidepressant, and before long started doing her homework and stopped carving DIE MOTHERFUCKER into her forearms with a razor.

It struck me that medicine had the potential to both ameliorate and impair. At the time, I tended to be mistrustful of psychopharmacology. Yet over and over again I saw that it was often the first-line treatment for psychic distress in this group of disadvantaged kids. They did not have health care that would pay for them to be in twice-a-month psychotherapy, but they did have coverage that paid for their daily doses of new, expensive psychiatric medications whose effects had only minimally been researched in children. Sometimes the medicines helped my students, and other times they didn't. I wondered wherein the difference lay.

In the midst of these questions and observations (and in the midst of my undeniable failure as a high school teacher) I found myself thinking more deeply about the territory of the mind. For years, I had written poems that flirted with madness. A yearning love poem had in it the figure of a cryptic madwoman:

> . . . down the hill the old widow has laced her river
> birch with bottles, some clear, some green, all clouded.
> They stay without string or fixative, each thin neck
> encircling a sturdy twig. *Pieces of wind inside*
> she croons at me one day. *A piano for the rain*
> she confides the next, grinning, and just yesterday,
> solemn, *You see, I'm making a deal with God.*

Another poem explored the fractured logic and linguistic associations of madness:

> the woman comes to your door and knocks.
> Nothing about her looks wrong but something
> does not look right. *Do you have*
> the padlock's key? she asks and points
> to your coat closet. *I have to get upstairs*
>
> delusion, illumine,
> lumière, solution,
> illusion, lunacy,
> luz; there's light

in all of it.
Light at the end
of the tunnel,
lights are on
but no one's home.

The social worker is new. The man speaks
steadily without crying. *Mother left*
first. Father stuffed my rolled
socks into the tailpipe of a rented car. She smiles
her best empathic look, writing
absent parents, childhood trauma thinking
four more minutes he says *so I'm a bird*
and I've come to you for help
because my brother just won't bring seed

sedate, seduce, sequester,
kestrel, guillemot, tern.

My struggling high schoolers helped me begin to understand
that this poetic and intellectualized view of madness was removed,
romantic, and simple. Just as, for them, Holden Caulfield failed to
reflect a realistic picture of adolescent angst, so my own poetic mus-
ings about the mind's failings largely missed the point. I was beginning to learn that real-life fractures of the mind were fascinating, and
at times poignant, but they were not lovely. Instead of providing a
window to an elusive realm of wisdom, mental illness more often was
a flagrant display of confusion and fear, of misery made plain.

Increasingly I felt drawn to a career investigating the mind. I considered training as a social worker, or as a psychologist, but my students demonstrated what I already knew from talking to a range of
therapists and doctors: the current of mental health treatment was
increasingly running toward medication. If I wanted to be an educated voice that could speak to the complexities of the brain's neu-

rochemistry and make a cogent argument for or against medication when I believed a patient did or didn't need it, I'd first need to learn anatomy and pharmacology. I'd have to go to medical school.

My partner, Deborah, looks back on the years prior to that decision and jokingly calls them "the years of false advertising." It is a story she loves to tell at a dinner party when new friends ask how we met or whether I had always known I wanted to be a doctor. "Keep in mind," she'll say as a teasing accusation, "that when I met Christine in graduate school, she was a *poet*. Poets don't have *pagers*," she'll continue. "Poets are never on overnight call."

When I finally decided that—despite being a poet—I wanted to go to medical school, I uprooted our lives from the twentysomething dreamland of San Francisco to the somewhat less entrancing suburbs of Philadelphia in order to take a year of premed courses at Bryn Mawr College. I was met with a rude awakening and a dose of self-doubt.

The awakening came in the form of my first physics exam. In college and graduate school I had studied little, breezing through a scintillating range of humanities courses with passion, great enthusiasm, and a minimal expenditure of energy. Nonetheless, I knew my year at Bryn Mawr would pose a different set of challenges, a kind of learning with which I was unfamiliar. So I studied. Hard. And when my first physics exam was handed back to me, a large *28* was scrawled across the top. I hadn't remembered that there had been as many as thirty questions. I flipped to the final page. There hadn't been. I was puzzled. I tried to determine the point allocation per question and how it would add up to 28/30 or perhaps even 28/35. Then the professor projected the range of scores on the screen in the front of the room, and I saw that my lone 28—on the far left side of the bell curve—was, in fact, a 28 percent. Failure was 60 percent. I hadn't just failed the test, I had bombed it.

This does not become a story of redemption and physics success. I did pass the course in the end, but just barely. I say without hesitation that if I were asked today to explain even the simplest relationship between force and velocity, or the concept of vectors, or whatever the hell else is in physics, I couldn't attempt to tell you without breaking into a fit of uncontrollable laughter at my own ineptitude.

And yet, despite my physics failures, I am, today, a practicing physician. I'm a psychiatrist and a writer. I love my job, and I think I'm good at it. I speak with some frequency at medical schools across the country, and as deans and faculty members brag to me about the staggeringly high MCAT scores of their matriculated students, I think only of how poorly I would have fared on the MCAT and how certain my rejection would have been from any medical school that required it.

Thankfully, Brown did not. Instead, the admissions committee asked me about my poetry and seemed to ignore my dismal physics performance. When I wrote about my high school teaching experience and how it had led me to want to practice psychiatry, they trusted my curiosity and commitment. They wanted to know more.

When I learned that I had been admitted and expressed shock to a friend of mine who had done her undergraduate work at Brown, she grinned widely and shrugged. "A doctor poet? Of *course* you were admitted! That's just the Brown way."

I began writing *Body of Work*—a memoir about the experience of dissecting a cadaver—as a first-year medical student at Brown. In the summer after that first year, when students could apply for competitive funding to support bench or clinical research, Dean Donald Marsh created and granted me a Summer Fellowship in the Arts and Humanities. While my peers worked with cell cultures and pipettes in basic science labs and crunched data for clinical trials, I used my funding to tramp around Italy researching anatomical theaters, underground crypts, saintly relics, and creepy wax museums.

In my second year, I scurried from pathophysiology lectures over to the literary arts building, where I was permitted to take an independent study writing elective with literary arts professor Carole Maso. Though our buildings were less than a block from each other, the talks I had with Carole about dissection were otherworldly and provided a necessary contrast to the medical lens of anatomical science. Those conversations allowed for more poetic and dreamlike intrusions to be woven into *Body of Work* in a way that mirrored the weird and unsettling mortal dreamscape of cadaveric dissection.

In my clinical years, I received medical school credit—just as I would have for a dermatology or neurosurgery elective—for researching and writing about the wild history of anatomy with its body snatching, grave robbing, and defiance of church and law. The pages I wrote during those electives formed the central historical component of my book manuscript.

In the years that followed, Brown has continued to be an academic home that has supported my own individual career priorities rather than forcing me to rigidly adhere to traditional expectations and pathways. I have now written a second book—*Falling Into the Fire*—about my most compelling clinical encounters as a psychiatrist. My earliest inclinations to explore mental illness through both literature and science have been allowed to take root and indeed nurtured here. I think back to that high school classroom confluence of psychopharmacology and Holden Caulfield, and the progression from there to my current faculty position in Brown's department of psychiatry seems almost linear, if not conventional. The shape of it has something to do with momentum, with trajectory. It's beginning to feel like some kind of a vector.

Cursing My Way to Enlightenment

A. J. JACOBS

I remember embarrassingly little from my classes at Brown. Among the flotsam still drifting around in my skull:

- My Nietzsche professor Martha Nussbaum's astrological sign is Taurus (one of my classmates raised his hand in the middle of a lecture to ask her, "What's your sign?")

- The important literary fact that James Joyce had an irrational fear of thunder

- All the distinctive grammatical properties of the word *un-fucking-believable*

That last one came from my intro to linguistics class. My TA was a grad student with shoulder-length hair and a sneering disdain for schoolmarmish prescriptive grammar (he would say, without irony, that linguistics is the "funnest" social science, using a word that still puts my computer spell-check into code red). But he loved what he called descriptive grammar—the study of how language actually works.

During one session, we were discussing suffixes and prefixes, and how they change the meanings of words. He told us there's another way to alter a word: the infix. This is when you insert a sound into the middle of a word, not the beginning or end. Arabic and ancient Greek have infixes, as does Khmer, the language of Cambodia. But English? We have but a single infix: *fucking*. As in *in-fucking-credible*. Or *un-fucking-believable*. *Ala-fucking-bama*. It serves as the ultimate intensifier.

Why do I remember this fact while 99 percent of my Brown education has faded to oblivion? Why does this stay with me while I've forgotten all four of Buddha's Noble Truths, all seven spectral classes of stars, all sixteen Habsburg monarchs?

Obviously, the human brain loves a good curse word. At least mine does, which is why I can recall offensive anatomical terms in most of the Romance languages and yet can't recall the name of my freshman dorm.

But to make myself feel better, I'm going to argue there's a greater significance to *un-fucking-believable*. I'm going to say that those five minutes discussing the *fucking* infix were the most quintessentially Brunonian five minutes of my education. They encapsulate everything wonderful and progressive—and simultaneously lampoonable—about this great university. I've broken it down to three reasons:

1. Intellectual Inquiry Has No Limits

For this essay, I read a book called *The History of Brown University*, which traced the evolution of Brown's curriculum. Thank God I was not a graduate of the class of 1850. The curriculum was eye-glazingly narrow, a mix of basic math, Roman writers, and more Roman writers. Livy, Horace, Tacitus, and on and on.

As a 1990 grad, I read my classics. But I was allowed to write papers about the umlaut over the vowels in heavy metal bands and the sexual politics of the Smurfs (why only one female, and why was gender her defining attribute?). And most proudly, I wrote about the ritual of the bong hit in twentieth-century colleges. Naturally, for that one, I had to do some serious participant observation, as all good anthropologists do.

This type of study is easy to mock. E. D. Hirsch Jr. made a career of railing against it. And newspapers have written hundreds of articles about the absurdity of college courses that dissect Keanu Reeves's oeuvre. Some of the ridicule is probably deserved. While I was at

Brown, there was an actual course called "John Locke, the Rape of the Lock and Matlock."

Even Ira Magaziner, creator of the New Curriculum, talks about the danger of trivializing college, quoting a critic who says it leads to "the belief that all knowledge is so good, that all parts of it are equally good."

But the general idea is true: All of life is a petri dish. We should bring a critical eye to everything, including bong hits.

2. It Helped Erode My Provincialism

I got the word *provincialism* from Magaziner's famous 1968 report on the New Curriculum (which I had never read before I was asked to write for this book). He argued that battling provincialism—our own slender view of the world—is one of the primary goals of a Brown education. It's a good point. We need to know that other cultures solve problems differently. There's more to this world than the prefix and suffix.

And just as important, we need to be reminded that our own rituals and rules would make other cultures scratch their heads (or whatever their gesture for confusion might be). What would they make of the Super Bowl halftime show? Or even odder, the Brown marching band?

Of course, this can be taken too far. It can slide into total moral relativism. It can lead naïve college students (like I once was) to believe that all ethical systems are equally valid—a notion that causes fear and loathing from pastors, Republicans, and parents. It can cause dorm room discussions like *How can we judge the Taliban? Aren't they just operating by their own culture's rules?*

At Brown, I became too smitten with moral relativism. In the years since, I've gotten older and either wiser or more closed-minded, take your pick. I'm no longer absolutist when it comes to relativism, but some remnants remain.

3. There Are Patterns Among the Chaos

During his lecture, my linguistics teacher explained that the *fucking* infix cannot be inserted randomly. You can't say *incredi-fucking-ble*. You can't say *Al-fucking-abama*.

You have to obey the unconscious infix rules. (My attempt to articulate those rules: the *fucking* must come immediately after the prefix, but if there's no prefix, then before the first stressed syllable.)

That's one of education's most important jobs: shining a light on the mental rules of which we are barely conscious. The infix rule may not have a huge real-world impact. But what about the unconscious bias that attractive people are morally superior? Or our tendency to interpret neutral data as supporting our preconceptions?

Well, that's my argument. As with many of the essays I wrote at Brown, I'm not sure I've totally proved my point. But I had a fan-fucking-tastic time trying.

The Entropy and the Ecstasy

MARY CAPONEGRO

> *To find a name for this function [Rudolph] Clausius said: I*
> *prefer going to the ancient languages for the names of impor-*
> *tant scientific qualities, so that they may mean the same*
> *thing in all living tongues. I propose, accordingly, to call S*
> *the entropy of a body, after the Greek word "transformation."*

—Leon Cooper, An Introduction to the Meaning and
Structure of Physics

Brown is such a part of me that any attempt to articulate its essence feels as tautological as using a word to define that word. The institution thoroughly shaped my life, as for nearly a decade I had the privilege of both being educated and becoming an educator there. The university, and by extension Providence, was one of those places that in retrospect one realizes was the place *to be*—both superficially, in the trendy sense, and profoundly, in the existential sense: to be and to become, i.e., to be transformed—and I am inclined to concur with Roger Williams, christener of Providence, in associating the city with the divine.

The shadows of benevolence eventually crept up on civic life, and in the eighties, Providence politics were always juicy with scandal. I arrived toward the end of Buddy Cianci's first mayoral stint (terminating with that infamous assault charge) and left shortly before his second (punctuated by the four-year jail sentence for racketeering).

Nationally these were of course the Reagan years, and down from College Hill, some graduate students joined Providence citizens to demonstrate outside city hall in Kennedy Plaza, chanting, "No more fights, no more war / US out of El Salvador," and on occasion we boarded a bus to Washington to do so on a larger scale. Still in high school as the Vietnam War wound down, I experienced this picketing as my first concrete political gesture—beyond voting for the first time that prior year. At an institution that formalized the sponsorship of international dissident writers, it was natural to get at least a little bit involved.

By the time I was leaving Brown toward decade's end, the picketing was happening up on the hill itself, in response to the creative writing program's inaugural Unspeakable Practices conference and the fact that its assemblage of metafictional masters had inadequate female representation. The repercussions of this sentiment were discernible many years later in the Sunday *New York Times*, when critic Wendy Steiner would declare the bloated male world of metafictional hijinks as used up, and female realists and the "commonplace of love" in clear ascendancy. My quarrel with her assessment was that it held no place for *female* metafictionists, or irrealists or postmodernists, as if the meta were intrinsically and exclusively a male domain. And yet for a budding female metafictionist like myself, and for a host of female writers whose fiction was more traditionally oriented as well, there was, in fact, no more congenial or inspirational place to be than Blistein House on Waterman. Those postmodern males with their textual swagger were not bloated merely with bravado. They were incubating us. Their distention was our procreation.

Overlapping with Reagan's eight years and Cianci's double decade was the reign of more specific relevance to me: the John Hawkes years. Of the thirty-three he taught (a mythically charged number), thirty were at Brown, and I was blessed to have his mentorship and friendship for the entirety of his final teaching decade—not to mention the post-teaching decade—during which he advised me on almost everything, ranging from the mundane to the metaphysical:

from matters of art to matters of the heart. Jack—as Hawkes was called by all who knew him well—would essentially teach me how to teach, sharing strategies pioneered at special conferences at Stanford; he even helped me navigate the vertiginous subjectivity of student evaluations. (In two sections of the same class the first year I taught, one student compared my personality to Clark Kent's, i.e., before his apotheosis, while a student from the other section said, "I thought she was an angel, or maybe God.")

But when I first arrived in Providence, I felt acutely mortal. Due to a bad case of transition jitters, I was conflicted in a dozen ways. A dozen solutions were arrived at, courtesy of Jack, within a week. He convinced me to trade poetry for fiction, rather than to straddle the two genres, since he was sure that all of the lyric gestures I prized could be housed comfortably in prose. Regarding a more literal housing comfort, I lamented that my apartment was directly in front of Brown's football practice field, and Jack, in his pragmatic way, proposed that I "get earplugs" and assured me that the karmic coincidence of Angela Carter's having occupied that space the prior year, while guest-teaching at Brown, would offset any negativity. (She was the queen of metafictional unspeakable practices and often pulled the weight of all her gender.) Besides, he said, it was the perfect size to hold our graduate fiction workshop. And it was only blocks away from Elmgrove Avenue, where the Waldrops lived—which led to his most sweepingly generous proclamation: that if I felt uneasy about anything at all before nine p.m., I should call him. And if I felt uneasy after nine, then I should call the Waldrops.

A convenient enough prescription, given that many nights after nine, one found oneself chez Waldrop anyway, participating in Providence's premier literary salon hosted by the divine city's most erudite and gracious literary couple, and publishers of Burning Deck Press. Keith possessed encyclopedic knowledge of both esoteric literary facts and Providence lore; he'd take you to see Poe's abode or Lovecraft's grave, or 111 Westminster, the tallest building in the city and spitting image of the *Daily Planet*, hence affiliating Providence with Superman. The Waldrop hospitality—and hyperliteracy—was another cornerstone of Providence beneficence. Tea was always brewing in a beautiful glass pot to serve from glass teacups, alongside wine and words, exchanged amidst towering stacks of books. Not one book was for show; all of them were read or being read, some written or translated by the hosts, others published by them, on letterpress, in their humble basement. Their night-owl schedules somehow allowed astonishing productivity, even on the heels of entertaining all of us!

Presumably from two a.m. to dawn they wrote, and that's when I would do my penance in the now-defunct mainframe computer space in the basement below the Science Library—the graveyard shift allowed the possibility of a longer session—the only competition being undergraduates playing what might have been an early version of computer games. I was learning to input my evolving thesis stories onto the computer, since Robert Coover wanted all the grad students to employ this nascent technology. I remember the frustration of spending hours trying to get the damn *accent aigu* over the *e* in *The Star Café*, as well as the triumph of walking out to see the May sunrise with a completed thesis in hand. (Well, almost in hand; it was waiting in the queue to be printed off the mainframe.)

The final thesis reading each creative writing graduate student gave, because of Jack, felt equally exhilarating. When he introduced me at the elegant Spanish House on Prospect Street, he spoke the words he had requested I provide. Jack had an idiosyncratic, utterly commanding style of delivery that to the naked ear might fall between histrionic and stentorian but was truly marvelous and inevitably generated both hilarity and pathos. I can still hear that mini-bio of a lapsed Catholic. "She fell from grace"—he paused for laughter— "and then further from poetry into prose"—another pause for yet more laughter as he worked the crowd, a crowd consisting of Brown undergraduates as well as grad students, some of whom were destined to become the country's most renowned contemporary writers. Many were unknown to me then, but I now think of them as family, because of the mentorship we shared under Jack's tutelage. They were in that room for him.

My words uttered by Jack and colored by the inimitable inflections of his comic genius elevated them so far beyond their worth that they became priceless to me—I who had barely opened my mouth all through college, though once I arrived at Brown and started Jack's workshop, seldom shut it. Among the scriveners of unspeakable practices, I had finally found the wherewithal to speak.

Evenings not spent at Keith and Rosmarie's might be spent at Jack and Sophie's or at Bob and Pili's. In fact Jack's slightly early retirement was, as I remember, precipitated by a dinner conversation during which my then companion Sheffield—a painter whom I had met one evening at the Waldrops'—who cherished, as we all did, Jack's work, urged him to embrace a more luxurious future and create a more capacious writing space within his life. Shortly after this discussion, Jack declared he would retire. Given that there would only be one decade left for him, I am all the more grateful Jack took this suggestion to heart, though the loss to the writing program was devastating.

All this took place before Providence was "discovered"—when it was dismissed as that funky little city on the way to the Cape, identified primarily by what it wasn't, i.e., *not* New York and not Boston, although Jack referred to it affectionately as the sepulchral city, and its thousand-and-some streets of hidden gardens and colonial charm and painted-lady Victorians were, to those of us under its spell, as ensorcelling as the thousand and one nights conjured by Scheherazade, she the muse and her narrative the urtext for the renegade fabular writers who presided over Brown's, and in fact the nation's, avant-garde literary culture, and who were to be for me the seat—or might I take the liberty to say the teat—of nurture.

Even as the Semiotics and English departments were about to declare irreconcilable differences, it was to us more exciting than distressing, as we children derived the benefits of joint custody. In fact, creative writing graduate students had offices in Adams House, ostensibly pedestrian spaces covertly designed for the voluptuary. Extending from our third-floor offices were slender overhangs, just wide enough to hold a body or two. Thus, even if grad students were crammed four to an office during the week, on Saturday we could selectively sneak back up and climb out the window onto the make-shift deck to view the skyline of downtown Providence, the ersatz *Daily Planet* its most salient structure, then make ourselves supine with no ambition but to bask in the sun, whose rays had not yet acquired the status of carcinogen.

Alliances across the divide, i.e., between Blistein House and Horace Mann, between the faculty writers and the scholar-critics who sometimes were the honorary subjects of each other's work, were robust regardless, and the galvanizing energy of Robert Scholes or Albert Cook or Arnold Weinstein and so many others made yet clearer what a major center Brown was for contemporary American letters. Initially I had applied to Brown's creative writing program believing it to bestow a doctor of arts degree, but that degree was now defunct and someone had neglected to remove it from the catalog. I still yearned, irrationally, for some version of that D, and started a PhD in English twice, but when offered the chance to teach instead and skip that step, I forfeited that fantasy, loitering far longer than your average doctoral student.

But both times, I found deciding agonizing. I am eternally grateful to Robert Scholes, who shared a personal anecdote about a time in his life when he struggled with twinned aspirations of creative work and scholarship. He was in the middle of composing a story, and each time he tried to work on it, he was interrupted by studying for prelims or the demands of his dissertation and he finally had to abandon the fiction. He was giving me permission to make what should have been the obvious choice, for me, i.e., to be content with the degree in hand and be a writer. There were, after all, only a fraction of the MFA programs that now exist and we, with no small hubris, thought of ours as the corrective to the prestigious one amidst the cornfields of the Midwest that represented the opposite aesthetic pole.

Among all these remarkably supportive presences I found safe haven to develop, ad infinitum, one of my earliest short stories, a retelling of Greek myth, in which a man transforms into a woman and then back into a man, experiencing all the sensations that he visited upon women but *as* a woman: a fictive exploration of empathy as afterlife that had arisen from my reading of the philosophy of Rudolf Steiner; Jack perpetually defended it against assumptions that it was too esoteric or too pornographic—he had much practice given the controversial nature of his own fiction—even as a critique penned by a young male peer read, "read it to me in the shower." I suspect at most other MFA programs such aspirations and such fiction would have been regarded as pretentious and self-indulgent, and met with ridicule or at best bemusement, but I gained confidence from the voluminous *good*s with which Jack littered the margins in each successive draft of the story.

When, several years after my degree, through the grace of C. D. Wright and Forrest Gander's Lost Roads Press, my first book was published, and the undergraduate reviewer in Brown's *Issues* magazine perceived a series of fabular narratives I had intended to be tender love stories, devoid of any ideological bent, as strident feminist narratives, replete with antimale sentiments, I retained my confidence because of Jack's support. The tales had arisen from an ingenious, customized assignment he had given me: to write a hundred Chinese fairy tales so as to become comfortable with the nuts and bolts of narrative cause and effect. The reviewer put forth a challenge: only when I delved into male consciousness would my work fully evolve. I dismissed this, and yet my next long project did feature a male protagonist, concerning whom Jack again came to my aid, by coaching me on how to stay inside a comic novel even in grief, since I had lost my father while immersed in writing it. A haunting stand of birch trees at Swan Point Cemetery—much nearer to the entrance than was Lovecraft's grave—seemed more mesmerizing and more worthy than my contrived fictive world, and I wanted to abandon the novel. But I stayed with it and shrank it to novella size, finding solace in its comedy—and yet more solace knowing that Jack, deep in the process of his own novel, had once contended with the persistent image of his deceased father in the mesmerizing palette of a fireplace's flames.

But I have jumped ahead. The novella was composed well after I graduated from Brown, when I was teaching there and down the hill at RISD, in the latter years of my Providence sojourn. In the spacious two years of the master's degree, little was required of us except to write. We were left free to sample any course within the university and made to take no more than one beyond a workshop. That only fueled in me the lust to audit everything—including, very briefly, an introduction to physics by Nobel laureate Leon Cooper. Professor Cooper happened to be of great interest to Jack because of Jack's career-long infatuation with the concept of entropy; the author of *Travesty*, *Second Skin*, and *The Passion Artist* believed his narratives investigated randomness and chaos in the realm of the unconscious—and he dreamed of some profound interdisciplinary meeting of the minds. A colloquium was arranged, Professor Cooper invited as the honored guest. Thus my apartment became an interdisciplinary laboratory for an afternoon, with complicated results. Had I read more closely then the textbook Cooper authored and used for the introductory course, and which I still possess, I might have seen the following statement and gleaned its function as a kind of literary foreshadowing.

It is part of the occupational hazard of being a physicist to be asked questions about time dilation at cocktail parties, just as doctors are expected to write prescriptions, psychiatrists to give analyses, palmists to read in an outstretched hand the future erotic monkeyshines of the owner.

Our workshop, never held in a classroom and always serving wine, might well have seemed, in Cooper's eyes, the equivalent of a cocktail party, which he perhaps attended as a form of community service, and Jack's infatuation with the concept of entropy may have been considerably less flattering to him than we presumed it would be.

Would entropy be demystified or remystified? By evening all would become clear.

As the afternoon wore on, it became demoralizingly obvious that worlds fashioned in fiction should only cautiously make a claim on rigorous scientific principle. One couldn't blame a Nobel laureate for being protective of a concept prone to the vagaries of metaphorical elaboration when interrogated by a roomful of benighted, metaphor-besotted writers. Perhaps the very conference itself served as a metaphor for entropy. In any case, before our eyes and lacking agency, entropy had somehow transformed ecstasy to agony. Jack seemed quite dejected for the next few days.

And yet when Jack himself served as a guest speaker at Harvard (his alma mater), it appears that he was equally capable of leaving his audience mystified—or so I gather from a brief anecdote within an eloquent *New Yorker* article John Updike wrote approximately ten years ago called "Mind/Body Problems." Updike refers to Jack as a "conspicuous avant garde libertarian" and seems bemused to recount the following capsule *ars poetica* Jack offered to their Harvard class: "When I want a character to fly, I just write 'he flew.'" Isn't it quintessentially Hawkesian that pedagogical instruction, and in fact fictive construction, could be both so pragmatic and so permissive, as unostentatious as it was outrageous—not unlike the spirit of Franz Kafka's opening of *The Metamorphosis*, in which, with analogous lack of fanfare, Gregor Samsa is transformed into a giant insect?

Updike honors the "dizzying freedom" available to a fiction writer that Jack's straightforward statement implies, even if a reader gets the sense the former finds the latter reckless and might himself opt for a method more respectful of the laws of physics. Or perhaps that's my projection, given that Updike was presumably the American author least likely to denounce plot, character, theme, and setting as irrelevant, as Jack had famously done. In truth, all those Updike stories that appeared in the *New Yorker* through the seventies were precisely the catalyst that prompted me to seek an alternative fictive avenue, one not mired in the suburban or the secular, one that took flight from the real, inspired by and aspiring toward the visionary.

A few years after studying with Jack, I wrote a story of a girl who turns into a mythic bird: a phoenix. The narrative was a bit more elaborate than the formula "she flew," but that was essentially its synopsis. She could have served as mascot for our transformative endeavors, she and that guy with *S* emblazoned on his chest, the one perpetually leaping over 111 Westminster Street as we scanned the skyline before closing our eyes to commune with the sun, two at a time, on the overhang of Adams House. Though we appeared no more than indolent voluptuaries seeking solar gratification, the supine status of our bodies was entirely misleading. With our imaginations we could truly leap tall buildings in a single bound, thanks to Jack. Or to quote the narrator of *Travesty*: "But see how we fly."

DIVERSITY

I came to Brown direct from three years of working on half-mile racetracks, hardly a literary milieu. I was too used to a solitary writing habit by that time to be a model member of a writers' workshop, but the great thing about that MA program, that English department, and indeed the Providence literary climate, is the extent to which diversity and eccentricity are permissible.

—**Jaimy Gordon** ('72)

Though there are no Jewish quotas in the Ivies today, policies of geographic diversity and legacy preference still serve as de facto quotas. In the 1980s, Asian American students at Brown raised concerns that their admittance rate had declined because they tended to be concentrated in large cities and because interviewers stigmatized them as boring, grade-grubbing nerds, similar to the "carpetbagger" stereotype of Jews in the 1920s . . . [The] Brown Report on Slavery and Injustice [*sic*] concluded: "We cannot change the past. But an institution can hold itself accountable for the past, accepting its burdens and responsibilities along with its benefits and privileges. This principle applies particularly to universities, which profess values of historical continuity, truth seeking, and service."

—**Amy Sohn** ('95)

The influence [Augustus A.] White '57 has had on Brown's racial and ethnic diversity reflects the steady, deliberate effort of an unlikely pioneer. A groundbreaking orthopedic surgeon, he was the first African American medical student at Stanford, the first black surgical resident at Yale, the first black professor of medicine at Yale, and the first black department chief at a Harvard teaching hospital. . . . White and his colleagues spoke to hundreds of students, faculty, and staff about diversity at Brown, and compiled, synthesized, and analyzed what they heard. The resulting report, *The American University and the Pluralist Ideal*, was released in 1986. It made seventeen recommendations, including broadened course offerings on race- and ethnicity-related subjects (the ethnic studies concentration was born as a result) and increased support for minority clubs and organizations.

—**Beth Schwartzapfel** ('01)

What Are You, Anyway?

AMY DUBOIS BARNETT

It was a muggy day in September of 1987. The dense New England humidity of a stubborn Indian summer had forced most of us pre-freshmen back into our skimpy August clothes. We'd hung the crisp new college outfits in our narrow dorm closets, and had retreated into the baggy shorts and long tank tops that all high school students wore that year.

Brown shoulders abounded as we nervously gathered for our first group event of the Third World Transition Program, or TWTP, as it was commonly known. All nonwhite members of the incoming freshman class were invited for a four-day orientation that was meant to acclimate us to our Ivy League surroundings. We were meant to commune together and develop bonds so that we felt comfortable and at home when the "snowstorm" (our term for the arrival of the Caucasian students) hit.

Upon arriving at TWTP, my first question had been: What's up with the name? I'm from New York, not a third-world country. Apparently, the program had been created to appease the mostly African-American students who famously organized a walkout in 1968 to protest their lack of representation among the classes and faculty. Therefore, the nomenclature was not to be trifled with (even though the majority of students who gathered under its banner had graduated at the top of their classes from some of the best high schools found in the Western Hemisphere).

Chastened by the explanation of TWTP's genesis and shamed by my lack of knowledge about what it took to make the program a reality, I took my seat in Andrews Dining Hall next to a cool Indian girl in an all-black outfit who was wearing only one enormous earring. In typical teen girl fashion, we became fast friends in about fifteen minutes, but were quickly parted when the program organizers announced that we would be gathering in ethnicity-based groups. She trotted off to join the Asian students and I was left alone to face a difficult choice: Did I join the large fun-looking group of black students at the far end of the room who were already laughing, high-fiving, and forming cliques? Or should I join the small sad group of biracial kids whose only unifying characteristic was parents of two different races?

Technically, I belonged with the biracial kids as my mother is black, while my father is white and Jewish. But that characterization did not feel like home to me at all. I had been raised black, felt black, and had never once called into question my racial identity. There was no confusion or conflict in my home either. My dad had always told me, "It's simple. I am white and you are black."

So, I made my decision and trotted off to join the black group. I sat down in a circle of girls who were complaining that the humidity was jacking up their straightened hair. My own curls were pulled back into a ponytail, so I had little to contribute to the conversation. They looked at me a little oddly until finally one girl asked, "You sure you're in the right group? You look like you're mixed with something. What are you, anyway?"

The dreaded question. I'd been asked "What are you?" my whole life as, apparently, my long nose, tan skin, and curly hair did not immediately indicate the identity I felt so strongly.

"I'm black, but my dad is white," I replied.

"Well, aren't you supposed to be over there?" The girl gestured with her chin in the direction of the biracial kids, who were in the middle of choreographing a skit that involved standing on either side of a rope and pulling back and forth to indicate their racial confusion. Ugh. Nevertheless, I knew I was too conspicuous to avoid grabbing a piece of that rope, so off I went. But I left feeling determined that would be the last time I would be deemed "not black enough" at Brown University.

I set about my focused overcompensation immediately. I joined most of the black groups at Brown, pledged a black sorority, mostly hung out with black students, and only dated black guys. In the middle of a Third World Center meeting that somehow devolved into a heated discussion about relationships, I even made a firm public declaration that I would never date a white guy.

By my sophomore year, I had successfully erased any doubt about my relative blackness. It had been a challenging process as the black student population at Brown was notoriously judgmental. The worst possible label a black student could have—and one that we threw around with relative ease and impunity—was *incognegro*. An incognegro was a black student who we did not feel "acted black" enough. Perhaps that person had too many white friends or, god forbid, hung out with the "Eurotrash" crowd. Perhaps the person didn't listen to "black music" or preferred Wriston Quad frat parties over black Greek step shows. Maybe the hapless incognegro simply couldn't shake his or her lifetime of prep school education and upper-middle-class suburban upbringing to develop a cultural bilinguality like the rest of us. No one thought twice when the black salutatorian from Exeter gave a pound (fist bump, for the uninitiated) to the Phillips Academy lacrosse team captain and said, "Wassup, bro."

Yes, I successfully avoided the dreaded incognegro label and was a fully accepted, card-carrying member of Brown's small but highly opinionated black community, until the unthinkable happened: I fell in love with a white student. Before Brown, I'd had an equal number of white and black boyfriends—a fact I had certainly not made public at college as I expressed my singular love for the "brothers." But sophomore year, I got swept away by a half-Danish student from Vermont. In other words, I fell for not just a regular white guy, but the whitest white guy you could possibly imagine. I simply could not help it; we had a powerful chemistry and I was head over heels within weeks.

At first, I tried to keep the relationship a secret, but that didn't last. We were nineteen-year-olds in love, which necessitated the requisite hand-holding between classes, sharing meals at the Ratty, and making out on the Green. Soon, everyone knew that we were a couple, and the shock reverberated across campus. I expected and received some ribbing related to my anti-interracial-dating comments of a few months prior. And I knew the black men of Brown would be less than thrilled that one of "theirs" had strayed from the fold. Interestingly, for as much as I had desired to have a place in Brown's black society, I found myself not giving a crap what anyone thought. I was comfortable in my own skin and I had nothing left to prove. I was who I was: a biracial black girl who loved a white man.

It was during this time that I learned one of the most important lessons that Brown University can teach: Being yourself is more important than anything else. And dichotomy is okay because one extreme does not have to preclude another. I was African-American and Jewish. I was a member of a black sorority yet my best friend was Asian. I loved both hip-hop and classic rock. I liked hiking and camping and I also loved to go clubbing in New York City. And I loved my white boyfriend (and white father, for that matter) but never had any doubt about my black identity.

My boyfriend and I were together long enough that the campus got completely used to seeing us. He would come with me to step shows and I would play hacky sack on the green with him and his Deadhead buddies. The more confident and comfortable we were, the more Brown felt like my real home. And I finally realized that I had never been in danger of being labeled an incognegro, because their main distinguishing characteristic wasn't actually lack of interest in the black community; it was lack of comfort in their own skin.

Sadly, the perils and temptations of junior year proved too much for my boyfriend and me. However, while he and I didn't exactly stay ever true to each other, I remain ever true to Brown for helping me to understand that I could be anything and everything as long as I was true to myself first.

Mix Tape

ANDREW SEAN GREER

I t was a very strange time to be in love.

I arrived at Brown in the fall of 1988. I was the now-impossible-to-recall age of seventeen, every bit the boy from the Maryland suburbs, looking wide-eyed around the dorm room in Morris-Champlain that I was to share with a yet-unmet roommate. My parents bought me a Thanksgiving sandwich at the Meeting Street Cafe and a Brown sweatshirt and drove away, leaving me quite perplexed as to what I was meant to do now. I was a tall, skinny redhead with jeans still short from my growing spurts and a steamer trunk filled with old T-shirts and sweatshirts. Years later, when a college friend moved to Washington, DC, he called me to say, "Now that I've seen the people out here, I understand the way you used to dress."

I was, as they used to say in the sixties, a "grind." A bland adolescent used to pleasing my teachers. Other high school kids seemed angry and tearful about something, but I had no idea what. They skipped classes and showed up bleary-eyed. They blinked vacantly when asked questions about the reading. They went to Fugazi concerts and dyed their hair black and dropped acid. This way of living seemed as foreign as that of a desert tribe. What I didn't realize was that they had already tasted life.

Reading over my diary from that freshman year is an embarrassing experience, and I will save us all the shame of quoting from it. Most are recountings of drinking blanc de blanc and playing card games in dorm rooms. Joining an a cappella singing group. Meeting with my advisor, Harriet Sheridan, and watching her smile patiently as I described my dreams. I still wrote papers a week early and finished every page of the reading. I was friendly, efficient, and numb. But I recall writing, deep in winter, that it was so strange everyone on my hall was having breakdowns. Coming to me asking for love advice. They all seemed to have such problems! *I must be asexual*, I decided. *I must be some kind of rock when other people are falling apart.* I ignored the very dark periods when I would stare at the floor in the shower and time would pass without my knowing. Time in which my mind blocked up some passage I had discovered in myself.

A rock. It shows my mind-set, that I would come up with such a myopic interpretation of what was going on. To others, it was already obvious that I was gay. Not, quite yet, to me.

Recall that it was 1988. Nobody was out. Absolutely nobody. The only gay people I had ever seen were Paul Lynde and Charles Nelson Reilly on TV. Gay sex was illegal in most states, including Rhode Island. Two years before, Californians had voted on a proposition to quarantine everyone with AIDS (it lost, of course). Ronald Reagan, president at the time, had only mentioned the existence of adults with AIDS the year before. There were clowns on TV, and there was silence. Behind the silence was death.

A cold, slushy winter in Providence; saving my breakfast meal credit to be used late at night at the Gate for pizza. Wearing a white tuxedo jacket and singing tenor with the Jabberwocks under Wayland Arch. Hoarding leftovers in a dorm room fridge so that my roommate, who was pledging Alpha Phi Alpha, could give his pledge brothers something to eat when they snuck away from their endless chores. Hiding cigarettes from my hallmate from Flushing who wanted to quit smoking. Taking a creative writing course where the teacher herself openly smoked. And Campus Dance, back in the days when you had to sneak in your own booze. I saw of Brown only the fantasy I had already made of it. I did the same with myself.

Cut to two years later. I was faltering in one class and about to fail another. Bs were more common than As. I had given up on my goals of taking a science class every semester and of learning a second foreign language. I had scandalized my singing group when they noticed a boy's name written on my Converse high-tops with a heart beside it (the scandal was compounded by the fact that he belonged to a rival singing group). I was never going to graduate magna cum laude. And I didn't care. I was in love.

I was a very irritating person to be around. I mooned around the Pembroke Campus like a ghost and wrote love notes in the snow below his window. I created terrible poetry. I played a particular mix tape at all hours in my off-campus housing. I wept and lost sleep and ate badly. I dressed all in black for Valentine's Day. One particularly sad day, I found myself behind the women's center crying and crying into the grass. In short: I did all the things that everyone else had done in high school. I acted like a teenager—which, in a way, I was. It always seemed a shame to me that gay kids back then got to progress in a normal way—with mash notes, and pulling pigtails, and chaste dates and prom and all that—the wading-in that straight kids got with love and sex. Back then, we had to throw ourselves into the deep end, which often proved complicated for those around us.

And, as I said, there was death. I remember reading the *New York Times* obituaries for young men who had died of "pneumonia." There were dozens every week. Graduate students at Brown, those older than us who hadn't the luck to be born a little too late, were dematriculating from their programs to go home. To go home and die, to be frank. The AIDS Memorial Quilt came to Brown and my friend Moore made a panel for Marco Clarke, a high school classmate who had died of AIDS. I remember walking downtown to the Providence clinic to have blood drawn and waiting a week before returning to hear my results. Imagine that horrible week!

All of that, laid on top of the awkwardness of courtship and dating and sex. On top of frat boys yelling *faggot* and boys refusing to date me because I was too "out" and the generally absurd politics of the era. On top of simply being young.

On top of that terrible mix tape blaring out the window on Meeting Street.

I am probably among the few who didn't get royally trashed before our graduation. That's because, along with my friend Alaraby, I was one of the commencement speakers. We walked at the head of the procession, through the gates, and down College Hill to the meetinghouse. We stood in front of President Vartan Gregorian and changed our speech without informing the graduation committee. We spoke out for need-blind admissions. We spoke about how hard it had been to be gay or of color or different in any way, even at liberal Brown. My classmates stood up, shouted at us, furious that we had ruined their graduation with politics yet again. A riot was beginning in the church. I suppose I froze up there, confused. I only remember feeling Gregorian's hand pulling at my gown. "Keep going," he said to me.

It's funny to think back on it now. What a different person I had become from the skinny boy in a sweatshirt my parents had left behind. Hard to picture that boy in a black gown and mortarboard before his class, hearing those things shouted at him. That boy never wanted that. He had only come to school because it was what had always been expected of him. He wanted to join a singing group, and wear J. Crew blazers, and visit his new friends at their parents' Cape Cod houses, and write a novel or a play or a story. That boy: he had a fantasy of Brown. That boy: he wanted to be loved by teachers and fellow students. That boy: he wanted finally, at last, to be popular. And this young man had spoiled that early dream so badly that he would have to skip graduation parties, for fear of people accosting him. This young man had spoiled everybody's fantasy.

"Thank you," a fellow classmate told me over a decade later. "I couldn't tell you then, nobody knew, but it meant a lot to me."

Of course it didn't help on that summer day back in 1992, standing in front of people who hated me, trying to start my speech up again. And to be honest, I hadn't done it for him. Or for the boy I used to be.

I spoke out that day, my graduation day, because I thought that out there, on the green, where our words were broadcast from the meetinghouse to all the parents, grandparents, friends, and professors, the boy who had recently dumped me might be there, sitting with his friends, listening. Maybe he would think me brave. Maybe I would win him back.

I was very young. Very young.

It was a very strange time to be in love.

The Wheel of the Fuji Goes Round

DILIP D'SOUZA

The magazine, I remember, was *Playboy*. After I had ogled the yards of bare feminine flesh, feeling mildly guilty, I noticed an ad for Cutty Sark whisky. It had a sweepstakes coupon at the bottom: first prize, a DeLorean car, the sleek silver beauty in the news that year for reasons I no longer remember. Not unlike many others of my gender, I drooled over the women in that magazine, but damn, I wanted the DeLorean!

Not that I really expected to win. Still, I scribbled my name on the coupon and tossed it into the nearest postbox.

This was 1981, and I was in my first few weeks at Brown—my first few weeks outside my home country of India as a student in the two-year-old computer science department. So new to it all, I was still extrapolating with faultless logic from the word *undergrad* to tell people that I was a "new grad." I couldn't understand why they looked bemused.

I caught on, eventually: *undergrad*, but *grad student*.

One time I called a friend—a member of the Brown women's squash team who regularly thumped me on the court—and burbled, "I've got music in my life," because I had just bought a basic clock radio. She didn't quite get my delight. And then there was the time I confessed to my landlady, "I really like Jews."

Like, you know, I really like toffee. I really like redheads. I really like Jews. The prince of fresh-off-the-boat, cringe-inducing, suck-me-into-the-earth-please naïveté? That was me.

And so it was fitting that I sent in that coupon and lived, naïvely, in hope. Oh, the dreams I had! I'd drive down Thayer Street in my gleaming DeLorean with all of Brown staring as I pushed up the door, casual-like, to pick up the Sunday morning *ProJo*. Folks would admire the machine and when they walked up for a closer look, I'd say, cool to the max: "It's mine! And get this, I'm a grad on a five-hundred-dollar-a-month fellowship!"

I mean, I was a student of computer science. Of all people, I should have been fully aware of the impossible odds of winning a sweepstakes. I should have known how futile the hope was. But I hoped nevertheless.

And then I did win.

Got home from the department late one evening to find my landlady waiting for me on her stoop, her teeth visibly chattering. Hopping about to keep warm in what they told me was Providence's coldest winter in years, she was nearly beside herself with excitement. "You got a big carton in the mail!" she said, even before I could ask what she was doing outside. "Really big!"

The DeLorean arrived in a carton?

No, the Fuji arrived in a carton. Second prize in the Cutty Sark sweepstakes, a Fuji ten-speed bicycle.

I could hardly believe it. Not six months into my time in the States and I owned a handsome bike! Nearly for free (I had to take it to a store to have it assembled)! What a country!

After the first few minutes, I didn't care that it wasn't the car. Once I got on the Fuji, it was DeLorean enough for me. Every Sunday morning, I rode it in style—well, as much style as dropped handle-bars allowed—down Thayer Street to get my *ProJo*.

Several months later, someone stole the front wheel, and only the front wheel. What a country. At the store, I learned that a replacement would set me back several times what I had paid to put the whole bike together. So my Fuji spent the rest of my grad experience resting (sans wheel) in the stairwell in the department. There were complaints and snide remarks, but there it stayed.

That swift machine gave me plenty of joy, yes. But when I couple that to its forlorn state in that stairwell, I know why—for me—the Fuji has always been a metaphor of sorts for my own time at Brown.

My first two semesters went astonishingly well. I threw myself into work like never before, actually enjoyed the courses and programming assignments, and met some of the warmest, keenest folks ever. My undergrad college was one of India's best, and I mean absolutely no disrespect to my buddies from there when I say that some of these Brown kids—Alex, Jeremy, Janet, Matthew, Jeannette— were the sharpest I had ever known. How did so many congregate at Brown? And mostly because of them, I felt constantly stimulated, like I was learning every single day. Every single moment. Nothing in my twenty-plus years in India had prepared me for this heady mix of hard work and intellectual smorgasbord.

Until the wheels fell off, hard.

In my first year at Brown, I had earned six As and a B. In my second year, I registered for a total of eight courses; I actually finished just one, earning a C. I had a research assistantship in which I produced nothing; by the end, I was hunting desperately, every day, for excuses to avoid meeting my professor. What could I tell him when I had nothing to show him? I failed my PhD qualifiers. To tell the truth, I didn't even try, because I had counted myself out before the start. I took to slinking in and out of my office, unable to face my colleagues. My best buddy in the department walked in one morning to berate me. "Do you know," he said, "we just can't understand what you're doing with yourself!"

His words make me quail even now. I couldn't understand it either. I was overwhelmed by a strange lassitude that, to this day, I cannot explain to myself. Through it all, the bike stayed in the stairwell, as forlorn as I had become.

Frantic to escape but unwilling to face what I had inexplicably become, I applied for a job halfway across the country. Somehow they made me an offer and I finally left the department. Finally moved the bike too. With my new salary in a distant city, I bought my Fuji a new wheel. Perhaps the surroundings where I didn't know a soul helped; the lassitude slowly lifted and I felt functional again. Life was looking up.

Except for one little detail: I hadn't actually finished my degree at Brown, and to this day, I cannot explain why I thought I might get away with that deliberate oversight. One morning, I got a call from a Brown official: "You had better return and finish, or we'll have to revoke your immigration status."

I flew back to Providence with minimal clothes, gritting my teeth in newfound resolve. I took along my Fuji. What followed was a brief throwback to my first year at Brown, with those pleasures and rewards I had nearly forgotten. It was three weeks of the hardest slogging I had ever done; it was how I renewed bonds with—and regained the respect of—my fellow students, because I was no longer slinking about. For three Sundays in a row, I set out on my old friend, the Flying Fuji, to collect the *ProJo*. To me, that bike felt like a DeLorean.

Oh yes, and I no longer needed to avoid my professor. When I was done, he shook my hand, smiled broadly, and whispered in my ear: "You did well!"

I blushed.

I had that Fuji for several years, riding it all over bike-friendly Austin, my new home. Those were good years: friends, satisfying work that I got recognized for, a handsome dog, lots of music in smoky blues bars. But something was always missing, and what started as gentle pangs grew over time into a yearning I could no longer ignore.

I had to return to India.

By the time I was ready to go, the Fuji was still serviceable, but only just. Rust had set in; the seat was falling apart. Nobody would buy it; there wasn't much point in refurbishing it or lugging it halfway across the world, and it was too much of a family member to fling on a scrap heap. What was I to do with my bike?

Just days before I left, the decision was taken out of my hands. One morning, it disappeared. Stolen. I was despondent but also relieved. Altogether, a curiously bittersweet and wholly appropriate coda to its time in my life.

There are times, even now, especially when I'm struggling with some daunting assignment, that I remember my Fuji. I imagine the thief discovering my beat-up prize, liberating it from my garage, and, bent earnestly over the dropped handlebars, riding like the wind down a leafy Austin street.

Strangely, I wish him well.

How Brown Turned Me into a Right-Wing Religious Conservative

DAVID KLINGHOFFER

Here's a confession you are unlikely to hear at your next class reunion. Brown turned me into the right-wing religious fundamentalist I am today. That's not the way I would describe myself, but it is how, very likely, many Brown alums would describe me. In brief, I'm an Orthodox Jew who has argued for seeing political conservatism as a reflection of the blueprint of moral reality found in the Bible. And this happened to me at Brown, notwithstanding its reputation for secular liberalism.

After graduating in 1987, I went straight to work at William F. Buckley Jr.'s *National Review*. By now I'm a seasoned professional conservative. I've been the literary editor of *NR* and now serve as a senior fellow at Discovery Institute, which, thanks to its advocacy of intelligent design, is probably the country's most hated think tank. Among my six books, this title stands out, if nothing else, for its forthrightness: *How Would God Vote? Why the Bible Commands You to Be a Conservative*. I've mellowed out a bit since writing that one, but you get the idea.

No parents, I assume, ever sent their child to Brown in the hope of inspiring a radical political and religious turn to the right. That would include my own liberal and secular Jewish parents, who were startled to realize the effect college was having on me. In high school, I wasn't content to be just a liberal. In the very Republican suburb of Los Angeles where I grew up, I wore hippie attire and a long beard, though I got rid of the facial hair in time for orientation week at Brown. By that time, I considered myself a socialist and was present, in Birkenstocks, for the school year's first meeting of the Democratic Socialists of America, held in a room in Hope College. Over my bed in Emery-Woolley hung a poster of Karl Marx. My freshman roommate, a lacrosse player from Long Island, seemed to think I was a pretty asinine seventeen-year-old. He was probably right.

By the summer of 1984, still asinine, I found my politics had been transformed. I was a youth delegate to the Republican National Convention in Dallas, which nominated Ronald Reagan for a second term. A noteworthy incident at the convention was the burning of a US flag outside Reunion Arena by a Communist Youth Brigade member. He was arrested (with my hearty approval) and took his case to the US Supreme Court, which ruled, in *Texas v. Johnson*, that anti-flag-burning statutes were unconstitutional.

What had happened to cause this political conversion? When I was a sophomore, a junior on whom I had a mad crush had a theory on this question: "You're just a contrarian," she said. "You're an anti-chameleon. Whatever other people around you say, you'll say the exact opposite." I laughed and half agreed.

We'll call her Tamara. Back then she was a semiotics concentrator who despised Republicans, took offense at being called a "girl" instead of a "woman," smoked cigarettes over cups of greasy coffee at Louis's, and consumed books by such French theorists as Derrida, Barthes, and Foucault. By Tamara's own measure, these habits would make her a regular conformist at Brown in 1984, at least among students in the humanities.

For Brown at that time was pervaded by a delightful atmosphere of addled liberalism. I loved it even as I opposed it, and still look back with fondness and nostalgia. I wouldn't rule out sending my own kids to such a college. That may seem paradoxical coming from someone who today is a very conservatively inclined father of five, but as I hope this essay will show, an atmosphere of provocation and challenge does not necessarily lead to one political or religious end.

For a lot of students back then, Brown in 1984 was the platform for sticking it to everything that is traditional in our "patriarchal" culture, as they called it. If you think of a father as a symbol—or a "signifier," as the semiotics crowd liked to say—then knocking him on his back was exactly what lefty campus activism boiled down to.

When I arrived on campus in 1983, for example, the boiling controversy was over whether to invite the Naval Reserve Officers Training Corps back to campus, almost twenty years after it had been abolished there. In 1984, students voted to demand that Health Services stock suicide pills in case of nuclear war—a theoretical measure since everyone knew Brown officials would never terrify our parents by going along with the plan. But again, upsetting Dad was the point of the whole episode.

Nor was the revolt against the paternal limited to politics. The theme of the most fashionable humanities scholarship was to indict the patriarchy by accusing the great fathers of literature—the classic authors—of racism, sexism, and homophobia. This may sound like a cartoon, but at Brown in the mid-1980s, it was commonplace. Yes, I delighted in all this craziness. What I most value in it now is that it provoked me, arousing my suspicion. If so many people were so intent on decrying the patriarchy, on insisting that every traditional idea transmitted by Western tradition was arbitrary and meaningless, then maybe the precise opposite was true. The more I was told that there was no singular Truth to be obtained from the great tradition that went before us, the more I was inspired to seek out the forbidden.

This is, I think, an overlooked aspect of a good education that conservatives, not least the religiously conservative, often forget. Education is not indoctrination. The purpose of college isn't to program students with accepted doctrines, turning them into clones of their teachers and parents, but to provoke them to think for themselves. Brown, true to its best tradition, did this for me.

Beginning with my sophomore year, everything that happened confirmed my new direction. I became the lone and reviled conservative columnist for the *Brown Daily Herald*. In my inaugural column,

I wrote about an experience I'd had at the Third World Center. One afternoon, Tamara and I had wandered in and discovered that President Howard Swearer was in the building, about to have a meeting with students. We ambled down the hall to the entrance of the room where the meeting would take place, only to be stopped by a young woman. She looked us up and down. "Sorry, you can't come in," she said, adding that because Tamara and I were not "third world" students, we were not welcome. We were barred from entering a university facility because we were white.

With a barely concealed glee at having discovered liberals in the act of discriminating on the basis of skin color, I wrote an inflamed column denouncing this antiwhite racism. I invoked Martin Luther King Jr. and the ideal of race-blindness. Warming to the subject, I pointed out that there was something wrong with Brown's—and many other universities'—approval of exclusively black fraternities and sororities. I lamented that at mealtime in the Ratty, you would see students of different races sitting at separate tables.

Why couldn't we all be friends? Why did no one protest politically correct racial separatism?

After the article appeared in the *Herald*, I returned to my room in Andrews Hall to find obscene graffiti on my door: F**K YOUR RAC-IST A**. Students poured forth enraged letters to the editor, almost every one condemning me. Because I was a resident counselor for a group of freshmen living in the basement of Andrews, the dean in charge of first-year students called me into her office to chastise me. As I understood it, I stood accused of racism for protesting racism. Subsequently, the dean appointed a student committee to oversee my counseling. The last name of the undergraduate who headed the committee was Kafka, proof that God, or possibly the dean of first-year students, had a wicked sense of humor.

I was shunned. I was a pariah. And I thoroughly enjoyed almost every minute of it.

Political conservatism often leads to religious tradition. We live today in a world stripped of what was, in the premodern era, an instinctive awareness of the sacred. Thanks to Darwin and other influences, from the mid-nineteenth century on, the truth of religion could no longer universally be taken for granted. My own emerging conservatism at Brown drove me to reexamine my inherited faith. I took my search to the Brown Hillel. At this Jewish gathering place, which was then housed in a barnlike white building on Brown Street, students of various denominations would gather. It was a sweet, humble, welcoming place without pretensions. Its emphasis was less on religion than on culture. I was brought there at first by, of all people, the object of my unrequited infatuation: Tamara.

Most people whose college experience changed their lives will tell you that their fellow students had the profoundest effect on them. That's what happened to me. Raised secular Jewish in Texas, Tamara had as a high school student lived for a year in England, where she'd fallen in love with a boy who was an Orthodox Jew. This led to a wild crush on both him and on traditional Judaism. As a result, she'd become an Orthodox Jew and exchanged her English name for the Hebrew Tamara.

To me there was something irresistibly exotic about Tamara. Here was a girl who addressed groups as "y'all" and scorned the liberal Judaism we had both grown up in. Yet politically she was left-wing, and she enjoyed shocking me with her opinions. Bisexuality was a favorite theme of hers. In this, she had been influenced by her study of "theory," which made a big fuss of romanticizing unconventional sexual practices. I remember once pointing out to her over lunch at Hillel that in the book of Leviticus, homosexuality is prohibited as an abomination. She was so offended by this that she rushed out of the building in tears.

I was charmed by the contradictions she encompassed, no less than by her adorable freckles. We would be sitting in Louis's, the surrounding air thickened by fumes of stuff frying in lard, with her latest incomprehensible semiotics paper about some dead Frenchman between us. While I joked about how impossible I found it to understand the jargon-heavy writing that was considered the norm in her classes, she would delightedly sneer at the nonkosher food in front of me. "Even the coffee here is *trefe* [nonkosher]," she would say.

It was partly my envy of her commitment and partly a simple desire to have an excuse to spend time with her that motivated me to try out Orthodox Judaism. I started attending religious services at Hillel. There, I perceived that the Orthodox prayer group, or minyan, had something in its loud-spirited worship that I hadn't come across before. A friend of mine who is an art critic once told me that he first came to appreciate the most austere abstract painting when he was visiting a gallery that had some highly praised but in fact mediocre specimens on the wall. By chance in his pocket he had a postcard with a Jackson Pollock painting on the front. He held the postcard up beside the painting on the wall, and the difference immediately struck him. The Pollock had a "buzz" to it, he said, a buzz of crackling energy and life.

Orthodox prayer buzzed. When Tamara and her friends sang the sixteenth-century mystical hymn "L'chah dodi" ("Come, My Beloved"), welcoming the Sabbath on Friday night, the urgency of their singing was that of the bridegroom running to meet his bride, which is exactly the symbolism that the hymn was written to evoke. This was nothing like the staid, dutiful singing at the Reform temple where I had grown up, which recalled not the excitement of the bridegroom but the boredom of grade-school kids reciting a multiplication table. Tamara and her friends stirred something in me spiritually that previously had lain asleep.

My attraction to Tamara led me to take first halting steps toward rethinking my assumptions about what makes for religion that lives, or buzzes, and religion that seems already dead. The Bible, I've since realized, has a precedent for everything that's really interesting in life and this is no exception. My discovery of my Jewish religious roots, however, raised disturbing questions about my personal identity, questions that would drive me to further rethink basic questions about faith, questions that Tamara, true to form, didn't hesitate to boldly, even rudely, articulate.

"You're not even Jewish," she sneered at me in her arch, teasing way. And she was right, strictly speaking. Though I had been raised in an ethnically Jewish home, I had been adopted as an infant, and my birth parents were non-Jews. Tamara advised me to visit a local Orthodox rabbi for advice on the question of my converting formally to Judaism.

When I went to visit the rabbi, he gave me a book to read but little other encouragement. Conversion in Jewish thinking is not a light matter, and I'm sure he could see that I was not ready to make any radical changes in my way of life, the kind that Judaism asks. That would come later.

What was important for me was the irritant that Tamara had planted in my soul, the question about myself—was I a Jew or not?—that stayed with me until I finally resolved it years later. At Brown, though, Tamara suggested that since I was staying in Providence for Passover—she would be out of town—I should share a seder meal with a local Orthodox family. Always eager to ingratiate myself with her, I did so, joining a family associated with the outreach-oriented Hasidic sect Chabad. I can't say I was enamored of the experience, but something one of the other guests told me turned out to trigger a turning point in my life. He was a young man from Brooklyn, studying to be a rabbi.

He noticed that I understood little of the Haggadah, the seder text, and he tried to explain a fundamental point of it. At Passover, he said, every Jew should see himself as if he is part of the Exodus from Egyptian slavery that the festival recalls. Judaism, like Jungian psychology, postulates a sort of racial memory passed down through generations, not in books but through something like spiritual genes. Nervously, I broached to the young man the subject of my adoption. It seemed that, as far as racial memories go, I was out of luck, I said. I had no claim on Jewish genes, but I realized at that moment that I wanted them.

My new friend looked warmly at me and issued a sort of prophecy. "I'm not sure what God has in store for you," he said, "but I've got a feeling that someday you may become a convert. Do you know what a *neshamah* is?" I said no. "It's a soul. Every soul contains a spark from God. All the sparks belonging to all the Jews who would ever live were present at Mount Sinai. All the converts who would ever live were there, too. When one of these sparks is born in the body of a gentile, it seeks to return to God."

That was the first time the thought entered my mind that God might have a particular plan for my soul. In Hebrew, the word for this minute divine attention to and involvement in the details of our lives is *hashgachah*. In English, it is, of course, Providence.

The unexpected influence of Brown continued to follow me when I left the city of Providence. I was still a spiritual dabbler, not yet committed to Judaism. But after graduation, a batch of clips from my columns for the *Herald* got me my job at *National Review*. At the time, *NR* was a haven of traditional-minded Catholics, a tribute to the spiritual influence of the founder, Bill Buckley. A young woman I met and dated there, the daughter of a professional right-wing Catholic antiabortion activist, filled a Tamara-like role for me. Once again, I was involved with a girl whose spiritual life I envied.

Wanting what she had, a relationship with God, I considered Catholicism but ultimately was provoked by spiritual envy to look more deeply at the religion I had inherited by default from childhood, Judaism.

Now that I'm a father, I wonder whether my children would benefit from going to Brown. A conservative and religious parent might prefer to see his son or daughter attend a piously traditional college. But a parent shouldn't expect a smart and independent young person to emerge as if from a printing press, inked with exactly the same thoughts and impressions every other student emerges with.

Education, as Judaism understands it, is both provocative and unpredictable, as the case of Abraham, the first Hebrew patriarch and prophet, demonstrates.

Shortly before Abraham's wife, Sarah, gave birth to his son and spiritual heir, Isaac, Abraham and Sarah moved to the Philistine city of Gerar. Why would this father of all Jewish fathers subject his son's earliest upbringing to the influence of a city that was urbane, cosmopolitan, and secular, a city where Abraham observed, "There is but no fear of God in this place"? Apparently, as Jewish rabbinic interpreters have suggested, it was because Abraham valued the challenge the city would pose to Isaac. Spiritual growth is aided by provocation.

But as with any growth, a good education takes unexpected twists and turns. Educators may wish to plant certain ideas in their students, but what happens, in fact, is unpredictable. Ideas can grow in the most fantastically unexpected directions. I believe that a traditionalist father or mother should consider the advantage that Abraham saw for his son Isaac in being challenged by neighbors holding views diametrically opposed to those of his parents. There is a danger in this, of course. But so too is there a risk in subjecting your child to a monotonous upbringing surrounded by mirror images of his parents. The risk is boredom. The risk is also the possibility that the child will never learn how to defend his tradition. When he finds it challenged after formal education is over, he may discover that he lacks any intellectual armor to ward off blows from hostile secularists.

For my children, I hope for a firm commitment to their tradition, but one grounded in independent thought and strong enough to answer critics. Maybe Providence will lead them to Brown.

Townie

ROBIN GREEN

When people today act all impressed that I went to Brown, I always feel compelled to set the record straight. Yes, I went there, but I was a townie. In other words, a category apart, and a lesser one. I suppose I assumed Brown had some kind of quota for townies, a pact with Providence to let some of its natives in. How else with my not-exactly-earth-shaking grades and test scores did I squeak by? What other explanation could there be?

Of course, I never took steps to find out if there was any truth to my theory. To be admitted at all was a coup for my family. My grandparents were immigrants, and though my own folks were funny and smart and assimilated, I was the first generation to go to college. And an Ivy League one no less. So who cared why I got in there?

Thus, in 1963, armed with an inferiority complex and inchoate resentments, I arrived on campus. Campus was a mile from our house on Wayland Avenue, near the old Brown gym, but I had never set foot inside. It was a world I had never imagined being admitted into. I knew even then that I was fulfilling my parents' yearnings.

I had some scholarship money from the state, and my own earnings. My parents sacrificed for the rest so I could live at school and have the full experience they dreamed of. I soon learned, however, that townies were not consigned to Andrews or Metcalf or a real dorm; instead, we were ghettoized at West House, a rambling 1885 wreck that I can't believe still stands on the corner of Meeting and Brown Streets and is, today, the green dorm, a vegan palace, special.

Back then it seemed like the outward manifestation of my gut feeling: *See? You can come here, but not really.*

Fine with me. Who were these Pembroke girls anyway? (Remember, it was a women's college then, and stayed that way well beyond my four years there.) What did these young women have to do with me? I had gone to a public school across town, a college-prep high where other go-getting grandchildren of early-twentieth-century immigrants went—Italians, Jews like me, a handful of Irish, maybe your random WASP. Most of the WASPs had fled the East Side for places like Barrington and Bristol when the Jews started to make money and move in.

I had learned about the WASP aversion to Jews firsthand, having spent days of my childhood summers with my family and their friends at the cabanas on Canonchet Beach in Narragansett Pier, aware from an early age that the much nicer Dunes Club down the beach did not accept Jews as members. I don't know about Italians. And blacks? Forget it. Same with the country clubs. Not that my family had the money even for the fancy Jewish country club to which their friends belonged.

And now, here I was at the regular Tuesday morning convocation, where all eight hundred Pembrokers were made to gather. Before me was a sea of blonde hair, more blonde hair than I had ever seen in my life or imagined. Dunes Club girls. Who had all gone to private girls' schools, like my rich Jewish girlfriends right here in Providence (I did not reserve my envy and resentment solely for WASPy blondes).

I soon found that I could compete with them in the classroom—well, maybe not with the New York Jewish girls who had gone to places like Fieldston and arrived on campus having already read the entire American Literature 101 syllabus—but did they even care about the classroom, other than the fact that there were Brown men there, prospective husbands?

Oh, the social opportunities in those years! The mixers and frat parties and football games and who knew what else? Certainly not me. Not having gone to a private girls' school, I had never been to a mixer and wasn't about to start now. It wasn't exactly a philosophical stance; what most likely kept me away was simple fear and social ineptitude.

To be sure, I had new and eye-opening cultural experiences at Pembroke—my first pork roast and chipped beef on toast, served by fellow Pembrokers in hairnets while I, a summer restaurant and factory worker, sat like a princess. I wasn't the lowest on the totem pole after all. I eventually had the genuine dorm experience, at Andrews, enjoying the luxury of weekly maid and linen service and sharing a room with three roommates I didn't much care for (see paragraph above on socially driven girls). After that, I was given a nice single in Metcalf, the serious (to some weird and geeky) girls' dorm, where I actually made a few good friends.

But for the most part, and much to my parents' disappointment, I stuck with what I knew, including my townie boyfriend, a handsome Greek-American who was now working as a parking lot attendant in Boston. Also my townie friends, the ones who hadn't gone off to college somewhere. I spent a lot of off-campus time with a friend who was a telephone operator and had a cool basement apartment across from Prospect Terrace Park. She was the sometime girlfriend of the son of an extremely high-level Mafia chief, a boy I had known since junior high. He had money and motorcycles and jailbird thug friends as bodyguards. We delivered messages from his father to other thugs at a nightclub in Boston's Combat Zone. We were wined and dined (despite being underage) at a now-defunct steakhouse downtown by staff who fawned over my friend the Mafia prince. It was all impossibly romantic—Valachi had recently testified about the existence of Cosa Nostra, but Mario Puzo's *Godfather* was not to be published until 1969, so who even knew about this stuff?

I remained an outsider at Pembroke. And Brown. I wasted four precious years maintaining a social distance, even as I became immersed in my studies—English and American lit with the incredibly handsome Mr. Van Nostrand and the passionate David Krause, and art classes down the hill at RISD. However, when I started writing short stories, which I did sophomore year after a professor identified in me a talent for writing and recommended I apply to John Hawkes's fiction seminar, my townie life actually paid off. It became my subject. And my stories were pretty good. Good enough to put me at the helm of Brown's literary magazine, and good enough that when an editor at the *New Yorker* magazine came up to campus, it was one of my stories that was chosen to be read and discussed by him before students packed into that very same sea-of-blondes Tuesday convocation hall.

And again, much later, those long-ago townie Mafia experiences came in handy when I spent six and a half seasons as a writer and producer on *The Sopranos*.

I know now how lucky I was to go to Brown—er, Pembroke, I mean. How it helped me to find myself. How it opened doors for me and gave me the wherewithal to venture out into other towns. And as Brown's stature in the Ivy League and the world has grown, so has mine when people learn I went there. But I always, still, for some reason, tell them I am a townie.

The Dyslexic Brain Kicks Ass

JONATHAN MOONEY

I wasn't supposed to make it to a place like Brown. I was the dumb kid. I didn't learn to read until I was twelve years old. I was one of those kids who couldn't sit still. I spent elementary school chilling out with the janitor in the hallway. Couldn't keep my mouth shut, so I spent middle school on a first-name basis with Shirley, the receptionist in the principal's office. And high school? I spent much of it hiding in the bathroom to escape reading out loud with tears streaming down my face. I was diagnosed with dyslexia in fourth grade, dropped out of school for a time in sixth grade, and had a plan for suicide when I was twelve years old. The only thing I was successful at was playing soccer.

I had transferred to Brown from Loyola Marymount University in Los Angeles. I went there only to play soccer. But the universe had a different idea—the fourth game of my sophomore year I broke my leg and ankle, ending my season and possibly any potential career. It was a relief, soon followed by emptiness and confusion, followed by an act of pure will that I still don't quite understand: I decided to do the one thing I was never supposed to be able to do: school. I took every literature course I could and declared to anyone who would listen that I was transferring to an Ivy League school. And what a dismal Ivy League applicant I made: spelled at a third-grade level, read in the thirteenth percentile, had the attention span of a gnat. I was a mediocre high school student; I had average test scores and a single-minded focus on one subject. They all said no. Brown said yes.

Transfer orientation went down in the basement of Mo-Champ on Pembroke and began with an icebreaker. We were handed a list of anonymous fun facts and our job was to match the facts with other transfer students. I was terrified. Here I was, with the "smart kids," the kids who sat in the front row, hands raised, the ones who got the gold stars. That wasn't me. I was the kid in the stupid reading group. In my school the smart and stupid tracks had been thinly veiled. There were the blackbirds, the bluebirds, and then my group, the sparrows. Might as well have named this group after a bird that did not fly: the ostriches. We read *Fun with Dick and Jane*. The other kids were reading *War and Peace*, and we all know that reading is what makes you smart. Getting As in a few literature classes at LMU didn't sew back up where I was split in half. It didn't help that kid in the hallway feel like he had a place in the classroom. Didn't help the ostrich feel like he had a mind that mattered.

That first night at Brown, I stood in the corner when the ice-breaker began and thought about heading to the bathroom. When I looked up, another student was standing in front of me. I don't know why he sought me out, standing alone in the back of the room, staring at my Sambas and pulling my white hat down over my eyes, but he did. He had purple hair, bicycle chains around his wrists like bracelets, paint-stained pants, and the elongated consonants of Hanover, New Hampshire.

"My name's Dave," he said as he ran his finger down the list of fun facts. "I got it," he said. "Circus performer."

I didn't get the joke and said very seriously, "No, I played Division One soccer."

"No way!" he shouted. "Don't buy that for a second."

"You?" I said.

"Investment banker," he deadpanned. "Now," he said, waving his hands wildly, "tell me something else."

I thought about my mom. She had walked me to my dorm room to say good-bye. I didn't want my mom to leave. I survived school because of my mom. No one messed with Colleen Mooney. She wasn't a tall woman—five four in high heels on her tiptoes. Not a rich woman. Raised my brother and two sisters on welfare in San Francisco. And she had a high-pitched voice like Mickey Mouse. But mom cursed like a truck driver and if you were a teacher or a principal not doing right by her, you did not want cursing Mickey Mouse in your office. But that is where she was. Every day. I said good-bye to my mom on the stairs of Pembroke, on the seal that supposedly put a curse on you if you stood on it. My mom was always a woman of few nonprofane words. She told me she was proud of me. That nothing was wrong with me. Then she left.

I told Dave that I had not learned to read until I was twelve years old. He stopped moving. "Now, that's cool," he said.

"Cool?"

"Yeah. Are you kidding? The dyslexic brain kicks ass."

Then he told me his story: high school dropout; struggled with substance abuse; graduated from a two-year college for students with learning disabilities and attention deficit disorder. Dave was the first of many truly singular people I met at Brown. I also met Becky, my Patrick Ewing–adoring, John Starks–worshipping, West African–dancing, fluent–in–American Sign Language–and–Spanish, tough–little–New Yorker future wife. People like Dave and Becky are exceptional, not in the trite way that word is most often used—as a proxy for *successful* or *accomplished*. No, they were two of the many rare breeds of mutants who populated Brown, people whose interests and passions radiated in diverging and overlapping concentric circles that couldn't be squared. They, and I, found a home at Brown. I had felt like a freak my whole life. But at Brown, difference was the norm.

It is common to tell kids that they are all special snowflakes, then in the same breath tell them to sit their special-snowflake asses down and learn the same way as everyone else. Not at Brown. I did over half my education as independent study. Took time off. Wrote a book. Developed a nonprofit. Went to a naked party and wrote about it for a literary theory class. At Brown, I wasn't the dumb kid anymore. I learned that I never was.

Neat-Hairs

ARIEL SABAR

I first spotted her in the slop line at Verney-Woolley. We were on opposite sides of the buffet. She wore a white apron and a hairnet, ladling turkey tetrazzini onto the passing cafeteria trays. I wore Bermudas and a vintage Hang Ten surf shirt, and I lingered, hoping to catch her eye as she flipped the glop du jour onto my plate.

It wasn't just the Marcia Brady hair—long, sandy blonde, parted in the middle—or the wide-spaced gold-green eyes. There was also an air of either hauteur or indifference. *If you want to judge me because I look like a slob in this grease-stained kitchen uniform, go ahead*, she seemed to be saying. *Because, you know what, I* am *a bit of a slob.*

I was judging from a distance, but I saw—or maybe idealized—her as a rebuke to those preening girls from Manhattan prep schools who glittered on the campus greens: the ones with artfully blow-dried hair, closets full of Guess jeans, and ancestral estates in the Hamptons. On a superficial level, I might have been their West Coast analogue. I grew up in West Los Angeles, sculpted my hair with mousse, gave thought to clothes. At Brown, because I performed in bands and was a Modern Culture and Media major, I often found myself among musicians, actors, and wannabe filmmakers. It was a milieu toward which Brown's wealthy, famous, and royal (as in the actual offspring of foreign nobility) gravitated, perhaps because it was the closest a college campus came to glamour. In two separate bands I had drummed for, the singers were the daughters or stepdaughters of sixties- and seventies-era rock icons (one was also a countess); the leader of a third band was the daughter of a leveraged-buyout wizard, and, grooving beside me in the rhythm section, on bass, was the son of a Manhattan publishing titan.

I wore black and went to their campus parties. I accepted invitations to weekend sleepovers at family homes in the Hamptons and on Cape Cod. I faked like I belonged. But deep down, I often felt like a fraud, moments from an unmasking. My father was a penny-pinching Middle Eastern immigrant professor with embarrassingly disheveled hair, and my mom, a geeky social worker who rarely wore makeup or fussed much about fashion. And so when the conversations at those parties turned to weekend jaunts to "the city" or spring break in some European capital, I fell suddenly—and self-consciously—silent.

The buffet girl at the V-Dub was every bit as alluring as the women at those parties. But I'd never seen her at one. How could someone like her not aspire to that bright world? What kind of nerve did it take to always—and unapologetically—be yourself? I wanted to know. But when I straggled in line, hoping to meet her eye, she seldom seemed to notice.

A couple of months later, I was eating at the V-Dub when a friend approached and said he wanted to introduce his new girlfriend. My heart dropped: it was her. It was apparently her day off, and she and my friend had just finished dinner.

Her name was Meg, my friend said. She was a sophomore, like us. Wasn't she great?

Sure, I said.

I'd thought we'd exchanged at least a few moments of significant eye contact in the buffet line in the preceding weeks, so I was trying to play it cool. But when she shook my hand, she gave no sign of ever having seen me before. I'd been, I saw now, just one more undergrad with a cafeteria tray.

I tried to be happy for my friend. But his constant bragging about "the greatest girl" he'd ever met made me angry at myself for not acting sooner. For being naïve and timid enough to think that with enough eye contact from a stranger—a cool one, who played in bands—she might suddenly decide she was in love with me.

The only consolation was that I now saw a lot of Meg, both in the slop line and on social outings with my friend. She noticed that I was shy and perhaps safe, and made sport of flirting with me when the three of us were together. It was an early-1990s ironic kind of flirting: dramatic eyelash flutters, overlong hugs, hand-on-hip Betty Boop poses. I told myself it was probably just a game for her and maybe for my friend, too: tweak the shy kid.

I acted positively Buddhalike in her presence, responding to her provocations with a poker face and turning away from temptation. It wasn't just out of loyalty to my friend. I worried that if I let on about my feelings, she'd laugh. *I'm just toying with you*, she might say. *You thought I actually liked you?*

So for a long time, I didn't call her bluff.

And then, finally—when she and my friend split—I did. I waited a respectful few weeks before telling my friend how I felt, and how I thought Meg might feel, too. Would he be okay with my asking her out?

Go for it, he said. (He let me know later that he recalled the conversation differently, and he decided, to my lasting regret, that we could no longer be friends.)

The next time I saw Meg, it was again at dinner at the V-Dub, on one of her evenings off. She took a seat next to me at one of the long tables near the kitchen. I'd just finished a jog and was in sweatpants and an old T-shirt. She had not just finished a jog or any other form of exercise but was wearing an even rattier T-shirt: a tattered relic from some long-ago family trip, with an illustration of grazing cows and the inscription HOLLAND.

This time, when she gave me a coquettish sidelong glance, I held her gaze. "Why don't we go up to your room?" I said, with what I imagined to be a 007-like cool.

The shock was visible on her face. After a very long moment, as if recovering from an uppercut, she said, "Uhhhh, I gotta go now."

I returned to my dorm crestfallen and hit the showers. I was certain I'd screwed everything up.

I was lonely that sophomore year and living in Spanish House. I'd wanted to bunk again with my freshman roommate, an heir to a drugstore-chain fortune. But he had chosen to room with another of our friends, the roguishly handsome son of an international banker who vacationed at a family compound on the Cape whose stone walls, he had informed me, were originally built by Miles Standish. So I applied solo for a spot at Spanish House. My assigned roommate was a short, muscle-bound Red Sox fan with a mealy Boston accent and the nickname Ballsy. We had nothing in common, except perhaps for a shared search for belonging at Brown. (One of the first things I'd noticed on move-in day was the ten-peg hat rack he'd mounted to the wall; it was positioned so that he could select from among his vast collection of baseball caps before getting out of bed.)

Late every night, once the lights were out, Ballsy called his high school sweetheart from back home, and their cooing often kept me from sleep. Other nights, he'd badger his friends about their shortcomings at the gym. "You gonna work out tomorrow?" he'd bark into the room phone. If he found the answer wanting, he'd respond, "What are you, a woman?" To outsiders, Brown could sometimes seem like a monoculture of political correctness and privilege. Ballsy was evidence of Brown's truer ideological diversity, which showed up in neither its marketing materials nor in the prevailing media narrative.

When I got back from the showers that evening, he'd just put down the receiver. "Hey, some chick named Meg just called. She says to call her back."

I had never been happier to hear Ballsy's voice.

After months of buildup, our first weeks together were ardent and nearly all-consuming. I soon saw that I'd been right about the things

I'd intuited in the buffet line. Her father, like mine, was an oddball immigrant—a Dutch farmer who tilled the patch of land they lived on in Connecticut. Her mother was a small-town librarian who cared even less than my own mom about clothes and jewelry.

To afford tuition, Meg required loans, grants, and a regular paycheck—just as my father had when he was in college. She worked three days a week, cleaning the women's locker room at the Olney-Margolies Athletic Center at dawn and working the V-Dub buffet in the evenings. But her future was bright. As a high school senior she'd been accepted into Brown's Program in Liberal Medical Education, which meant she'd go straight from her undergraduate studies into medical school.

While Brown had its share of Doogie Howsers—students whose teenage identities hinged on future lives as doctors—Meg staked her self-worth on other things. She had a sense of whimsy about the world, and a gift for storytelling that lifted me out of my laconic moods. While I holed up in the library for hours, obsessed with perfecting papers and maintaining a high GPA, Meg often coasted on her native intelligence and took most of her classes S/NC. She devoured young adult novels for pleasure, giggled at goofy movies, and padded for hours along forest paths, and these were as enriching for her as any classroom grade. As I see it now, she was modeling for me a life rooted less in prestige and achievement than in everyday relationships and experience.

One day, not long after we'd started dating, the conversation turned to those willowy Manhattan girls whom I'd seen as her antitheses.

"Oh, the 'Neat-hairs'?" Meg said with a knowing smile. I laughed, not just because I admired the phrase, but because of how effortlessly she dismissed Brown's social elite as irrelevant to her life at Brown.

Meg had a motley collection of friends: financial aid kids who worked alongside her at the V-Dub, a few geeks and misfits, all fiercely smart and independent. Many she'd met simply because they lived on the same hall in whatever dorm Res Life had assigned her to. She belonged to no scene. If she had any broader renown at Brown, it was only because of the quirky personal essays she wrote for the *Brown Daily Herald*, in a recurring column she'd titled "Life Near the Bone," after Thoreau. ("It is life near the bone where it is sweetest," he had written in *Walden*. "Superfluous wealth can buy superfluities only.")

Meg never complained about having to work; nor did I feel any particular guilt that I didn't. She went off to her jobs, and I went off to band practice, and neither errand carried any moral charge: such were the demands college made of ambitious students. Still, when I groused about a one-week summer stint scrubbing the kitchen at the East Campus Dining Center (the "Greasy Dee-Cee"), Meg rolled her eyes. "Try spending a year picking women's hair out of shower drains." That shut me up for a while.

Common sense argued against our getting serious. I was a Jewish boy from Los Angeles, she a gentile from rural Connecticut. I played drums in MuthaFridge, an eight-piece ska-funk band that drew hundreds of fans to its gigs on Spring Weekend and at Campus Dance. She played an autoharp she kept in a cardboard box under her bed and regaled me with recordings from *Annie*, *West Side Story*, and other Broadway musicals she had on vinyl.

I read Thomas Pynchon, Don DeLillo, and Joan Didion, she Jane Austen, A. S. Byatt, and Miss Manners.

At Brown, however, our differences were not obstacles but fuel for adventure. I took her to a Jane's Addiction concert at the Rocky Point Palladium; we rode together in the back of my freshman roommate's red Porsche. (Though no longer roommates, he and I remained friends.) She took me on hikes through Lincoln Woods, taught me to make rhubarb pies, and recited Robert Frost poems as we cuddled in her single bed. I tried to impress her with semiotic theory from my Modern Culture and Media classes, explaining how *The Cosby Show* and *Rambo* were not just entertainment but coded representations of the dominant ideology; she called that a bunch of pretentious nonsense and cutely told me to get over myself.

Meg came to my bands' shows but rarely felt comfortable at the cool-kid parties I dragged her to. She didn't drink and often wanted to go home early. Only occasionally did she mortify me. Straining for small talk with the neat-hair host of one house party, Meg rolled out an expression more suited to a Victorian novel than a house of hipsters.

"So who's the founder of this feast?" Meg asked earnestly.

The neat-hair gave her a look of utter incomprehension.

Graduation put our relationship under strain. Maybe we had only made sense on College Hill, which had shielded us from the headwinds of the real world. Maybe it was smart to see other people, to test whether what we had was genuine or whether hormones had just gotten the better of us.

After graduation, I moved to California with four other members of MuthaFridge. Our new band, Cleveland Lounge, found a foothold in the emerging "acid jazz" scene, signed with a small record label, and gigged at nightclubs across San Francisco and LA. There were lots of late, booze-fueled nights, and the women I went out with were—on paper anyway—more like me.

Meg, for her part, stayed back in Providence, for medical school, and dated men who'd shoveled farm soil and composed verse in their spare time.

But after two years, neither of us had found happiness. Our separation was clarifying: whatever love was, it wasn't a product of overlapping census data or matching answers on a questionnaire. I parted with the band and moved back to Providence. Four years later, Meg and I were married, on her family's farm, in Connecticut.

A decade and a half on, we are not quite as disparate as we once were: our tastes in movies, for instance, have converged, which means she is a little less fond of *The Princess Bride* and I a little less crazy about John Cassavetes. And though the coexistence of Julie Andrews and Funkadelic on our iPod betrays an abiding rift in our relationship, it has given our two children unusually broad musical tastes.

In essence, though, we are little changed. Meg is still the early-to-bed country girl, I a party-hardy (LA slang, circa 1989) city boy. As we've grown older, we've had to work harder to straddle those fault lines. We lived in Providence and Baltimore while I wrote for newspapers in those cities. Then we moved to rural Maine, to a sprawling 1830s farmhouse with a woodstove, giant barn, and sloping field. Meg hoped we'd stay there forever. I felt isolated and missed professional colleagues, and when I turned in the manuscript for my first book, we sold the house and moved to Washington, DC, where I had friends and a new job.

Meg, who completed her residency at Brown and Yale, works now as a psychiatrist at a mental health clinic in DC, treating immigrants and the poor. She likes her hard-luck patients—the strugglers and the strivers—but I don't know how long she will survive the city. She longs for the lush quiet of the countryside, and the National Arboretum—though picturesque and a short drive from our Capitol Hill row house—is no match for the ever-unfolding woods of her childhood. We are still searching for a place we can both call home; it is a search we are resolved to make together.

Looking back, I'm not sure we would have taken a chance on each other were it not for Brown. It was the one place where none of our differences seemed to matter. For a few precious years, we were free enough from the gravitational forces of family and faith and history to see through to the core of another person—to the part that snickers at the neat-hairs of the world, smiles at the well-turned phrase, and values trueness-to-self over status in the world. This last—this living of life near the bone—I know I will always struggle with. When I succeed at all, it is only because of that strange and beautiful girl who ignored and then found me in the V-Dub.

Beautiful Girls

KATE BORNSTEIN

I t was a cavernous New York City Hilton ballroom, September
1986. Well, it was roughly 1986, and it might not have been the
Hilton. But it was a ballroom, and everything you're going to read
here really happened, except for a few little stretchers.

It was late afternoon. I'd come up to the city by train from Philadelphia and arrived at the party half an hour early. The two ball-
rooms were empty except for myself and two friends I'd not seen
or spoken with for over twenty years. Jon Charnas and Martin
Broomfield—the two most delightfully flaming fags of Brown University theater in the sixties. I myself was not a flaming fag—not
then, nor now. I was a closet tranny in those days, and today I'm an
old dyke—in all of which identities I've endeavored to be delightful, which is an important quality in any gender or sexuality. Was I
a fag? A straight guy? Am I a dyke? Which is the truth of gender and
sexuality? Which is the lie? I'd only begun to explore that while I was
in college at Brown.

Jon, Martin, and I had all been leading men in our day. We were
the first to arrive at the party honoring Professor James O. Barnhill,
the charismatic master who'd built Brown's theater department. JOB
was retiring that year, and decades of his students, actors, designers,
playwrights, and directors were gathering to say thank you to the
man who'd opened their minds and hearts to theater. We hung out
mostly with each other, so it wasn't purely coincidental that many
of us in Brown theater had had sex of some sort with one another. It
was mostly heterosexual sex, but many of us enjoyed the new era of

177

sexual freedom with partners of all genders. Why, I could tell you the most wondrous story of a boy so beautiful he looked like a girl—she and I in the back of my VW Squareback. I miss her to this day. But telling the tale would be too much of a distraction to this story we're in the middle of.

Jon and Martin were delighted to be spending time with me, the newly out ex-Scientologist and transsexual lesbian actress and director. They fussed over me like a pair of doting older sisters at a debutante ball, fixing my hair and adding flowers here and there to girl up my androgynous lesbian outfit. We talked about the old days, the in-the-closet days. The only place gays and lesbians could be somewhat out was in the theater. Even so, trannies like me remained hidden. The only way to be transgender and out in those days was to be a drag queen and I never thought I was pretty enough to pull that off. It had taken me more than fifteen years to create a gender that was as close to female as I could manage. Now, only five months after my sex reassignment surgery, Professor Barnhill's retirement celebration was also my coming-out party.

In the mid-1960s, there was no theater program at Brown—there were less than a dozen theater-related courses hidden away in the English department. Those of us who were die-hard theater nerds quickly found English 23–24, "Play Production"—eight hours a week, not counting all the rehearsal time outside of class hours, two semesters a year. You could repeat those classes every year. There was no classroom, there was Faunce House Theatre: a fifty-foot proscenium stage that seated an audience of up to four hundred. During class hours, twenty to thirty of us students draped ourselves over seats in the first three to five rows of the theater. James O. Barnhill had studied with Stella Adler at the Group Theatre. Miss Adler's other students included Marlon Brando, Warren Beatty, and Robert De Niro. Professor Barnhill stood before us and sat among us, training us as Method actors. He didn't treat us as students. He treated us as professional theater people, and we all loved him for it.

Jon and Martin and I looked up from our reminiscing to see that scores of people had already arrived, and hundreds more were about to arrive. JoBeth Williams—star of stage and screen—would be one of them. In 1967, I was a sophomore. JoBeth was an incoming freshman. It had taken me only a year, but I was known across campus as the university's Richard Burton—right down to the heavy drinking and reputation with the ladies . . . and with more than a few gentlemen. JoBeth was beautiful, talented, smart, kind, and strong. One look at her, and you'd know that stardom was her destiny. I, too, wanted to be a star, but my gender/sexuality conundrum drove me heavily into weed. I played most of my roles stoned out of my mind—somehow I was able to make it work. And JoBeth and I were madly in love, looking forward to a future together in theater. We were a powerful couple—the "it" couple of Brown University theater—and we burned out brightly in less than one year. She was a star. I was a stoner. That's how those things go.

Back in the ballroom, Jon was confiding in me.

"JoBeth just found out about you last night, and . . ."—he stretched out the word with dramatic effect—"I hear she had a bit to drink at a small gathering for Jim, and she told everyone there what a wonderful lover you were."

I have no idea if Jon's rumor was true, but I do like to remember it just the way he told it to me. I was still blushing and we were all laughing when from behind me I heard, "Al!" I still responded to my guy name. So, I turned to see Jack Rose approaching me at a trot. He was a big man, bigger than me. He'd played Kent to my Lear.

"It's Kate now."

"Kate it is!" Jack picked me up in a bear hug. My feet didn't touch the floor. He swung me in a circle. Part of me felt girlish and delighted. Most of me felt trapped.

"Put. Me. Down."

To my surprise, that's what he did, and backed away. Hundreds of people around us had grown quiet, all heads turned to the door.

JoBeth Williams had just walked into the room. Her eyes locked on to mine. I turned to Martin, but he and Jon had backed off as well. So had nearly everyone else within twenty or thirty feet of me. JoBeth walked slowly and regally through the crowd, joining me in the open space. We stood eye to eye. JoBeth is tall; I'm slightly taller. That evening, she was wearing heels, a gown of forties noir. I was wearing cowboy boots under the skinny legs of my jeans, and a slightly frilly gingham cowgirl shirt. She was standing in front of me, her hands around my waist. She smelled the same. I was disarmed.

"Are you happy now?" she asked. "Are you finally happy?"

Happy? No, I didn't think I was happy. But I was looking right into the eyes of my once true love, and I was grinning ear to ear.

"You look beautiful," she said, and leaned forward and lightly kissed me on the cheek.

I bathed in her compliment. On good days, I looked like a tomboy. Kids in passing cars were beginning to yell "Lesbian!" out the window at me more often than they yelled "Faggot!" So I was more girl in the world than boy. That made me happy.

"Yeah, I'm happier," I told JoBeth truthfully. "I'm glad to be alive."

"Oh, Al! I'm glad to hear that. I mean . . . Kate? I'm sorry."

"It's okay."

I wanted her to take my cheeks in her hands and pull me forward into a kiss. I wanted the gathered theater tribe of mine to gasp and clap their hands. I wanted JoBeth to be a lesbian. I was sober, and I wanted another chance. But she was already backing away from me.

"It's been good to see you . . ." She paused. Would she say Al or Kate? The ring of people around us could not have been more silent.

". . . hon!" she concluded with a laugh. Her timing had always been perfect. Friends and strangers laughed and cheered for us. She walked off with her friends. I walked off with Jon and Martin.

As with all theatrical parties, the later the hour, the merrier the festivities, and the better the performances. That night, with the encouragement and acceptance of the Brown theater community, I gave one of my finest performances. I played girl better that night than I ever had in my life.

I took the early morning train back to Philly. The cats were stand-offish, glaring alternately at me and their empty food bowls. I fed them and sat down at my desk to study the script of Jane Chambers's *Last Summer at Bluefish Cove*, the show I was directing with an all-lesbian cast. It was early afternoon, and rehearsal was set for seven that night.

SELF-DISCOVERY

I was surrounded by fashion-conscious people, and I loved their influence on me. I wrapped myself up in an old black oilcloth rain cape that I found on a trip to New York in a Secondhand Rose sort of store in the East Village; I decorated that cape with black tassels removed from an old curtain. I pulled a big, black marauder hat down on my forehead and sauntered off to class, just the way Mrs. Vreeland had Veruschka (that German countess with feet almost as big as mine) photographed as Garbo in the film *Queen Christina*.

—**André Leon Talley** ('73 AM)

Senior year I moved into the House of Drinking and Smoking, took the cheap room, almost a pantry. It had a futon, some books, a desk, a chair, a Fold 'N Play record player. I screwed a blue bulb in the ceiling and slept there, mostly alone. I listened to old records and stared at the blue light. I worried I might go crazy, but I also felt on the verge of something important . . . I stayed many hours in that room.

—Milo Burke in *The Ask* by **Sam Lipsyte** ('90)

My own epiphany—more like a break, really—occurred senior year of college. I was mid job interview with Quaker Oats, explaining why I wanted to work there (it had something to do with Crunch Berries). Suddenly, I saw myself from a distance. Is this what I'd gone to four years of college for? What happened to my dreams of writing, of public service? I ended up interrupting myself by saying, "I'm sorry, I've made a mistake—I actually don't want to work here." Then I walked out.

—**Pamela Paul** ('93)

Sleepwalking at Brown

MEG WOLITZER

The combination of excitement and loneliness that can describe the experience of beginning adulthood can also describe the experience of writing a first novel. The two experiences will always be braided tightly for me, because I wrote my first novel as an undergraduate. Over the thirty-two years since I graduated from Brown, whenever I've had reason to go back I've felt a familiar, reactive blend of excitement and loneliness, in equal parts. I picture myself at age twenty, alone and walking across the quad wearing one of the very soft thrift-shop flannel shirts that I used to like. (Or that I used to "favor," as I might have written in my first novel.) In the picture my head is tilted down, my chin tucked in. Maybe I'm thinking about a sentence in progress, silently saying it over and over to myself. In all probability, the sentence has been overly polished, though with a little luck I'll realize it later, after I've typed a few pages and then taken them somewhere, perhaps a local burger joint on Thayer Street, in order to sit with them awhile. Mostly, walking around the Brown campus thinking about writing, or sitting in a diner, or at the quivering blue, blender-loud Smith Corona that I brought with me to Providence, I feel very much alone in my little enterprise, the way any writer does, but I don't understand yet that such extended aloneness is to be expected, and that there will almost never be a way around it.

I'd transferred to Brown that fall and didn't know too many other students on campus. In the beginning, all of us transfers continually collected in an odd little heterogeneous flock, the way people on the same floor of a freshman dorm do, except we were older and already knew what college life was like. So we were sort of jaded, too, and those meals we ate together weren't nervously boisterous, but were instead kind of melancholic: five wary, measured, disparate students poking at eggplant and soft-swirl, then hurrying off in different directions as soon as we could.

I had something I really wanted to hurry off to, and I spent a lot of time in my tiny Pembroke single, writing the novel that I'd begun before I arrived at school. My closest friend there, and really one of the few friends I'd made so far, was obsessed with Virginia Woolf. He was like a one-man Bloomsbury show, doing drop-dead impressions of Duncan Grant and Vita Sackville-West (though how would I know they were drop-dead? How would almost *anyone*?), and when I haltingly admitted to him that I'd been trying to figure out how to write a novel, he gave me *Mrs. Dalloway* and *To the Lighthouse*, both of which I tried to love, though really I was nowhere near ready to love them. Loving Woolf would come later, when I wasn't trying to pillage every novel I read for potential "writing tips."

I wonder why I decided that now was the time to do this, when I hadn't read enough great books yet, and when my tastes were only beginning to form. Maybe it was because my mother, Hilma Wolitzer, a novelist, regretted that she'd begun writing relatively late. She'd started publishing short stories in her midthirties, and her first novel didn't appear until she was forty-four. Her parents hadn't thought it was important for her and her two sisters to attend college, but she'd taken art classes and read a lot, and I've always thought of her as an autodidact. Second-wave feminism had altered her life; it had given her the bravery to write, and to go into New York City from our suburb each week and take fiction classes at the New School with the critic Anatole Broyard. I was intensely proud of my mother's accomplishments, but I also knew she felt she'd lost time as a writer, and I didn't want to do the same thing.

My novel, I thought, as I straightened up the mass of pages at the end of a day. It was as if the thing itself—and it could barely be con-

sidered a *thing* at that point—had already been finished and published and translated into other languages. Between bouts of writing,
I did my course work, reading Victorian novels and Japanese novels
and the Romantic poets. I felt as if I were standing under a waterfall
of pages, some of them my own, most of them not.

The word *ambition*, which comes to mind here, tends to have an
unpleasant tang to it, which can be unfair. While I do feel that maybe
I was in a kind of rush back then, it wasn't a rush to be famous or
rich, but just to be a novelist. Which maybe meant, to me, a rush to
be *formed*, when in fact I felt so unformed. Somehow, I knew that I
could treat the university like a laboratory in which writing experiments could be attempted. That first year, I studied with novelist
John Hawkes, whose workshops were an inspiration and a comfort.
We'd meet each week in the living room of someone's off-campus
house for a couple of hours and talk freely and frankly about one
another's work. Jack, as he was known, was a generous and thoughtful teacher who treated every piece of writing with careful consider-
ation, though most of our work had nothing in common with his
deeply experimental writing. There were none of the tense moments
that seem to happen in some workshops—moments in which someone suddenly attacks someone else, and there's a crackle of shock
and excitement, as everyone sits back like a literary version of Kitty
Genovese's neighbors and just watches.

Jack's class was an open, unguarded, and charitable environment.
We were a group of twelve sitting around showing each other what
we had. And Jack's comments, in class and on the backs of our sub-
missions, were essential. Once, late in the day, I ran into him when
I was leaving the library and, without thinking, I said, "Jack, I just
finished a new chapter!" It wasn't true; I hadn't finished a chapter but
had been struggling with one. "That's wonderful," he said. "Bring it
in tomorrow." And then I hurried home and finished the chapter,
just so I could bring it to him.

This worked well; as long as Jack expected writing from me, I produced it. But then, in my senior year, Jack was gone, off in Europe on

leave, and though I took another workshop it wasn't nearly the same. I was left by myself at the moment in a book's development when you have to make the shift from what you originally thought the thing was going to be to what it actually is. I'd moved to an off-campus apartment in Fox Point with two friends, and we'd set up a teetering, makeshift household. All three of us were trying to figure out how to live on our own in a close approximation of adulthood. One day I ironed a shirt by spreading out a towel on the used glass-topped table I'd just bought. Within seconds, the glass split with a shockingly loud crack, as if I'd chopped it with an axe. I hadn't known any better.

I could hardly live as an adult, but I kept writing my novel, which was itself an adult thing to do. I tried to remember all that Jack had told me; there was something to do with adverbs, I recalled. Something to do with metaphor. Something to do with being truthful. When you start out as a writer, you often write *for* another person— a mother, a friend, a teacher, or even a metaphorical person—the idea of the dream reader. And this can carry you a very long way. But finally, inevitably, you have to stop caring what that other person thinks and write the way you instinctively feel is best for you. Clearly, Jack Hawkes had done this himself—at least the second part—in his own work.

In my bedroom with its white-painted garage-sale child's writing desk, near the split-in-half glass table that I hadn't yet thrown out, I worked seriously on this new, frustrating, slippery part of my novel. Without Jack, I began to treat Brown as if it were a combination university/arts colony. I took all my courses pass/fail so that I wouldn't have to worry about anything as anxious-making as grades. Brown allowed all of that. The requirements toward my concentration were flexible, and I had time to write fiction and a great deal of time to read it. My advisor didn't intrude, and a student at Brown in 1980 (and maybe even now, though I wouldn't know) could decide to use her time there in a way that might be idiosyncratic, but would still fall under the general overhang of a serious undergraduate education.

I wrote a novel at Brown because I wanted to, and because Brown let me, and because Jack had encouraged me. I did it because I was lonely and excited and had an idea: a novel, of course, about college students. Had I really understood that there would be no other time in my life when I'd be allowed just to read (and write papers) and do little else, I might have decided that writing a novel was not what I should do yet. But that first novel, *Sleepwalking*—not only how it turned out, but what it felt like when I was writing it—retains a strange, small power for me. When I picture myself at twenty walking across campus in an old flannel shirt, my lips maybe moving a little, the image is of someone on her own and vulnerable and single-minded. But really, of course, it's just who I was. It's who I was when I was there.

Help Me Help You (Help Me)

LISA BIRNBACH

I hadn't been at Brown too long before I noticed a clique of *really* cool kids—the cohesive group of juniors and seniors who comprised the sexually liberal acolytes of Reverend Richard Dannenfelser, a handsome WASP minister, antiwar agitator, and sexuality counselor. In the aftermath of the Vietnam War, Watergate, and the New Curriculum, you couldn't invent a charismatic figure more perfect for his time than Dick Dannenfelser, Brown's Presbyterian chaplain (from 1965 to 1980). You just couldn't. (Although I have a fuzzy memory that perhaps Garry Trudeau tried with his Rev. Scot Sloan.) An outspoken Vietnam veteran, Dannenfelser had studied with the couple from Yale (Philip and Lorna Sarrell) who had studied with Masters and Johnson. Dannenfelser made sexuality sound as important as American history. Fine with me! I mean, we were at Brown University, the most liberal of the Ivy League schools in the midseventies, before the discovery of HIV/AIDS. It was a time of innocence. One feared unwanted pregnancy but not life-threatening disease. We understood our moment as one of very few consequences and a lot of exploration.

Those of you who remember the seventies are probably . . . my classmates. Those of you who don't—a few highlights: Bonnie Raitt at Spring Weekend. Semiotics. President Jimmy Carter. The bicentennial. The year of "Born to Run." Off-campus parties at Lupo's, and the first fancy dressed-up one in Newport. The blizzard of 1978. Martial law in Providence. The corner of the Ratty where the Europeans ate and smoked. (Yes, you could smoke in the Ratty. And almost anywhere else.) You could buy lunch at Big Mother for thirty-five cents. Other than survey courses like Engine 9, "Introduction to Religious Studies 1," or Champa's "Nineteenth-Century Art," classes were fairly intimate. I still recall classes of just six to twelve people as being quite the norm.

Those cool kids had somehow figured out that by taking Dick's (he was on a nickname basis with them) and Carla Hansen's team-taught seminar, "Topics in Human Sexuality," an ungraded, un-S/NCed, uncredited eight-week program, they would be encouraged to talk about sex and sexuality as much as they wanted—at least with other students in the program. To be fair, "Topics" was freighted with values and ethics too, but sex talk was the obvious draw.

The structure was patterned after Masters (a he) and Johnson (a she): the optimal way to conduct these sexuality and gender conversations was to have them led by a man and a woman together. Following weekly presentations, Dick and his partner, Carla, an MSSW, would divide their students into small discussion groups. And here, there was a hierarchy. There was a "head couple," whose names were Steve and Wendy. (They were so merged that I thought Wendy's last name was "Andsteve." I don't think I was the only one who did.)

Eventually, perhaps because of my lifelong quest to become cool or at least to be thought of as cool (a struggle that continues to this very day), I wanted in. I signed up to be a "Topics" facilitator. I was paired with a fellow I barely knew, and soon we were deputized to be sexuality discussion leaders.

This was probably 1977. It sounds like the dark ages, and in many ways it was. There was a gay group at Brown at the time, but I was unaware of any other organization to support lesbians or other sexuality and gender preferences. I was hardly a sexual daredevil. I wasn't really even an adventuress. I was silly and spontaneous enough to be considered fun or "crazy," at least compared to many of my classmates. I did take *everything* S/NC, which provided a little audacious swagger, but daredevil? Not by most standards. Still, in my mind, I was an adventuress of a sort. For instance, as a nondriver I sometimes sought rides home and would accept rides from people I didn't know. I didn't get, at first, that one should always ask one's driver whether he or she is planning to drive straight or stoned; I once got a ride from New York to Providence with a driver who had ingested LSD before we got on the FDR.

I wanted to LIVE in all capitals. I was the one who would go to the Silver Top Diner or on an all-night drive to L.L. Bean at the drop of a hat, because acting on impulses was living out loud. Talking about sex, which was novel for me, was part of this experiment in a new identity.

Maybe I was on the (in retrospect, annoying) continuum that starts at faux Bohemian and stretches to attention-seeking. (How Bohemian are you if your daily uniform includes a Lacoste shirt?) Nevertheless I was one of those people who had all the time in the world to talk (meaning to listen) to friends and acquaintances who needed to vent. I would justify this by thinking, *Oh, I'll remember the night I spent four hours listening to Mitchell talk about his bad relationship more than I'd remember studying for four hours.* Looking back, I think I was addicted to empathy.

Once a week all the facilitators and students, and Dick and Carla, would gather in an auditorium to listen to the scheduled speaker, who could be a transsexual, a cross-dresser, or a prostitute; a combination of those three; or someone even *more* advanced. Then we'd divide into our little couple-led groups to talk and talk and talk.

Did one of the students in our "Topics" section have a problem in her relationship? I wanted to help. Did another one have an inkling he was homosexual? I wanted to help him come out and feel okay about it. In my awkward and gentle way, I wanted to help—or maybe I just wanted to be liked.

In my little pocket of time in Providence, the thing that exclusive couples did was called "going out." The word *date* was far too square, too hetero-normatively conventional. The mossy smell of pot was discernible many evenings in the quads. The 1970s were a time of sharing. (This was before that word became corrupted by the

Internet.) People would turn their large stereo speakers toward their windows and blast their records outside so that others could enjoy the music. Headphones only existed in language labs. I think back to Friday afternoons, which were marked by so many—what can I say—warm and sharing impromptu window concerts to help us herald the weekend.

The draft was over. The economy was healthy. Upon graduation one could absolutely get an "interesting" job—which was far more important than a well-paying one (in my crowd, anyway). You could break your heart or cause someone's heart to ache, but you didn't worry about STDs, drug overdoses, paying back loans that would cramp your life through middle age, whether there were peanuts or peanut oil in your food, or where you left your cell phone. In fact, now I marvel at the fact that we could lead full lives without the crutch of total round-the-clock connectivity. We didn't have it. We didn't need it. We probably talked to our parents about as much as today's students, but since it was part comforting ritual and part checking in with one's parole officer, it was generally a weekly scheduled event—more newsletter than fund-raiser. Our parents didn't decorate our college rooms for us; we put them together (and didn't use the word *decorate*). We were kind of on our own, a bit adrift, and absolutely fine.

Did I tell my parents that I was a gender and sexuality facilitator? I doubt it. What would have been the point? My being a "Topics" counselor didn't take away from my classwork, my main extracurricular activities, or my social life.

During my tenure as a sex talker, I became involved with a guy who was the opposite of me: a Southern Christian athlete who once asked me if I owned a skirt. He wasn't being sarcastic or *Christian*, he just wanted to see my legs. That was the year I mostly wore my taller brother's hand-me-down Levi's. I had neglected to pack a skirt, makeup, or jewelry when I came to campus. It had just never occurred to me that I might want those things. But, eager to please, I decided to surprise him and show up in a skirt. In the late 1970s, unless one wanted a floor-length Indian skirt-slash-bedspread, one could not purchase such a thing in Providence. A trip to Boston was called for. I was pleased to find the perfect skirt in the first store I went to. It was a burgundy fine-wale corduroy skirt in the semipopular midi length. It looked not unlike a pair of my brother's jeans sewn together and hemmed at midcalf. I thought it was fetching.

I mention this because I had my own ideas of what attractive and sexy were. They might not have been accepted as attractive or sexy by others, but I was in "Topics," so yeah. I think I might have become more confident myself by offering counsel to students who were even less secure than I.

I was delighted when one of the seniors in "Topics" sat down at my table one day in the Airport Lounge in Faunce House. At once, I felt helpful, feminine, empathic, and upperclass (as in—a junior). I didn't know he knew who I was. We had a conversation about how fantastic "Topics" was and eventually, how great sex was—in an abstract, intellectual, S/NC kind of way, of course. Then he asked me which gadgets I preferred to use in the act. Oh God. Were we supposed to use electronics and handcuffs and things? Were we supposed to have sex with people *and objects*? What did the objects want? As being liked was very high on my agenda, if I became acquainted with these objects, I would need them to like me too.

This was a test of my inner prude. I hadn't been trained for this, and I was not half as experienced or curious as the senior. I was not only out of my depth, I was even turned off by the conversation. How could I help others talk about sex when I clearly didn't know anything about it? To me, sex was about love, passion, and commitment between two people. I was not a recreational sex player. Needless to say, I brought nothing—no *shred* of knowledge—to the Southerner. What we had together never even became an actual relationship in the technical or S/NC sense; I was a Jewish woman with a corduroy skirt and he was a guy with a big cross and we were each killing time with someone new and different.

While I concentrated in Semiotics, I minored in Figuring Out Who I Was and Making My Own Decisions. When I think about my years at Brown it is with pleasure and surprise that life was ever so simple. Of course, at the time, I didn't think my life was simple. I thought I'd never finish my papers on time, never pass my exams, and never be cool. I was scared that I wouldn't be chosen as class speaker at commencement, then I was scared that I would be (I wasn't). I was scared that I really didn't know what semiotics was or were and that someone would ask me about it during a job interview. And all this was before I'd ever met a Republican.

Jump Shots

BILL REYNOLDS

I remember the exact moment when I first realized that basketball was no longer the simple game I had played as a kid.

It was February of 1968.

We had just been annihilated by Princeton, then one of the country's top college teams. The five-hour bus ride back to Providence seemed as bleak as nuclear winter. While the bus crept along through the dreary New Jersey meadows, I leaned against a window, feigning sleep. All around me in the darkened bus were teammates slumped in their seats. The air smelled like failure. If we had had any illusions about ourselves as a team, this drubbing had shattered them.

As it had shattered any illusions I had about myself as an athlete. The game had been a defining moment, the night I first came face-to-face with my athletic mortality, the painful realization that I wasn't as good as I wanted to be and never would be.

What was I going to do with this realization?

I didn't have a clue.

For I had been brought up to believe in the most American of convictions: that if you worked hard enough, desired something enough, sacrificed enough, your dreams could come true. I had grown up surrounded by inspirational clichés and simplistic slogans that began seducing me at an early age. These slogans were deeply embedded in the culture, forever hanging from locker room walls, essentially unquestioned, unchallenged.

So I sat by the window, running the past through my mind as if it were some newsreel, my despair increasing with each passing mile.

Eventually, as if I had crossed some emotional fault line, the despair turned to disgust.

Basketball had always been more than just a game to me. It had been a way of life. It had determined who my friends were, where I went to school, what I studied once I got there. For nearly a decade there hadn't been a day when I didn't think about it. Without it, I certainly wouldn't have been at Brown. Without it, my life undoubtedly would have been very different. Now I suddenly wondered what it had all been for.

I had arrived at Brown with no confidence in myself as a student, and for four years, I had consistently taken the easiest courses I could find. Now I was a college senior, two courses short of graduating with my class that spring, without any idea of what I wanted to do in the future. It was 1968, three-quarters of the way through one of the most turbulent decades in American history, when it often seemed as if the country was undergoing a national nervous breakdown. It also was a time of dizzying social change, of the civil rights movement, the antiwar movement, the rise of the counterculture. Cultural tremors were shaking our society, growing into shock waves that would change it forever. Here it was—going on all around me—and I knew too little about it.

Why?

Why didn't I know anything about politics or theater? About history, literature, or art? Why, in the past decade, had I only read a handful of books outside of school, when I had been a voracious reader as a kid? Why was my life so one-dimensional? Why was my life both defined and shaped by a childhood obsession with a game? My life was a mélange of empty gyms and taped ankles, pregame pep talks, echoes of muted cheers. My life revolved around whether my jump shot went in or not.

Was there life after basketball?

At twenty-two, on a cold night in the winter of 1968, sitting on that bus and watching the future unfold ahead of me, headlights illuminating patches of the darkened highway, I wasn't sure.

*   *   *

Twelve years later, I often found myself on the third floor of the Rockefeller Library at Brown, always in a small carrel by a window that overlooked downtown Providence. I was trying to eke out a living as a freelance writer at the time, which—in the real world—was a euphemism for being unemployed.

After returning from six months of active duty in the army, I had taught high school English for three years. I had quit the teaching job to write a novel about a teacher with nothing to say, in front of a class that didn't want to hear anything anyway. But now that novel was in some drawer somewhere, right along with the rejection slips. My new project was a memoir about my basketball journey, which would eventually become the book *Glory Days*. It would begin with that night on the bus coming home from Princeton.

Every morning I would sit in the library, wallowing in the irony of it. Could you make up the fact that I was now spending more time in the library than I ever did in my time as a Brown student?

Did I wish I could go back and do my college years over, get up every morning with my notebooks and my sharpened pencils, then come back and study deep into the night, like a scene from some sepia-toned movie?

No doubt.

I was haunted by sketchy memories like this one: I was in a study group for a course I was taking—it was either "The Philosophy of Literature" or "The Literature of Philosophy," but to this day I'm not sure which, because I rarely went. I was a senior at the time, and there was a peace rally on the green every Wednesday; my student deferment was about to run out, and everything was as up in the air as a long jump shot. So there I was, at a study session one night, trying to play catch-up before the next exam.

I had listened to all the talk, trying to absorb it, until one guy said, "I guess that does it. It should be no sweat."

"Wait," I said, flipping through my notebook. "There's one more. It's in my notes. Yeah, here it is. Doctor Zay-goon."

There was a silence.

"It's right here," I said. "Doctor Zay-goon. Or something like that."

More silence.

"You don't mean *Darkness at Noon*, do you?" another kid asked.

Oh.

But I've come to realize that Brown taught me things I didn't know I was learning. At the most obvious level, it put me around highly intelligent, motivated people, and they did what good team-mates always do: they pushed me up, opened up my world in ways that would once have been unimaginable. Could any college student ask for more, regardless of his grade point average?

Brown also taught me a certain confidence that I'd never had before. Never again would I be intimidated around academic people, never again would I be impressed with pretensions. That, in many ways, was Brown's gift to me.

It was not an insignificant one.

After I'd freelanced at the *Providence Journal* for seven years, they finally offered me a job as a reporter. At the time, I didn't want to write about sports. It was the early eighties; I had evolved and was ready to accept the possibility that there was life after basketball. I was covering town council meetings that would make my eyes glaze over. Then one day a sportswriting job opened up at the paper.

"Why would anyone give up being a reporter to be a sports-writer?" asked the top editor.

"Because the worst game in the world is better than the best town council meeting that ever was," I said.

The editor shook his head in disgust and walked away.

That was thirty years go.

But even though I've been writing professionally for over thirty years now, and have written twelve books, I still consider myself a basketball player first and a writer second. Having played basketball at the level I played at is still the thing I take the most pride in. Shooting a basketball is still the thing I did the best.

I know this is foolish.

But it's never changed.

And there are still days when I find myself in some pickup basketball game somewhere, when reality gets distorted and I am still young and strong, off in my own world, oblivious to everything else around me. And on those rare occasions, which come like gifts from some benevolent god, the only thing I care about is my jump shot.

Faith and Doubt at Brown

KRISTA TIPPETT

I came to Brown in the late 1970s from a small town in Oklahoma with an immersive religious universe. The spiritual patriarch of our family was my Southern Baptist, hellfire-and-brimstone preacher grandfather. He was able to make some peace with my crazy leap far away when he learned that Roger Williams had founded the first Baptist church in America in Providence. I'd grown up hearing that only *Southern* Baptists were going to heaven—but my grandfather seemed to grant Roger Williams a posthumous exception, if his lineage would keep me safe.

As it turned out, I only entered that white church once or twice, and only with any reverence on graduation day. So simple. So reserved. Not at all what I was looking for on this whole new planet, this new beginning to my life. My only religiously observant friends at Brown were Jewish. I found their rituals exotic and lovely in equal measure to their disconnect from me.

Was there a cathartic moment when I began to doubt the existence of God? I don't think so. But in the exhilarating world of ideas and action opening up to me at Brown, I immediately doubted the relevance of religion.

Still, I signed up for a philosophy seminar on Kierkegaard my freshman year. I thrilled to Kierkegaard's lush imaginings. It felt nothing like piety to me when he took the biblical story of Abraham apart and retold it from every conceivable angle. I got an A on every paper I wrote in that class without understanding why. Meanwhile I was flailing in more secular subjects I thought I would love, like

"Introduction to Psychology." Pavlov didn't move me like Kierke-gaard's fear and trembling, his angst, his tortured "purity of heart."

Politics and history did captivate me. These, after all, were super-sized landscapes of fear and trembling, angst, and tortured purity of heart. The Cold War world carried its drama conveniently (in hind-sight) inside borders, ideologies, and armies. Its political battles were overtly cast in grand moral terms of Good versus Evil, transposing the religious sensibility of my childhood into a geopolitical key. I threw myself at one of the most unlikely Brown accomplishments of the early 1980s—an unprecedented exchange program with a university on the Baltic coast of Communist East Germany. I hadn't studied any languages in high school or traveled to any foreign country, as we so quaintly said then, but now I learned German. I was in one of the early groups to spend a semester of my junior year at the Wilhelm-Pieck-Universität in Rostock. Martial law had just been declared in nearby Poland. It seemed unimaginable that the Berlin Wall was not the shape of many lifetimes. I spent half a year among people my age who were crippled not so much by material want as by a poverty of possibility.

I now understood myself to be rich with choices and correspond-ing responsibility, and that gravity infused the political passions that drove my twenties. Eighteen months after leaving Rostock, I was back in Germany on a Fulbright and then on to divided Berlin as a journalist and diplomat until a year before the wall fell.

But first, back at Brown for senior year, I took a theology course. The late, dear Giles Milhaven let me into a graduate seminar on Dietrich Bonhoeffer, the Christian ethicist turned would-be assassin of Hitler. I still have my copy of Bonhoeffer's *Letters and Papers from Prison* from that class, marked up with Milhaven's favorite passages and my own. Like this:

> I'm still discovering, right up to this moment, that it is only
> by living completely in this world that one learns to have
> faith . . . By this-worldliness I mean living unreservedly in

life's duties, problems, successes and failures, experiences and perplexities. In so doing we throw ourselves completely into the arms of God.

I was still thinking of this foray into theology as respectable because it had relevance in terms of politics and history. But it pointed at a new religious sensibility taking root in me, not yet ready to name itself. So did my concentration in History—a decision I'd taken at the last possible moment before deadline. I fell in love with the study of history because it asked such large, interesting questions. I'd grown up thinking of this discipline as a matter of timelines. Now I was assigned a paper on whether the French Revolution was inevitable, or how West German foreign policy toward East Germany was a dance with the human trauma of the division. I can still physically recall my sense of the thrill and honor of such assignments. These were thought experiments about deep realities—inquiries into not merely what happened, but what mattered.

That's one way into describing the work I do now, a few lifetimes later, as a writer and the creator of a public radio project called *On Being*. I've come to see the great religious and spiritual traditions as a conversation across generations about the large, interesting, essential questions at the center of life: what does it mean to be human, and how do we want to live? My experiences in Germany after graduation finally left me pondering the limits of geopolitical maneuvering. They left me longing to grapple directly with the mystery of the human mind, heart, and spirit.

As I first learned at Brown, Bonhoeffer dreamed up the notion of "religionless Christianity" in the letters he wrote from a Nazi prison. He died in that prison and didn't live to develop it. But there it has rested in the annals of Christian theology ever since. From where I sit, this phrase is coming into its own as religious and spiritual identities intersect with the twenty-first century's global reformation of all of our endeavors. A third of adults under thirty resist conventional religious identity. But I have found so many of them to be ethically passionate and searchingly curious, theologically as well as spiritually.

Just as important, I see that new generations at Brown and elsewhere don't feel the need (as I did) to choose between curiosity about religion and politics or history or the arts or any practical sphere of action in the world. They don't see intellectual and spiritual grounding, reflection, and social action as separate endeavors. They are asking large questions of meaning from inside every discipline.

And here I am, uniquely equipped to trace their imprint on the world because of Brown's gift to me of a follow-your-nose education. I spend my days working with the power of questions, Brown's first great gift to me. In conversation with wise thinkers and actors— emerging Kierkegaards and Bonhoeffers of our day—I learn with ever greater nuance how we rise to (or fall from) the questions we are invited to meet. And I take delight in the paradoxical contrast between what I thought I was learning and the unforeseen ways the larger culture could use that learning later. In the world that has followed the Cold War's startling end, religious and spiritual traditions are as "relevant" as ever before—politically, culturally, globally. Even as Brown was fueling my undergraduate doubt, it was equipping me to reckon with faith's evolution in my own life and in the astonishing century that has unfolded.

Did I Really Found Production Workshop?

RICHARD FOREMAN

*Being an artist means ceasing to take seriously that very
serious person we are when we are not an artist.*

—José Ortega y Gasset

When I graduated from Brown in '59, it was a different and less progressive school than it is now. Back then, I had mixed feelings about my four years; I wasn't aware of how much I was learning and growing. And I didn't know that one day, I would be remembered as the guy who founded Production Workshop, Brown's student-run theater.

It's true that when I first arrived at Brown, I already had a strong interest in theater. I immediately approached Professor Florence Vandewater, the advisor to Sock and Buskin, which was Brown's theater club at the time. Back in high school, I had done lots of scenery and also acted in plays. So I asked Professor Vandewater if I could work in the scene shop.

She said, "Yes, of course—but why don't you come and try out for our fall production of *Much Ado About Nothing*?" So I did, and to my surprise, I got a big part. My fate was sealed. The next production was *Death of a Salesman* and much to everyone's shock, I (a mere freshman) was given the leading role of Willy Loman. After that, all through my four years at Brown, I played many great leading roles— everything from Shakespeare to contemporary French theater.

I soon became "known" at Brown. And one amazing benefit from this notoriety took place during freshman year, in my required French language class. In high school as well as at Brown, I had been an A student in all my classes—except for French, where I struggled to earn, at best, a C-minus. But the day after *Death of a Salesman* opened, I walked into the dreaded French class and my professor, a Frenchman whose name I have forgotten, announced to the class, "Gentlemen, we are honored to have a great artist with us. Last night I saw Mr. Foreman playing the lead in *Death of a Salesman*. What a wonderful actor!" What a shock it was to hear that from my haughty French professor. At the end of the class (it was winter) my professor came over to his C-minus student and helped him into his heavy overcoat! Needless to say, I passed the class.

But the very best thing that happened to me during my Brown career was my accidental enrollment, sophmore year, in a comparative literature course taught by Professor Juan López-Morillas. The course I had originally applied for was full, so as a second option I chose López-Morillas's course, knowing nothing about him. He was the most dynamic, stimulating, and inspiring professor I ever encountered either at Brown or during my graduate studies at Yale. He allowed me (as other Brown professors did not, in those days) to write very idiosyncratic papers for his class. He pulled the best out of me, and as an expert on the Spanish philosopher José Ortega y Gasset, he introduced me to the work of that great Spanish thinker, which led me to a lifelong obsession with contemporary European thought.

My gratitude to Professor López-Morillas goes beyond that one class. Shortly before graduation, when I was about to be married, he asked me if I was taking a honeymoon and where I was going. I told him my family had offered us a wedding trip to Europe, but I wasn't really interested. Professor López-Morillas looked at me slyly and said to me gently, "Well, Richard—I really think you should go." That persuaded me, thank God, for that trip truly opened my eyes and changed my life for good.

What made it especially ironic in retrospect (given my struggles in French class) was that after my first trip to Europe, I became enamored of, and seduced by, Paris and by everything Parisian. That love is still going strong; so far, I have directed nine French productions, all in French, at major venues from the Paris Opera to famous state theaters.

But let's return to my days at Brown and my legendary founding of Production Workshop. In my junior year, when I and a few friends generally avoided the offical dining hall and instead had long lunches with extended conversations in the cafeteria at Faunce House, some of those friends started showing me (the "Famous" Brown Actor) plays that they were writing for class.

After reading a few, I said to myself, "I can do better than this." So I switched from being an English major to being a creative writing major and I started writing plays.

I was still acting, and in my senior year, as a member of the student board of Sock and Buskin, I persuaded them to schedule a production of Bertolt Brecht's *Caucasian Chalk Circle*. Brecht was not well-known in America at the time, and unbeknownst to me, all Sock and Buskin choices had to be approved by the dean of the college. Well, there had never been a problem with this before, but we quickly got the message from the dean: "Brown is not going to allow performances of a play by a Communist!"

Needless to say, I was upset by this. I had believed Brown to be more open-minded at the time (1958). And, in response, I resigned from Sock and Buskin.

Where to turn? I went to the director of Faunce House and got permission to do a series of "art events" featuring readings of some of my own experimental plays. That all went well enough, and I graduated and moved on to Yale drama school as a playwright.

It was only years later that someone told me, "Oh, you never heard? Derived from your Faunce House events, we started something called Production Workshop that is now the major producing organization at Brown, and you are remembered as the founder." I was delighted, of course, that my efforts were apparently not forgotten, but I suspect that I'm getting more credit than I deserve.

Certainly, it was thanks to Brown that I began writing plays and then mounting them myself. And now, in my seventies, I have begun a new career as a film director, following another interest that began at Brown. Despite the fact that I was so involved in theater, I rarely went to films. But in my first two years at Brown, I began to review movies for the *Brown Daily Herald*. Now that my (very experimental) feature films are beginning to be shown at festivals around the world, I am somewhat shocked to remember that my obsession with film actually started at Brown when I accidentally "fell into the role" of film critic.

When I think about it, I owe many things to Brown, and it has been illuminating to take stock of my indebtedness. Having returned a few times in later years to speak to classes, I am impressed at how much more sophisticated and intelligent the Brown students seem to me today. All to the good, of course. I now believe that Brown lives up to its reputation as a top-quality school, even though, in my perhaps arrogant and overly demanding youth, I was not at all convinced.

Residential Life

DAVID EBERSHOFF

I n the summer of 1987 I called my future freshman roommate—
let's call him Ryan—to introduce myself. He was from Green Bay,
Wisconsin, and as I understood it, the Office of Residential Life had
assigned us almost randomly. I remember only two questions playing
a part in the decision: Do you smoke? Are you a morning or night
person?

If other information played a part in our assignment, I was never
privy to it.

"Do you play football?" Ryan asked on the phone. No one had
ever asked me that question before (nor has anyone since). He told
me that Brown's football team had recruited him, but he quickly
moved on. He asked what kind of music I listened to. In high school
I was a devotee of the Smiths. I had cut dozens of photographs of
Morrissey from magazines and Scotch-taped them to my bedroom
wall. In one, he was clutching a dozen daisies to his bare chest. In
another he wore jeans and no underwear. My parents tolerated these
pictures with more compassion than I appreciated at the time, but
what exactly they meant to me remained unsaid.

On the phone Ryan admitted he didn't know the Smiths. He
liked Led Zeppelin and Metallica but expressed a genuine interest in
listening to my CDs as well.

Ryan was modest in a midwestern, irony-free way that I have
always found endearing, probably because it reminds me of my parents. He didn't mention that the football team was grooming him to
be a future star. As long as I knew him—which would not be long—

he never once discussed his considerable athletic talents. That phone call was in July, and we had no further contact until we arrived on campus in the fall.

For three years I had been thinking of my arrival at college, and Brown specifically, as my own personal liberation. In my early teens I hated myself for being gay. I was lonely, distrustful, and certain the world would turn on me if it knew. The summer I was fifteen I felt especially isolated; I distanced myself from my friends, fearing their response to who I really was. For company I turned to books. I devoured every gay novel I could find at the public library and on the shelves of our local Waldenbooks. I read probably forty or fifty books that summer; it was one of the most powerful educational experiences of my life. I read Truman Capote and James Baldwin, Armistead Maupin and Rita Mae Brown, Gore Vidal and Edmund White. I read Oscar Wilde, André Gide, and the gayer books by Virginia Woolf. I tried to find the gayness in Marlowe, Melville, and Henry James. Some of this writing was beyond me, but it confirmed what I needed to know: gay people existed in the world and our truths were valid.

One day that summer, I realized I had read every novel in the bookstore's small Gay & Lesbian section. A certain satisfaction fell upon me. In that moment I saw a future where I was happy and finally accepted myself. I vowed to sit tight with this secret for three more years until college and then I would be free. This motivated me to study and it's probably why I had the grades to get into Brown. I chose Brown because of its liberal reputation. I assumed the most liberal college in America would be the best place for me. Sometimes our decisions are even simpler than they seem.

Our room on campus overlooked an alley and a Dumpster. It was ugly, with cinder-block walls and linoleum floor tiles, but I didn't care and neither did Ryan. We arranged our desks to face each other like an old-fashioned partners' desk. I taped up two or three Morrissey pictures and some poster board with lines from Joan Didion. Ryan didn't decorate his side. He had very few possessions and made his bed with a prison-y brown blanket. He was about six-three and had the strong but lithe body you want in a quarterback. He was ginger haired and his face seemed a little pushed in. With my dreams of the poetic, nerdy 140-pound Morrissey, I didn't find Ryan attractive, but I soon realized from the parade of young women who knocked on our door that many did.

"I'm out of here," he said that first day, throwing his backpack over his shoulder. The lock clicked behind him and I thought, *This is it; my life can finally begin.*

The next day, I went to Arnold Lounge for the Lesbian, Gay, and Bisexual Alliance's welcome meeting. About a dozen people stood around nibbling Chips Ahoy! cookies. A small woman with short blonde hair and Doc Martens broke off from a conversation to greet me. I'll call her Kathy. Almost at once she began stroking my arm and calling me sweetie, while sharing intimate details about herself. Kathy was bisexual and enjoyed masturbating while watching two men have sex. Kathy found my discomfort endearing and started calling me her little innocent. She introduced me to the others, most of them men, and I felt a certain gaze reminiscent of what happens when a stranger walks into a bar at two a.m. "Careful what you say around him," she said, standing on her toes to cover my ears. "He's very innocent."

The group was discussing a recent *Wall Street Journal* story depicting Yale as a haven for gay students, with a wide-reaching network among students, faculty, and staff—an environment I had expected to find at Brown. Yale's president had publicly denounced both the article and its author, a Yale alum. The group in Arnold wondered if Brown would have handled it any differently. Someone said Brown's president would never have dismissed its gay students so cruelly and someone else said, "Are you kidding me? When money's on the line?" Someone else noted that no one would have written such an article about Brown in the first place.

I left the meeting disappointed. Although I had met a handful of people who would become good friends, the open sexual banter and the cynicism didn't sit well with me. I had probably walked through the door of Arnold Lounge hoping to find a skinny, vegetarian poet-musician with black eyeglasses, so my letdown was inevitable. Still, I was so hungry for companionship that the next day I dropped by the LGBA office in Faunce House. The LGBA had a custom of propping a large pink triangle in its window whenever someone was there. The university prohibited other student groups from posting anything in their windows but made an exception for the triangle's welcoming pink beacon.

"It's my little innocent!" Kathy patted the sofa for me to join her. She was barefoot, her coltish legs tucked up beneath her. She touched my knee and said, "I know a lot of men who are dying to get in your pants." I was both appalled and intrigued. A few others were there, organizing an AIDS rally, and one of the men, a senior wearing a SILENCE = DEATH button, indicated he was HIV-positive. I didn't say much on that visit and felt separate from them and their activism. Before Brown, I hadn't thought of being gay in any political or social terms; for me, it was personal: I just wanted a cute boyfriend. Still, Kathy and her friends were warm to me and asked nothing in return. I left the office both relieved to have spent time in a place where I felt accepted and, I'm afraid, feeling somewhat cool toward people who had been warm to me.

During this time, the *Brown Daily Herald* published a story about the dean for freshmen and sophomores; he had been arrested at an I-95 rest stop in Attleboro for "lewd and lascivious" behavior with another man. Dean Donovan, a married father of two, was well respected on campus. He was a round-faced, red-cheeked, jovial recovering alcoholic with an admirable history of supporting groups that needed friends in the administration, including the LGBA. The arrest was the main topic of conversation on campus that week. A number of professors and students expressed support for Dean Donovan, highlighting his many professional accomplishments as a classics scholar and administrator and arguing he did not deserve punishment or ostracism for such a "mistake."

Dean Donovan found less sympathy than you might expect in the LGBA office, where there was a low-grade scorn for what they called closet cases. We weren't without feeling for Dean Donovan's turmoil, but we were hurt. We now knew our dean was one of us and yet many at Brown argued that all could be forgiven if he returned to the closet. The administration quietly reassigned the dean's duties while he sorted out his legal troubles.

Had Dean Donovan been in place (he eventually returned to serve Brown's students with distinction for another seventeen years), he probably would've played a part in what happened next. Maybe his good humor and empathy would have infused the situation with a little more grace. But Dean Donovan was otherwise occupied when my own troubles began.

One day Ryan said, "Hey, Dave"—he called me Dave, even though I never go by that—"a couple of guys on the team told me you were gay."

When I said it was true he said it was cool and didn't bother him.

"It doesn't bother me either," I said.

Soon after this exchange, it dawned on me that some people on my floor were treating me differently. A few acted awkwardly, as if they didn't know what to say when I passed them in the hall; others wanted me to know "it didn't matter"; and for a couple of women, this news suddenly made me a potential best friend. One day, returning to my room, I came upon Ryan on the phone with his parents. He seemed tense and quickly hung up. He looked at me somewhat helplessly and said his parents were acting weird. "I don't want you to take this the wrong way but they don't want me living with a gay guy."

I asked what he wanted to do.

"Don't worry, man. I told them I don't want to move."

I was surprised by how far this information about me had traveled. I wasn't ready to come out to my family or my friends in California and I began to worry; if this news had reached Wisconsin, how long before it hit the West Coast?

A few days later, two of the dorm's residential advisors—I'll call them Susie and Jeff—knocked on the door. Susie was one of those boarding school graduates who landed on campus with three dozen friends, a beat-up BMW, and the social ability to organize a coed touch football game any time of day or night. "Dave, can we talk?" she asked. "Ryan's parents are really upset."

"They want him to move out," Jeff added. I barely knew him but he gave the impression that he had filled out his RA application late one night with a pen in one hand and a bong in the other and was still a little stunned that he'd been accepted.

Susie explained that Ryan's parents had threatened to pull Ryan from Brown if they didn't reassign him and "obviously no one wants that."

"Ryan doesn't want to move but his parents keep insisting and the football team isn't going to risk losing him," Jeff explained, embarrassed about the whole thing.

"It's a big mess." Susie sighed. "Everyone wants to figure out the right thing to do."

I was stunned by the invisible flurry of phone calls, meetings, and "discussions" about me that had apparently taken place. To use one of the campus's favorite words of the era, I had become an issue.

"No one wants to see Ryan leave," Susie said. "We wish there was some other option."

That's when I realized why they were there.

"I'm not moving," I said.

Susie blinked. Jeff looked at his Top-Siders. I was about to cry but willed myself not to. I don't remember what was said after this, but they soon left. I imagined Susie calling someone—who?—to report, "He won't budge."

When I turned up at the LGBA, Kathy immediately sensed I was upset. I told her what had just happened and she said, "They can't do that." She picked up the phone to call the Office of Residential Life, but I told her not to. She set down the phone and warned me to be careful.

When I returned to the room late that night, Ryan said, "Hey, Dave, it isn't me. It's my parents. I told them you're cool."

I told him not to worry and went to bed, exhausted. I had begun to hope he would move. I had never shared a room before and, his parents aside, I didn't really enjoy sharing one now. Ryan was neat and often out, but still he snored and occasionally invited friends over to listen to *The Black Album*. I imagined turning our double into a single where I could hang more Morrissey pictures and a few ethnic scarves. I imagined inviting my future, hypothetical boyfriend over to be alone.

A couple of days later, Susie and Jeff returned.

"Ryan's moving out tomorrow," Susie announced. "People are really upset."

"I thought he wanted to stay."

Susie told me that the football team had requested the university reassign Ryan. I don't know if that's true, but I do know that after almost a week of private conversations about me that I was excluded from, he was moving out. "People need to process what's going on," Susie said. There was to be a unit-wide meeting that night but everyone agreed, she told me, I shouldn't be there. Apparently Susie, and quite a few others, blamed me.

Behind her, Jeff made a face that said, *Man, I so don't want to be here*.

My first reaction wasn't anger but relief. I would like to tell you that in this moment my personal convictions emboldened me and I spoke up for myself. I didn't. I was just glad it was over and began to think about rearranging the furniture.

Not long after, I got a call from a *BDH* reporter. "We're doing a story about what's going on with your roommate."

I hung up. Was I really going to come out to the world—*like this*? I was confused about all the people involved. Who were they? What were they saying? Even now I have no idea.

I found Kathy in the LGBA office. Before I could finish explaining, she was on the phone with Residential Life. "Answer this: is it or isn't it Brown's policy to allow someone to move just because their roommate's gay?" Followed by, "Then why is he moving?" Next she asked me what I wanted to do about the *BDH*. There's never a really great time to come out—at least there wasn't back in those days. No matter how awkward, this was my chance to leave the closet forever. I thought about it, then returned the door to its ajar position. "You sure?" Kathy asked one last time. I was. She called the *BDH* and convinced them to kill a story they didn't have all the facts on.

Looking back, my passivity frustrates me. Why didn't I assert my rights? I should have let the *BDH* open the debate. But I was young and afraid; in some ways my old fears from my early teens had played out. I didn't want to fight a public battle with rules and players I did not understand. More basically, I no longer wanted to live with Ryan. By then I was blaming him—he could've stopped everything by saying no. I wanted him out. And even more than justice, I wanted my single.

I returned to my dorm soon after the meeting had ended. People were hanging out in the hall. No one spoke to me as I passed. In one room, a woman was sobbing while her friend consoled her. Her red face, her unreasonable tears, her friend squeezing her shoulder is what finally sent a rod through my backbone. "Get over it," I snapped. Later, two women came by my room. "We just want you to know we don't blame you." They were reaching out with real empathy, but I was done. "Neither do I," I said, and shut the door.

Ryan slept elsewhere that night. The next day when I returned from class there was no trace of him, except the two desks pushed back-to-back.

How did this end? Not well for either of us. I never saw Ryan again. Our campus schedules were so different we never ran into each other. After winter break, he didn't return to Brown. I heard he had flunked out. I don't know if this is true. All I can say is he spent one semester at Brown and never returned. As for me, I've regretted this next part for twenty-five years.

Late in the semester, Res Life notified me I would have a new roommate in January, an unidentified transfer student. I had settled into my extra-large single and didn't want to share it. I enjoyed the freedom to write and study, to sleep when I wanted, to listen to Morrissey, and to invite over the new friends I was making, including my now-real boyfriend (a cute grad student from Houston). There was more: the experience with Ryan had so scalded me that I had vowed never to be so vulnerable again.

The night before I left for winter break, my best friend and I hatched a plan to drive away my future roommate. We gayed up the room, decorating it with rainbows, pink triangles, and, most insultingly, pages ripped from beefcake magazines. It was a desperate, passive-aggressive move: I wasn't going to let anyone reject me; instead I would reject him first, turning myself into a stereotype. At the time I didn't think of it in those terms, but certainly that's what I was doing. I'm still embarrassed by the scene: I imagine this hopeful transfer student entering the room and finding pictures of naked men next to the Morrissey posters. He fled to the housing office, which promptly assigned him another room. When I returned to campus the double was mine alone and Susie said something vague about my roommate deciding to live somewhere else. That transfer student I turned against could have been a friend; he could have been gay himself. After being so coldly unaccepted, I had turned around and done the same thing. A psych major would say that after being punished for being gay I used it as a weapon. It was worthy of disciplinary action and yet my own lewd behavior escaped punishment.

I sometimes wonder about Ryan, about what really happened and why he never returned. No one comes to Brown thinking they'll last only a semester. Certainly Ryan arrived in Providence with as many hopes as you and me. Yet something destroyed that version of Ryan's future and I wonder how I fit into the narrative of that destruction. For a long time I resented my roommate experience and was ashamed of how I responded to it. Now I look back on it as a relic of another age. In our first weeks in college, Ryan and I found ourselves in opposite ends of a boat caught on tricky shoals. Instead of helping each other, we both bailed. And here's what I really wonder: how is it that fate can bring two young men so close together that only a pair of desks separates their pillows, and then yank their paths so drastically apart that I cannot tell you if Ryan is now among the living or the dead?

POLITICS

On the morning of May 5th, awakening to the sound of a bullhorn on the street—"BROWN UNIVERSITY ON STRIKE!"—I pulled the pillow over my head. I think this would be the week I hung up on my gentle but still pro-Nixon father from one of those pay phones in the West Quad.

I stayed in my room or at the library, writing a long paper on Romantic poetry that I didn't really need to turn in. Everywhere else, at least for a while, the war protests thrived.

—**Thomas Mallon** ('73)

[At] Brown University, I was always someone who was a social activist, but I dabbled in experimental filmmaking classes. It became clear as I got into the real world that there was a way to combine these two interests.

—**Liz Garbus** ('92)

JEFF SHESOL

Talking 'Bout My Generation

IRA C. MAGAZINER

In 1965, when I became a freshman at Brown University, black Americans in Southern states could not eat at white lunch counters. They had to ride in the backs of buses and use separate bathrooms. Black Americans in northern states could not move into middle-class neighborhoods and were paid less for the same jobs than their white coworkers. Women made up only 2 percent of the student bodies at medical and law schools. A woman was raped and beaten in Central Park in New York and the news accounts led with the commentary that "she was asking for it because she was wearing a short skirt."

Some of my eighteen-year-old friends who could not go to college would die in a war in Vietnam whose purpose few of us understood. Though they fought valiantly for their country, they were not allowed to vote in elections because the minimum voting age was twenty-one. Rivers caught fire because toxic chemicals were dumped in them, and on some days soot from factories and power plants was so thick that breathing without coughing was difficult. And despite two decades of economic growth in America, many Americans still lived in dire poverty.

While America provided unparalleled freedom and opportunity for many people, many problems needed to be addressed.

At most American universities, education consisted of fact-filled lectures followed by rote regurgitation of those facts on tests that left little room for creative thinking. Students were passive learners moving from one required course to another. Knowledge was divided into separate compartments, and students had little responsibility for their own education.

There were only a handful of African-American students at leading US universities, and they represented less than 2 percent of the student body at Brown. Women made up only 20 percent of the total Brown/Pembroke student body. Students had no say in university governance. Men could not be in a woman's dorm room unless the door was open, and visiting hours were limited.

But in the space of six years, all of this would change—both nationally and at Brown—and students played a significant role in bringing about that change.

The student idealism of the late 1960s has been caricatured for its extremes—the "yippies" and the "hippies" and the "sex, drugs, and rock and roll." (I will not comment on the sex and drugs, but the rock and roll was and remains something special.) But there was a lot more to student life than this. The movements that students helped initiate and support transformed America in positive ways. And America, and Brown University, would never be the same.

Two events at Brown stand out: the commitment to affirmative action forged when black students walked out of the university in protest in 1968, and the adoption of the New Curriculum in 1969. In both cases, students conceived of the changes that were needed and organized political movements that forced those transformations. They were aided by a university administration that was willing to listen and engage and that had the courage to change.

My first attempt at student activism at Brown was born of necessity and self-interest. At that time, students were required to eat at Brown's main dining hall, popularly called "the Ratty." The food was awful and I usually bought my dinner from a truck called Pizza Pete that parked near my dorm. Pete eventually became the official caterer of the education movement at Brown.

One of my main projects as freshman class president was to organize a petition and hold rallies to eliminate the requirement to eat at the Ratty. Needless to say, it was a popular cause. I got the Brown student government to endorse the movement.

We thought we were making progress when another student and I were invited to meet then-president Barnaby Keeney. We showed up at University Hall ready to negotiate. His secretary ushered us into his office. He was sitting at his desk, which seemed to be elevated a good five feet off the floor. He never acknowledged us. Instead, he began dictating into a microphone. His dictation was a letter expelling us from Brown. We sat in amazement. When he finished, he turned to us as if surprised to see us and then said his only words: "You can go now." His secretary, who had been waiting in the back of the office, escorted us out.

We decided we had nothing to lose so we kept agitating, fully expecting the campus police to serve us with an eviction notice. But they never came. We did not win that battle that year, but eventually the mandatory contracts were ended and the food got better.

In the spring of my sophomore year, my peers and I became frustrated by the education we were receiving at Brown and we decided to act. Already accustomed to joining civil rights marches and demonstrations against the Vietnam War and against environmental pollution, we felt that we could have the greatest impact by reforming our own institution. We could help establish at Brown an education system that would encourage more creative and responsible leadership, and we could try to address racial and sexual injustices within our own community.

In the summer after my sophomore year, I drafted a four-hundred-page report that was then edited, in the fall, by a group of twenty students led by Elliot Maxwell. The report made recommendations on how to improve Brown's education system.

There were a few fundamental principles guiding our recommendations:

- Students should be actively responsible for their education, choosing what to study, aided by a strong counseling system, rather than being subjected to requirements that encouraged passive learning. They should have the choice to develop independent concentrations with a faculty advisor rather than having to fit a predetermined design of a concentration.

- The teaching of facts was less important than teaching students how different disciplines approached knowledge and learning. If a student knew how to learn, then he or she could engage in a lifetime of learning, including acquiring factual knowledge.

- Instead of large lecture courses in early years and then seminars in later years, students could benefit better from small classes in their early years and then more independent and group independent work in their later years.

- Interdisciplinary activities should be encouraged, going beyond the traditional compartmentalization of knowledge in departments.

- Letter or number grades were not particularly valuable methods of evaluation. Written performance evaluations that actually helped students understand in some detail what they could do better were more meaningful.

- Encouraging students to be more responsible for their learning—removing the props of requirements, letter grades, and spoon-fed course selections—would encourage better, more creative learning and a more meaningful form of rigor.

This philosophy of education was designed to produce leaders who would be entrepreneurs, who would question authority and have the skills to create new paradigms in government, business, and science.

The substance of our proposed reforms was important, but the grassroots process that we implemented was also crucial to the success and sustainability of the reforms. We had looked at other schools where small groups of students engaged in violent demonstrations or occupied buildings while the majority of students merely observed from across the street. We didn't think this was the best way to bring long-lasting change. Instead, we set out to mobilize the whole student body. If we had large numbers, we could achieve greater results with moderate tactics.

In September 1968, I pulled together a group of twenty students to mobilize the student body and to lobby faculty. Our aim was to get the faculty to pass fundamental reforms by the end of the school year.

What made us think we could pull this off? In part, our confidence came from the successful Spring Weekend I had spearheaded the year before. In my sophomore year, I had decided to organize concerts on campus on a scale that had never been attempted before. We brought in the Lovin' Spoonful, the Doors, Mitch Ryder and the Detroit Wheels, and the Paul Butterfield Blues Band, and thousands of students attended the concerts. This culminated—in my junior year—in the first large-scale Spring Weekend ever attempted in New England.

We had James Brown, Dionne Warwick, Procol Harum, the Yardbirds, and Dizzy Gillespie; for the poetry crowd we had Allen Ginsberg and Lawrence Ferlinghetti. We had classical musician Lorin Hollander, the comedian Jean Shepherd, and folk musicians Ian and Sylvia. We also set up a seventy-two-hour classic movie marathon. Allen Ginsberg and some other performers were so impressed by the lineup that they stayed for the whole weekend.

To launch the event, we chartered a small airplane to fly over the college green and dump thousands of colored Ping-Pong balls stamped with WELCOME SPRING WEEKEND. The university administration was already worried about the scale of our programming. They anticipated busloads of students arriving from schools as far away as Washington, DC. When they heard about the Ping-Pong balls, they said, "Absolutely not." They feared that a falling ball might hit someone and cause dire injury. We had some physics students prepare a treatise to show that no damage could be done, but the administration was not persuaded.

We had already colored and stamped thousands of Ping-Pong balls and could not get a refund on the chartered plane, so we told the administration that we would not yield. But in fact, after consulting with our engineering-student brain trust and learning that they, too, were envisioning potential car accidents caused by errant balls, we had decided to call it off. But we did not tell the administration. Instead, we instructed the plane to fly over the green towing a banner saying, WELCOME SPRING WEEKEND. When nervous members of the administration dashed onto the lawn to watch the plane, we had some students sneak in through the back of University Hall and dump the Ping-Pong balls in the dean's office.

Looking back on it now, I'd say that this wildly successful Spring Weekend, and the organization it took to pull it off, was a precursor to the organized effort we created to pass the New Curriculum.

One of our first tasks in the fall of 1968 was to get enough copies of the report we had written. At a time when dinosaurs ruled the earth, this was no easy challenge. We had no Internet, no copy machines, no electric typewriters, and the only computer at Brown—the IBM System/360—was larger than a railcar.

The student government had a small office with a mimeograph machine that had to be manually cranked. It produced copies with blue ink, giving off a fragrant, chemical smell. We worked day and night, in shifts, cranking out several hundred copies of each page, carrying huge batches of paper into the small room where the machine resided, and storing the pages wherever we could. In order to get a thousand copies collated and stapled, we decided to get one of the best rock bands on campus to play in Sayles Hall and we sponsored a collation dance. We set up four hundred chairs around the perimeter of Sayles Hall and the price of admission was to circulate around the hall once and collate and staple a full copy of the report. It was utter chaos—there was little room to dance in, once a few hundred people had gone through—but we did get several hundred copies collated.

We started visiting dorms to talk with students. Usually on the first visit somebody on our committee had a good friend in the dorm who could gather four or five friends together, so we could talk to them about the report. We were then able to motivate them to recruit more of their friends for another meeting a few days later. We kept returning until we had twenty or thirty students showing up to a meeting in a dorm. In all cases, the meetings included detailed discussions so that students truly understood the report and came to support it.

At the same time, we sent the report to all faculty members and asked for appointments to discuss it with them. We sent teams of three students to meet each faculty member, one of whom already knew the professor. Often when we showed up, faculty members had not read the report or had only skimmed it. So we actively engaged them in a dialogue, often leaving them a bit shaken. We then rated the faculty members on a scale of 1 to 4 as one would in a political campaign. The 1s were definite supporters and the 4s were a lost cause. We posted people outside of faculty meetings to take attendance, which helped us to target our efforts on the "likely voters," who were 2s and 3s.

In November, we started holding short rallies on the green. They were limited to thirty minutes. Student speakers were told to limit their talks to five minutes each, to be humorous and entertaining, but also to illustrate some problem with the curriculum as it existed. The number of attendees at our rallies grew over time, until over a thousand students were regularly attending.

We also visited student clubs and other places where students congregated and we gradually built lists of interested students, creating a large network so that eventually, if we needed to do so, we could turn out thousands of students on short notice.

We pushed for the creation of a high-level committee of administration, faculty, and students to consider the recommendations, with a mandate to produce a comprehensive reform package to be considered by the full faculty before the end of the year (prior to this, students did not serve on university committees).

Finally, in December 1968, when our rallies were drawing large crowds on campus and we had a petition signed by well over half the undergraduate student body asking for the committee to be established, I sat down with the president for a serious talk. Other universities were experiencing violent protests and occupations of administration buildings. We had produced a four-hundred-page footnoted report and were engaging in discussion and debate worthy of a university setting. We had broad-based student support. We did not want to engage in more militant tactics. We were simply asking that the university form a committee to consider our recommendations. The president agreed.

A high-level committee including some student members was formed under Vice Provost Paul Maeder. They met frequently and urgently and produced a set of recommendations broadly in line with those we had advocated.

Around this same time, in December 1968, black students at Brown took a courageous step. They orchestrated a walkout to press for greater minority recruitment and more African-American faculty and course work. We immediately utilized our network to mobilize widespread student support for their efforts through a rally and a petition that was signed by almost three thousand Brown students.

On the first night of the walkout, I was invited to the president's house to meet with senior administrators and trustees and discuss the situation. I told them that if they did not negotiate a satisfactory resolution and address the issues being raised, a massive walkout of white students would take place in sympathy with our black student compatriots.

To their credit, administration leaders like President Heffner, Provost Stoltz, Vice Provost Maeder, Dean Eckelmann, and corporation student life chair Judge Alfred Joslin were enlightened leaders who understood that "times were changing" and they became active partners in that process. Had they taken the hard-line approach of officials at other universities, Brown would never have undergone such a successful transformation. The Black Walkout yielded important concessions and we turned our attention back to education reform.

From January to April 1969, a committee led by Paul Maeder drew up a set of recommendations for curriculum reform based on the suggestions in our student report. In May, at the final faculty meeting in Sayles Hall to vote on the recommendations, only the three students who were on the Maeder committee were allowed to attend. But we persuaded the administration to set up loudspeakers so students might congregate on the green outside of the hall and hear the proceedings. Aided by fortuitous good weather, over 80 percent of the student body gathered outside. When a faculty member in Sayles Hall endorsed the reforms, the crowd loudly cheered, while a chorus of boos accompanied any negative statement. The reforms passed overwhelmingly.

The mobilization of students allowed us to bring other needed changes.

By the time my class left in 1969, Brown was on a course to increase its African-American student population dramatically, and also to increase admissions of other minority students. Pembroke was to be disbanded and women would soon make up half of all Brown students. An education system was established that put student choice and responsibility and more creative learning at the center of the educational process. Brown students were engaging in activities in the Rhode Island community to combat poverty, improve the environment, and fight for social justice. Students were also serving on university oversight committees and were allowed to run businesses through the Brown Student Agencies to serve other students. And parietal rules gave way to coed dorms.

Nationally, civil rights demonstrations—often organized by students—led to laws being implemented that would reverse centuries of racial discrimination; student-led protests had forced the president of the United States not to seek a second term, and large parts of society were calling for an end to the Vietnam War; the numbers of women admitted to professional schools were increasing dramatically; the roles of women were being redefined, and attitudes toward sexual harassment were changing to blame the harasser, not the harassed. Movements like Earth Day and protests against air and water pollution would eventually lead to the Clean Water and Clean Air Acts, and the voting age was moved from twenty-one to eighteen.

Brown and America transformed in ways that were positive and have endured. This is the legacy of the student generation of the late 1960s and early 1970s. As we now advance into old age (though I still think of myself as being twenty-one years old even if my body tells me differently), the legacy of our student days is one in which we can take great pride.

Today's Brown students benefit from the values that my generation fought for: civil rights, equality between the sexes, a cleaner environment, a more creative and open educational system at Brown, and the reduction of poverty. But there are important battles today's students should fight for the next generation. Problems of global poverty, climate change, growing income inequality in America, and equal rights for gay and lesbian Americans are among the issues that rightfully command the attention of today's Brown students. I wish today's student activists at Brown success as they take on these and other important issues.

Creating Change: Black at Brown in the 1960s

SPENCER R. CREW

Attending a school like Brown was not on my radar before my junior year of high school. I grew up in northern Ohio, spending my early years in inner-city Cleveland before attending a small suburban high school. My family had moved to the suburbs because my parents wanted my brother, sister, and me to live in a more racially and economically integrated environment. My high school graduating class had two hundred students, six of whom were African-American. The common path for most college-bound graduates was to attend one of the many private or public colleges in the state. Going out of state was rare, and attending an Ivy League university was even more unusual. My older cousin was attending Yale, but he was considered "the brain" in our family and not someone I thought I could emulate.

I expected to attend an in-state college. But because I had maintained good grades, held class offices, won several awards, and lettered in three sports, my high school counselor had higher aspirations for me. She arranged for a Brown admissions officer and the Brown football coach to talk to me, and I was recruited to play football at Brown as a member of the class of 1971. It was an exciting moment for me and my family. Neither of my parents was a college graduate, though my mother had graduated from nursing school and my father had attended Ohio State for two years before becoming one of only two African-American chemists in the paint industry in Ohio.

Going to Brown was a big step for all of us, as I was not just going to college, I was traveling more than five hundred miles to the East Coast to attend an Ivy League university. During the twelve-hour drive to Providence, my father spoke with me about what was ahead. He told me how proud he was of me. He expected me to apply myself and do well. Sending me to Brown was a financial stretch for the family and an opportunity that I was not to squander.

I arrived early enough to attend Freshman Week activities but spent most of my time in the twice-daily football practices. My new teammates came from around the country, as did my dorm mates in Caswell Hall. Living with people from such diverse backgrounds was a new experience for me. I had never gone away to summer camp, and in Ohio, I had lived in the cocoon of my extended family, high school friends, and other African-American families who lived in our community. Late-night dormitory discussions about our backgrounds and views on world politics were at once exciting and intimidating. Everyone I met had excelled in high school and they were dauntingly articulate.

There were only two African-American students in Caswell— me and Gregory Brown—and we both played football. Gregory had attended a city high school in Buffalo, New York. We hit it off immediately and remained very good friends throughout our time at Brown. Conversations with Gregory and with other black students in the freshman class broadened my perception of African-American experiences across the country. We were the largest class of African-American students to matriculate at Brown and Pembroke to date.

Upperclassmen in the African-American community made the freshmen feel welcome, drawing us into a close-knit community in which academic class was less significant than ethnic heritage. We created an active social and intellectual life for ourselves, which allowed us to interact both in the larger Brown community and within our own group. This community gave me an anchor, a home base to which I could return whenever things felt overwhelming or homesickness set in. My new friends understood the challenges and adjustments I was experiencing. They understood the pressures of being expected to serve as a spokesperson for all African-Americans whenever issues of race came up in dorm conversations or classroom discussions. Eating together in the Ratty at what came to be known as the "black table," or just hanging out together casually, offered needed relief from the burden of being one of the few black students at Brown in the late 1960s.

I developed a number of close friendships at the time, but the most important and enduring one was with a Pembroke freshman from Washington, DC, named Sandra Prioleau. Casual conversations sparked a friendship that evolved into a long-term relationship; we married four years later, right after graduation.

We were at Brown in a time of heightened civil rights activism across the country and our shared experiences sharpened our political sensitivities. Black Power was emerging as a movement that contrasted sharply with the nonviolent philosophy of Martin Luther King Jr. Students on campuses across the nation were protesting the Vietnam War, as well as racial issues. The longer we were at Brown, the more sensitive we became to issues regarding minority students. The most obvious deficiency was the dearth of courses on African-American issues at a time when they were at the center of many critical and heated discussions in the academy and across the nation. There were also very few administrators and faculty members of color. We all felt that these courses and faculty members would enhance the Brown educational experience—not just for us, but for all students. In addition, while the number of black students in the class of 1971 was a step forward, Brown needed to be more aggressive in recruiting African-American students from a broad range of backgrounds.

These issues were central to forging the creation of Umoja—the Afro-American student organization. Umoja meetings provided the platform for many thought-provoking discussions about how to get the university to address our concerns. These heated conversations made me think seriously about my own feelings concerning activism and confrontation. They made me question what I was willing to jeopardize in support of my increasingly strong beliefs.

African-American women at Pembroke took the first step by pressing Alberta Brown, dean of admissions at the college, to commit to a plan for recruiting more African-American students. When she failed to respond positively, the demands were pushed higher up the ladder. A letter signed by sixty-five African-American students was sent to the president of Brown, Ray L. Heffner; we demanded that the university make a long-term commitment to hire more minority faculty. In addition, we asked the administration to set targets for increasing the percentage of minority students; to offer academic courses focused on the history, culture, and politics of Africans in America; to set aside a house on campus for African-American student activities; and to develop a program to help students of color make the transition to the academic and social environment at Brown.

Heffner's response did not satisfy the signers of the letter and we decided to take more dramatic steps to attain our goals. On other campuses, students were taking over buildings to emphasize their demands, which often resulted in tense confrontations. We chose a different strategy. Instead of occupying a building, we would boycott classes in a very visible manner by leaving campus en masse and refusing to return until the university agreed to our demands. Consequently, in December of 1968, the black female students of Pembroke marched to Faunce House, where they were joined by the male students. There were sixty-five of us in the group, including me and Sandra, three-quarters of the black undergraduates at the university, who marched silently off the campus.

The decision to take this step was not easy. We knew we might be putting our careers at Brown at stake. The administration had the power to expel us; this had happened to many student activists in the South, and it was a sobering prospect.

Many of us contacted our parents by phone to tell them what we were planning. We were not sure how they would react. My father questioned me closely on our thinking and the issues. He wanted to know whether I believed what we were doing was right and to make sure I was not just following the crowd. I assured him that even with my high regard for the upperclassmen who were leading our protest, I knew this was a decision I had to make for myself. I reminded him that he had raised me to be an independent thinker. After our discussion he gave me his full support.

Others in the group had similar conversations with their parents, who worried about what might happen but understood how important it was for us to act on these issues we felt so strongly about. They were all too familiar with the impact of discrimination and knew that change did not happen easily or without pressure.

When we walked out, we headed over to the Congdon Street Baptist Church, which was less than a mile from campus on College Hill. Their minister, Reverend Dennis Earl Norris, and the congregation had agreed to provide shelter and food for us. It was very generous on their part. Only a few of us had prior connections to that church, but they supported us as fellow Christians and African-Americans. While we stayed there, the women upstairs and the men downstairs, they watched over us and tried to make us comfortable. Some members even took small groups of us to their homes for meals.

From the beginning of our action we had agreed to designate specific spokespeople who would negotiate for the group to ensure that we maintained a consistent public position. We needed the university to take our demands seriously and to adopt actions that would demonstrate a real commitment to changing their policies. Our negotiating team—women and men from different classes—included Sheryl Grooms, a sophomore, and Glenn Dixon, a junior, who was president of the Afro-American Society. Kenneth McDaniel, a senior, was one of our spokespeople.

Each day, our team met with the administration and then reported back to the larger group. Together, we fashioned responses that the team could use in further negotiations. The discussion lasted several days. Those of us at the church had only minimal contact with the outside world and we were not aware of the conversations taking place on campus. We spent our time at the church studying, discussing the negotiations, and keeping in touch with our parents. We later learned that there was a lively debate on campus over whether or not our demands were reasonable. The *Brown Daily Herald* argued in an editorial that we were demanding too much and that the administration had already done more than enough. In contrast, a petition signed by more than 2,800 students supported our actions.

After five days of talks, an agreement was reached. The administration agreed to recruit more black students. They did not, however, set the hard percentage goals we had demanded. Still, we decided to end our walkout, believing that substantial progress had been made. We had raised consciousness about important issues and had pushed the university to act more rapidly on these matters than they might otherwise have done. Our goal, on returning to campus, was to continue to push for more progress, but to do so as a part of the campus community, rather than as a separate entity.

The 1968 Walkout changed the environment for African-American students at Brown. In the aftermath, more courses were offered that related to issues of race and the roles of African-Americans. George Houston Bass came to Brown and created Rites and Reason Theatre as an outlet for the creation of African-American–oriented theater. I was a history major and was pleased that a course on African-American history was quickly established. In addition, two remarkable graduate students, Wilson Moses and Rhett Jones, were hired to teach history courses. They were the first African-American instructors I had at Brown. Working with them transformed how I thought about American history and elevated my understanding of the critical role African-Americans had played in the creation of this nation. I was drawn to their commitment to impeccable scholarship and the discovery of new sources of information. They saw history as a tool for social change—as a vehicle for better understanding the present and creating change for the future. This was a perspective I enthusiastically shared. During my remaining time at Brown, whenever the opportunity arose, I wrote my term papers on African-American or African topics. And it was largely because of those two gifted instructors that I went to graduate school with a focus on African-American history, going on to a life-long career as a historian of the black American experience.

Several months after the walkout, the Afro House was established by the university as a place for students to live, study, and plan programs. Soon thereafter, the Third World Transition Program was developed. Its goal was to help new minority students, prior to the onset of the academic year, to become acclimated to Brown and to prepare for the new experiences and challenges they would soon face. It would then continue to provide support during the course of the year. Both Afro House and TWTP were important demands in the letter we had sent to President Heffner.

The 1968 Walkout changed the makeup of the African-American student body. In the years that followed, during which time I "retired" from playing football and focused more on my studies, the number of students of color who were recruited and matriculated at Brown steadily rose. By the time I graduated in 1971 there were more than three hundred African-American students at Brown. Those numbers were still not representative of the percentage of African-Americans in the general population, but this bigger and more diverse group marked a substantial improvement.

It was a good change for Brown, but ironically, for those of us who had participated in the walkout, it marked the end of a special time for us. As the African-American community expanded, our sense of belonging to a close-knit community that was almost like family slowly dissipated.

But if that was the price we had to pay in order to stimulate such important changes, it was well worth it. Ultimately, the policies set in motion by the walkout helped to cement Brown's leading place among the universities of the world. Indeed, it set the stage for an environment in which the Corporation of Brown University, following the recommendation of a search committee of which I was a member, would eventually elect Dr. Ruth Simmons as its eighteenth president.

Need-Blind Now!

SARAH SHUN-LIEN BYNUM

I felt old and lonely when I started at Brown. It was January of 1992, and I was nearly twenty. Since leaving high school I'd lived on my own in Los Angeles and then Philadelphia, working at a video store, a diner, a discount clothing store, a café. College had delivered me from these jobs, for which I was deeply glad. At the same time, I was unspeakably depressed by the cinder-block walls of my freshman dormitory and the camaraderie of its residents. Having been for the most part a companionable person all my life, I was surprised to find myself incapable of making much conversation or finding new friends.

The absence of friends became most apparent whenever I entered the dining hall, so I avoided the dining hall by eating my meals in a dimly lit student lounge that had a sandwich counter. Almost every night I ate a sandwich for dinner, watching the television that hung from the ceiling. This is where, in the spring, I watched live coverage of the Los Angeles riots, and this is probably where I first learned about the protest movement that was happening on campus. I imagine that I picked up a flyer from the black laminate surface of one of the bistro tables near the sandwich counter.

On an April evening I went to a meeting held in Salomon Center, hosted by an organization called Students for Aid and Minority Admissions. There were easily over a hundred people in the room. At issue was the college's need-aware admissions policy, which took a student's ability to pay tuition into account as part of her application. This meant, from what I understood, that when choosing between two similarly qualified applicants, Brown picked the kid who could come up with the money, and more likely than not that kid would be white. We were the only Ivy League school still practicing this approach, maybe not surprisingly, given that our endowment was also the smallest. SAMA was demanding that the university add $50 million to its current $450 million capital campaign in order to address the problem.

I'd been ignorant up to this point of the need-aware policy, but its existence seemed to confirm an uneasy feeling I had about Brown: that exactly what made it so attractive to me (a lack of requirements, an absurdly generous grading system, a freedom to indulge one's particular interests and obsessions) was its luxuriousness, and this luxuriousness was reserved largely for those who could afford it. And while I had spent the previous year and a half folding sweatshirts and shelving videocassettes and dumping out coffee grounds, I had done so at will, and as soon as I'd tired of working minimum-wage jobs, going to bars, following rock and roll bands, as soon as I felt ready to resume my education, my parents had been ready to pay for it. They paid the full tuition, just as US senators and film directors and musical icons and minor European royalty had paid for their children to go to Brown. It no longer seemed a glamorous coincidence that they were among my classmates.

That night I signed my name to a petition circulating the hall. I signed my name to a list of those interested in attending future meetings and teach-ins. Every time a clipboard came my way, I seized hold of it and wrote my name. Never a joiner, suspicious of anything resembling a team, I felt suddenly, mysteriously, moved to take part. This I can clearly remember, this urge, but it's harder to put a finger on what actually stirred me as I sat there, signing up for everything. Was it the organizers themselves, their competence and seriousness, their air of experience, of having been seasoned in the service of other causes? Or did I feel, after several years of erratic volunteerism (tutoring kids, working at shelters, passing out pamphlets for Planned Parenthood), that it was time for me to commit meaningfully to the work of social justice? That it was time for me to commit to something other than rock bands and my long-distance boyfriend?

A few days later, I woke up early, walked from my dingy freshman dorm to the brick Georgian spread of University Hall, and joined a group of students sitting quietly on the polished floor outside the president's office. The plan, I think, was to waylay Vartan Gregorian as he came in to work that morning: the organization's leaders would insist on an audience and then formally present him with our demands. About seventy of us spent much of the morning waiting, cross-legged, or scooting up against the rotunda's walls and drawing our knees to our chests whenever a staff person needed to pass through. Vartan never showed up, and neither did the provost; it turned out that they were both out of town (conveniently, was the general conclusion). By the time this news filtered down to us, a SAMA rally had gathered force outside on the Main Green, with hand-lettered banners and bullhorns and chanting, swelling to a size and pitch much greater than anyone expected, and in an unplanned development, a spontaneous act of solidarity, the demonstrators surged through the doors and windows of University Hall, and our sit-in turned into a takeover.

Those of us already on the inside must have cheered when the others pushed and climbed their way in. We must have cheered and clapped and sung throughout the day as we asserted our presence along the halls and in the large, airy Corporation Room of Brown's administrative headquarters. Curiously enough, I remember none of this. I spent over twelve hours camped out in that building with more than three hundred protesters and I can recall almost nothing of the experience. It was a day that culminated in my arrest, in the arrest of 253 students, a day that ended with multiple misdemeanor charges and fingerprinting at the downtown Providence police station, yet the details and the feelings surrounding this singular episode in my life somehow refuse to be summoned. The event has for me the blankness of a day spent waiting in an airline terminal for an extremely delayed flight, or of an endless afternoon passed under fluorescent lights at the DMV. Maybe a few friendly, commiserating glances and remarks exchanged with one's fellow passengers? But mostly just a lot of sitting and waiting in silence.

There is only one moment I can clearly and perfectly recall: at some point during the day, students on the outside began passing food and water in through the windows, and I remember watching the handsome lead singer from a campus ska band I liked lean in and hand over an industrial-size carton of Goldfish crackers, with a huge smile on his face, and wishing badly that he were on the inside of the building with the rest of us.

When, a week later, the Rodney King verdict was announced, I was alone again in the dimly lit student lounge, eating a sandwich in front of the television, watching Los Angeles, the city where I had recently lived and worked and made friends, erupt.

I didn't come back to Brown after that semester. I returned to Philadelphia and enrolled in the African-American Studies program at Temple. I got back my old job at the café. It's funny to think that I didn't know, that I didn't have any way of knowing, what was happening with the protest movement for which I'd been arrested. There were no email blasts, no Tumblr posts, no Facebook updates, no tweets: none of the means by which we now communicate en masse existed then. As soon as I left campus, I lost all contact with SAMA.

I've been tempted at different points since then to think of the takeover as a brief burst of sound and fury that didn't end up signifying much. After all, the administration declined to meet SAMA's demands; need-aware admission continued at Brown; the student organization soon disbanded; I'd failed to find an opening into a new community of friends. Worse, the isolated nature of the event made me feel unserious, a dabbler, my activism ersatz. When I pictured myself being escorted out of University Hall by the police, a particularly self-damning phrase came to mind, the harshest possible insult from my days as an aspiring hardcore kid: *What a poser.*

The writing of this essay and the woolliness of my memory have compelled me to make use of the technology unavailable to us back in 1992; through Facebook, Google, and the online *Brown Daily Herald*, I've tracked down details I had completely forgotten regarding names and numbers and dates. In the course of doing so I've also learned something important about the students who organized and took part in that protest: many of them are still activists. Over twenty years later! Working for ACT UP and the Communist Party USA, for Barack Obama's presidential campaign, for language justice, for the movement to free Mumia Abu-Jamal. Knowing this makes me feel retroactively happy about having been among the 253. I was a late arrival to the cause and just another warm body in the occupation, but maybe enough warm bodies showing up at the same time can start someone on a certain path, or strengthen a conviction that the path they've already started on is the right one.

As for me, I did eventually circle back to Brown, and when I returned I found myself, a year after my first SAMA meeting, signing up again, this time not for a sit-in or a rally but for the Writing Fellows Program. I joined a group of students who loved to write, who loved to talk and think about writing, and who wanted to support others in their writing efforts. The whole program was built around the idea that all writers, no matter how inexperienced or how accomplished, would become stronger through the process of receiving thoughtful, one-on-one feedback. Our approach didn't single out students needing remedial help; we worked with undergraduates across all disciplines and all levels. I liked this equitable approach. Really, I liked everything about the program: the other Fellows, the cozy basement office, the road trips to Long Island for pedagogy conferences. My activism had shrunk to the scope of a well-wrought sentence, but I believed in the power of that sentence, and that its power could be available to everyone. I still believe that.

And as for Brown: eleven years after the takeover of University Hall, the college finally admitted its domestic freshman class on a need-blind basis.

A momentous change, truly, but this sentence still doesn't quite achieve the note of ringing finality that I was hoping for. The problem is its awkward qualifiers: *domestic* and *freshman*. Awkward, but necessary, because Brown's need-blind admission policy applies to first-year applicants who are US citizens or permanent residents. Which means that a significant swath of Brown's population—international, transfer, and RUE students—are not included. A new movement on campus is now advocating for universal need-blind admission, a policy that would provide equal access to all applicants, regardless of citizenship or transfer status. And this group is breathtakingly well organized: they've built a website, made a short video, established a network of alumni ambassadors, created a Facebook page, and presented a comprehensive report to administrators and members of the Corporation. They've also launched a succinct and forceful petition. No more clipboards this time around—just now I went online and signed it.

JOAN HILTY

THE TIMES — Joan Hilty

1986.

IT'S HARD TO BELIEVE THERE WAS A TIME WHEN WE DRAGGED A BIG WOODEN PINK TRIANGLE ONTO THE MAIN GREEN FOR GAY AWARENESS WEEK...

HARDER STILL TO BELIEVE THAT MEMBERS OF THE LESBIAN GAY STUDENT ALLIANCE WATCHED OVER IT ALL NIGHT LONG, CAMPING OUT IN SHIFTS ABOVE FAUNCE ARCH.

BUT THE TRIANGLE HAD BEEN DESTROYED FOR THREE YEARS RUNNING — TWICE TORN APART, ONCE BURNED.

I KNEW I WAS GAY BEFORE I GOT TO BROWN. MY FRESHMAN ROOMMATE AND I TOOK TURNS AT LONG-DISTANCE FIGHTS WITH THE BOY-FRIEND AND GIRLFRIEND WE'D RESPECTIVELY LEFT BEHIND.

BUT I WASN'T REALLY OUT.

THE PUBLIC FACE OF *AIDS* WAS ROCK HUDSON. WHILE EVERYONE PANICKED ABOUT WHO HE'D KISSED ON *DYNASTY*, THE WHITE HOUSE WAS SILENT.

THE FACE OF SAME-SEX UNIONS WAS KAREN THOMPSON. SHE'D EXCHANGED RINGS AND INSURANCE POLICIES WITH SHARON KOWALSKI; WHEN KOWALSKI WAS SEVERELY DISABLED IN A CAR CRASH, HER PARENTS TOOK GUARDIANSHIP AND CUT OFF THOMPSON'S VISITATION RIGHTS.

"OUT AND PROUD" WAS CATCHING ON, BUT IT WAS STILL EASIER TO BE PROUD THAN OUT. AND WHEN MY TEEN ROMANCE ENDED OVER CHRIST-MAS BREAK, IT WAS JUST PLAIN PAINFUL.

1987.

I WAS DRAGGING MYSELF TO LGSA MEETINGS, BUT LURKING IN THE BACK. EVERYONE SEEMED COOLER THAN ME. I GOT INTO EDITORIAL CARTOONING ON UTTERLY NON-GAY TOPICS FOR THE BDH....

...AND WHEN THE NATIONAL MARCH ON WASHINGTON FOR LESBIAN & GAY RIGHTS ROLLED AROUND IN OCTOBER, I DIDN'T GO, I'LL ALWAYS WISH I HAD.

THE NAMES PROJECT QUILT UNFURLED DOWN THE NATIONAL MALL IN ITS FIRST PUBLIC DISPLAY.

TWO THOUSAND GAY COUPLES THREW A MASS WEDDING IN FRONT OF THE IRS OFFICES.

BRAND-NEW CONGRESSWOMAN NANCY PELOSI MARCHED; PRESIDENTIAL CANDIDATE JESSE JACKSON SPOKE.

AS MARCHERS FLOODED THE MALL, WHOOPI GOLDBERG TOLD EVERYONE TO SHOUT THE CROWD ESTIMATE ALOUD SO THE PRESS WOULD GET IT RIGHT.

FIVE HUNDRED THOUSAND!

FIVE HUNDRED THOUSAND!

BROWN

AND OVER 100 PEOPLE FROM BROWN WENT DOWN TO MARCH.

SEVERAL OF THEM GOT ARRESTED AT THE SUPREME COURT, PROTESTING THE ANTI-SODOMY LAWS ON THE BOOKS IN 25 STATES. THE COPS WORE RUBBER GLOVES, OF COURSE.

SEVERAL MORE BRUNONIANS MANNED A HOTLINE FOR MARCHERS WITH AIDS. BUT ALMOST NOTHING COULD BE DONE FOR THE PWAs IN CRISIS WHO CALLED. REAL RESOURCES WERE YEARS AWAY.

1988.

I WAS FINISHING UP AN ILLUSTRATED GUIDE TO ALL 25 OF THOSE ANTI-SODOMY LAWS.

I'D STOPPED LURKING IN THE BACK OF LGSA MEETINGS. I'LL ALWAYS BE GLAD I DID.

THE MARCH HAD INSPIRED US; THE MEDIA HAD ALMOST TOTALLY IGNORED IT. WE DECIDED TO COVER IT OURSELVES.

THREE BREAKNECK MONTHS OF WORK LATER, WE HAD A LESBIAN/GAY/BISEXUAL ISSUES MAGAZINE.

SAFE SEX, ANTI-GAY VIOLENCE, QUEER BLACK AND LATINA IDENTITY, GAY FACULTY AND ATHLETES, GAY STUDIES, AN HOUR-BY-HOUR ACCOUNT OF THE MARCH; WE WROTE ABOUT EVERYTHING WE COULD THINK OF. AND MOST OF US USED OUR REAL NAMES.

SOMEONE COLD-CALLED KEITH HARING TO DRAW THE COVER.

NOT GUILTY

Volume 2, Issue 2 February 1988

© K. Haring 88

IT WAS OUT ALL OVER CAMPUS, AND SO WERE WE.

GREAT! THANK YOU!

HE SAID YES.

SHRIEK!!

YOUR PLACE OR MINE?   YOU'VE GOT FOUR ROOMMATES.

YOURS IT IS.

IN THE MAGAZINE'S WORDS, IT WAS TIME "FOR OUR PRIDE TO BE AS EVIDENT AS OUR RAGE; FOR OUR SORROWS AND FRUSTRATION TO NOT ECLIPSE THE VERY REAL JOY THAT OUR SEXUAL AND SOCIAL IDENTITIES BRING US."

AND IT WAS TIME, FINALLY, FOR ME TO FALL IN LOVE AGAIN.

INSPIRATION

I think one of the most inspirational figures in my life—certainly in my life as a theater artist—was a professor at Brown University named John Bass. What he taught me was the joy of ritual. He taught me that, through playwriting, we could discover our ancestors. We could explore issues. We could find our history.

—**Lynn Nottage** ('86)

Mostly I say, just write the poems you must write. And then write some more so you're ready; it's a marathon, not a footrace, so you have to train. Then buy a book, go to a reading, expect the unexpected—and poetry will surprise you.

—**Kevin Young** ('96 MFA)

[What] had the strongest impact on me were not valuable technical lessons but the, "Yes, yes, do more of that, keep going on, more, more, more." Paula [Vogel] really had this childlike enthusiasm for nudging me and pushing me on the path without telling me what that path should be.

—**Quiara Alegría Hudes** ('04 MFA)

[Robert Coover] taught a course called Ancient Fictions which included the Bible and Homer's *Odyssey*, Gilgamesh, Ovid; early works of fiction. He was enormously erudite, generous, challenging, fascinating, filled with ideas. He didn't seem to mind when a student did really well, he was extremely supportive of a whole range of younger writers to an incredible degree.

—**Ben Marcus** ('91)

To Be Young, Indignant, and Inspired

PAMELA CONSTABLE

On September 18, 1970, Jimi Hendrix died.

On August 9, 1974, Richard Nixon resigned.

I will never forget those two dates, which bracketed my four years as an undergraduate at Brown during a politically turbulent, culturally freewheeling time. Hendrix, whom I worshipped, and Nixon, whom I detested, represented two sides of a struggle that loomed large for us at the time—a struggle between generations, ideologies, and values. Hendrix reinvented "The Star-Spangled Banner" as an anthem of the counterculture; Nixon betrayed it.

I had applied to Brown mostly to please my father, a member of the class of 1939, who had gone almost straight from graduation to parachuting out of warplanes. By the time I entered college, he was a dignified gentleman in his sixties, proud of my good grades but appalled at my choice of music and friends. We disagreed about almost every issue of the day, but he was the rock of my life, and I was eager to succeed at his alma mater.

I expected to be academically challenged, but I had no idea how much of my education would spring from the atmosphere and ethos of campus life. Brown in the early 1970s was an ideal setting—both sheltering and stimulating—to be young, indignant, and inspired. The nation was reeling from war and revolution, and campuses from Kent State to Columbia had been torn apart by protests and strikes. In the wake of these upheavals, Brown took a wise, innovative path that absorbed and channeled conflict in healthier ways. In essence, it threw out the rules and gave students the freedom to study, express, and experience almost anything that didn't kill them.

Of course, the freshman dean of Pembroke College, as it was still called then, was far from pleased when I vanished from campus for a week during my first semester. I had run off to Cape Cod with a bunch of long-haired strangers for an instant introduction to Miles Davis, John Fahey, Anaïs Nin, Antonin Artaud, peyote, tequila, Luis Buñuel, the Dalai Lama, and other icons and indulgences of the time. I remember writing a lot of poetry on the walls of a seaside cottage, but not much else. This wild escapade provided a cathartic bridge between girls' boarding school and a brave new world.

Having gotten that out of my system, however, I quickly realized that Brown offered just as much opportunity to learn and explore as a psychedelic romp on the beach. Most specifically, my classmates and I were the immediate beneficiaries of the Magaziner Report and the New Curriculum, which did away with the traditional academic point system and gave students the option to take any course, in any department, for a grade of Satisfactory/No Credit.

That notion may sound quaint in today's hypercompetitive, money-conscious era, when many students hunch over laptops like robots and demand to know why they didn't get an A. But although some of us back then misused this license by coasting through semesters of astrology and music appreciation, for most it was a wonderful, liberating spur to intellectual curiosity.

In my case, it meant venturing outside my academic comfort zone, signing up for psychology labs and urban planning seminars, and attending lectures in constitutional law and Soviet studies by infamously brilliant but tyrannical professors. Knowing I didn't have to memorize treaty dates and legal opinions allowed me to enjoy pondering questions such as what three-fifths of a man really meant, or whether the policy of "to each according to his needs, from each according to his ability" was a nobler ideal than democracy.

I also took every writing and literature class I could squeeze in. I read Joyce and Yeats, Faulkner and Wolfe, Isak Dinesen and Frantz

Fanon, Pablo Neruda and Eduardo Galeano. I wrote bad poetry, pretentious film reviews, and earnest papers on public housing and urban riots. The best piece of work I produced in four years, though, may have been this twenty-five-word limerick: "The natives of tropical Amazon / Cavort without any pajamas on / And what's even worse / I've heard they write verse / With no semicolons or commas on."

Amid this heady academic feast, I discovered my muse and my calling. It was in a small seminar on writers of the Great Depression, which included Steinbeck, Faulkner, and the great *USA Trilogy* by John Dos Passos. The book that took my breath away, and that would ultimately become my bible, was James Agee's *Let Us Now Praise Famous Men*. It was a lyrical journalistic portrait of poor white tenant farmer families in Alabama in the 1930s—and a memoir of a young Northerner's self-conscious and aching efforts to connect with them.

Most Americans know *Famous Men* because of the accompanying photographs by Walker Evans—stark black-and-white portraits of people with pinched faces, haunted eyes, and flour-sack clothing that became instant, iconic emblems of rural poverty. But although I was moved by Evans's images, it was Agee's prose that gripped me like a potent cure for an ailment I had never been able to name. Like me, he had been a driven young student, full of theories and searching for a cause. I reread and underlined the book until I knew whole passages by heart.

Agee's gift was to find beauty and pathos in the mundane objects and activities of invisible lives. He wrote tender descriptions of cracked plates, rusty tools, and plastic vases on a farmer's fireplace mantel. He drew an excruciating portrait of what it feels like to pick cotton by hand, stooped over for hours in the sun, dragging a heavy sack by one shoulder, pinching and pricking your fingers on sharp bolls a thousand times in a row.

His few brushes with black Alabamians produced sharp insights into the harsh racial realities of the Deep South. He followed a young woman to ask her a polite question, but at the sound of his footsteps she instinctively jerked and "sprang forward into the first motions . . . of a suddenly terrified wild animal." He squirmed with horrified embarrassment when a white landowner ordered a group of dignified black men on their way to church to perform several sassy minstrel tunes for the visitor's entertainment.

By the time I read this book, the civil rights movement had shattered traditional Southern life. Fear and hostility still smoldered, but hope and change were on the rise. I yearned to follow Agee's journey, and Brown offered an opportunity to do so; the university established a student exchange program with Tougaloo College, a small, historically black liberal arts school in Jackson, Mississippi. I signed up to spend a semester there, but in the end I didn't go, partly because I was deeply immersed in college life and partly because my family disapproved. It was a decision I always regretted.

Without leaving Providence, though, I found more modest outlets for my budding journalistic ambitions and antiestablishment proclivities. One was the cooperative housing society, started by a group of students just ahead of us. Under an experimental arrangement, the co-op leased two houses owned by the university, which students occupied, managed, and maintained.

For three years I lived in Carberry House. It was a creaky old clapboard mansion, named after Josiah Carberry, an imaginary Brown professor of psychoceramics. There were about twenty residents divided among a dozen rooms, which we often repainted in fits of creative inspiration. Everyone had to sign up for a schedule of shopping, cooking, and cleaning. Dinners were communal, and the cuisine was dominated by spaghetti and tomato sauce. There were frequent group meetings to air grievances (no loud music at three a.m.) and suggestions (more variety in the dinner menu).

The cast of co-op characters ranged from studious to revolutionary to Carberry-esque. There were science majors whose class notes looked like mysterious scribbles and flower children who slept until noon. There was a waterbed room and a permanent rollicking soundtrack from the Allman Brothers and the Grateful Dead. There were sign-up sheets for every possible cause, from recycling campaigns to protests against Nixon's bombing of Cambodia. My parents visited once from Connecticut, smiled politely, and fled. I was never happier.

The other institution that consumed my energy and ambition was the *Brown Daily Herald*. One day during freshman year I wandered into its shabby office, with the old horseshoe-shaped editor's desk, and it became my after-hours haunt for the next three and a half years. The *BDH* was a semi-grown-up outlet for the campus zeitgeist of the day—irreverent and indignant but grammatically correct. I wrote book reviews and headlines and editorials, pasted copy after dinner, and occasionally drove the pages to our printer in Massachusetts at midnight.

My most enduring contribution to the *Herald* was an infamous senior-year poster, aimed at wooing subscribers, in which I and three male editors—one of whom went on to enjoy a vertiginous career in the financial stratosphere—appeared to be wearing nothing but copies of that day's edition. Alas (but not really), that poster from four decades ago is still the first thing people mention whenever I attend a Brown-related event, no matter how properly I am attired for the occasion.

Our years at Brown came during a relative lull after a period of explosive events that shook the nation and defined our generation— the rash of antiwar riots and protests in 1968; the assassinations of Martin Luther King and Bobby Kennedy the same year; the Woodstock concert in August of 1969; the shootings at Kent State University in May of 1970. I remember feeling frustrated that at eighteen, I had missed all the action while stuck in boarding school—that I had been born just two years too late to be part of the impassioned crusades of my era.

I needn't have worried. The reverberations from those spasms of conflict and creativity spread through the East Side like a drug. Music floated from every dorm window and suffused the campus with raucous harmony. Today, when I close my eyes and picture sitting on the Green between classes, I hear "Uncle John's Band" and "Blue Sky" wafting happily through the air, with an occasional jarring blast from the late Jimi Hendrix performing "Purple Haze."

There were peace petitions in the Ratty, political speakers in Sayles Hall, and occasional trips to downtown Providence or Boston to hear Jefferson Starship or Vietnam Veterans Against the War. At Brown, we felt safely ensconced in a carefree, counterculture cocoon—free to criticize the university president, join a strike by cafeteria workers, break china laughing, or kiss the sky.

Occasionally, reality pierced our sanctuary in the form of official, legal, or medical consequences for our behavior. One of my boyfriends, who had ignored numerous letters from his draft board, was detained during soccer practice and put on a bus to Fort Dix. Another got busted for trying to buy some marijuana from an undercover policeman at a campus party. Although the university health service provided low-cost contraceptives, one of my friends became pregnant and underwent a painful abortion. Another, who was studying to be a dentist, had her front teeth knocked out when she fell during an antiwar demonstration.

Eventually, most of us recovered in time to graduate, get haircuts, and turn to professional pursuits. During senior year I typed out application letters to more than three hundred daily newspapers across the country. That summer, I headed out in my 1970 Dodge Dart to visit as many of them as possible. It was a glorious excuse to tour America. In Birmingham, I visited the church where Dr. King had preached. In San Antonio, I visited the Alamo. In Berkeley, I stood on the corner of Haight and Ashbury Streets, surprised to see sidewalk craftsmen using credit card machines. In Oregon, I stayed with friends in a cabin in a dripping forest and encountered a solitary moose, silhouetted in the fog of a mountain highway at night.

Heading back east, I stopped in Chicago for an interview at the *Tribune*, then drove to the Lincoln Park Zoo to see the gorillas. When I returned to the parking lot, the Dodge was gone, along with my nice clothes, my résumés, and a trunk full of newspapers I had carefully saved to document my job search. The police assured me the car would eventually turn up, but I was shaken and despondent. I took a taxi to the home of a friend from Brown, and when I rang the doorbell, her entire family was riveted to the TV. Nixon was on the screen, resigning.

The next day, I accepted the first job offer that came in. A month later, I was a cub reporter at the *Evening Capital* in Annapolis, earning $125 a week. Still determined to become the next James Agee, I stole away from zoning board meetings and sought out social problems to chronicle. For the next decade, at a series of newspaper jobs, I wrote about alcoholics and mental patients, garbage collectors and tobacco pickers, refugees and runaways.

I reached for Agee's lyrical framing of the mundane, his eye for detail, his search for redemption amid suffering and failure. And occasionally, I came close to achieving these things—for example, in my portrait of a brilliant, haunted journalist who fled the superficiality of TV news but delved too deep in his quest for reality and became a homeless street addict. What drew me to stories like this, I finally realized, were the same tragic contradictions that had attracted me to Agee, a tormented genius who drank too much and died at forty-two. They were contradictions I also feared in myself.

One day in 1983, I was offered the chance to become a foreign correspondent in Latin America, which opened up a vast new canvas of life-and-death struggles—revolutions, dictatorships, natural disasters, and dire poverty. Over the next twenty-five years, I reported intermittently from more than thirty countries, mostly in the third world. I burrowed happily into the seething shantytowns of Port-au-Prince and Lima. I covered the tumultuous rebirth of democracy in Chile and the Philippines. I traveled with tides of ecstatic Hindu pilgrims and met shaken survivors of Taliban market bombings.

Always, though, it was the rare encounters with personal stoicism, faith, or kindness that inspired my best word portraits: the Indian family who took me on a journey to the Ganges to baptize their infant son; the Afghan teacher whose humble home contained the only library in a war-ruined village. When I sat down to re-create these experiences, Agee was always there.

But on another level, during all those years of far-flung and often dangerous travel, it was my father, Cheston Constable, who provided me with the moral support to go on. Whenever I called from some new disaster zone, he always answered with a calm and reassuring voice, no matter how awful it looked on the evening news. As I learned how cruel and selfish the world really was, I outgrew my adolescent disdain for his upper-crust ways and began to appreciate the quieter pain of loss and aging; the values of frugality, dignity, and compassion he upheld; and the strength of character that was his true legacy to me.

Several years ago, my father and I shared a unique experience at Brown that meant more to both of us than I can easily put into words. In the spring of 2009, my fortieth reunion and his seventy-fifth fell on the same day. By then, Dad was in his nineties and one of the few surviving members of his class. He had always been a loyal supporter of Brown but rarely visited in his later years. The frailties of old age were shrinking his horizons, and arthritis made it painful for him to walk. I knew he had little interest in attending his own reunion, but I had been asked to speak at mine, so I invited him to join us. Somewhat to my surprise, he accepted. Neither of us said so, but we both knew it would be his last trip to Providence.

We drove up from Connecticut that morning, and the class gathered under a tent on a Pembroke lawn. I had arranged to have Dad seated at the head table for the luncheon speech, but there was a cocktail party first, during which everyone mingled on the grass. Dressed in his jaunty jacket and tie, he insisted on standing the entire time, although I could see that he was in pain and barely able to keep his balance on the uneven terrain, while trying to hold a wineglass to boot. Someone offered to bring him a folding chair, but I knew he would refuse it.

I can hardly remember what I said at lunch, but I can still see Dad standing there on the lawn, stoically leaning on his cane and looking dapper as ever in his green linen jacket with a yellow silk handkerchief peeking from the pocket. Four years later, when he passed away at ninety-six, I was grateful to be at my father's side, having gone to his alma mater, traveled the world, and come back home—no longer young, but more indignant than ever, and still just as inspired.

And Yet Again Wonderful

ALFRED UHRY

I was in the class of 1958 at Brown. I remember that there was a photo spread on display, during my graduation weekend, of the class of 1908, in celebration of their fiftieth reunion. There were all these photos of young men wearing straw hats and high starched collars, smoking pipes and clowning around and apparently having a high old time. They seemed as remote to me as Mathew Brady photographs from the Civil War. And I wonder now if the pictures of my time at Brown would seem as archaic to current undergraduates as those pictures did to me.

I came to Brown from a high school just outside of Atlanta, Georgia. There were two more local boys in my freshman class, and no other Georgians enrolled as undergraduates at the university. It was a long way from home. We were met at the train by upperclassmen and bussed up the hill. They handed out little brown beanies that we were supposed to wear. I don't remember if we did or not. Hurricane Hazel arrived in Providence not long after I did. I remember stacking sandbags along the Providence River. People made fun of my Southern accent. I was homesick. I wasn't sure why I was there. I knew that this was what you did; after high school you went to college. But why? And why all the way up here? I was used to rolling green lawns and brick houses set well apart from one another. I thought Providence was hideous—all those frame Victorian houses mashed up against each other. And it rained all the time. And eventually snowed! I remember walking out of my dorm in the first snow and immediately falling on my rear end. I developed a crush on a girl named Barbara. She was a blue-eyed blonde and she had a pixie haircut like Audrey Hepburn. I never got up the nerve to talk to her. She went to study at the John Hay Library every night, so I did too. I mostly fell asleep there. I had terrible study habits; I flunked logic, but that figured because I was completely illogical. I don't remember feeling unhappy, or feeling anything really. I was just dazed.

There were three or four first-run movie houses in downtown Providence. I walked down the hill many afternoons and saw whatever movie was playing. And a few times I took the train to Boston to see whatever musicals were having pre-Broadway tryouts there. One of them was a Rodgers and Hammerstein show called *Pipe Dream*. I think it was their only flop.

I lived on the second floor of North Hope College, right on the main campus. It was a handsome nineteenth-century edifice and the room was large. There was a nonfunctioning fireplace and three big windows, all with window seats. There was a row of rusty showers two floors down in the basement. There was a pay phone in the hall outside the room. I think it was the only telephone in the building. My roommate was Mike from Pittsburgh. He was athletic and easygoing and popular. I was none of those things, but I liked him very much. I emulated him as much as possible, trying desperately to lose the Southern accent and sound like him. Of course, being from Pittsburgh, Mike had his own unusual accent, but I wasn't aware of that at the time. All Yankees sounded pretty much the same to my Georgia ears.

I enjoyed dorm life. The term *hanging out* wasn't in the vernacular then, but that's what I did quite a bit of the time, with Mike, with the guys across the hall, and with whoever happened by. Looking back, I think I learned more about life in those bull sessions than in any of the classes I took that year.

The classes were very different from my Georgia county high school's. Expectations were high. I was called Mr. Uhry. Before that, *Mr. Uhry* referred to my father only. There was a wonderful European history survey course taught by Professor Walter George. It was a big lecture class, meeting in Alumnae Hall on the Pembroke Campus. We had assigned seats, and a spotter in the balcony checked for attendance. Professor George was very dignified and very theatrical at the same time. He had the ability to hold the entire room spellbound.

Toward the end of that freshman year, I met a sophomore from Brooklyn named Robert Waldman. He had written the music for the annual Brownbrokers musical with a graduating senior. He asked me to collaborate with him on the musical for the next year. Brownbrokers was a competition. You had to submit an entire show—book, music, and lyrics—and a committee of upperclassmen picked the winner. The offer from Waldman was like a call from on high. He was a seasoned veteran, a pro in my eyes. Of course I said yes, overjoyed and terrified to be working in such rarefied climes.

I think my real life began during my sophomore year. I don't remember much about the courses I took, but I didn't flunk anything, so I must've done all right. What I do remember is writing the book and lyrics for that show. We called it *Barney 'n Me*. The title was an in-joke because Barnaby Keeney was the newly appointed president of the university. The Barney in the show was a set of fake dinosaur bones. I loved collaborating. I loved writing a draft, meeting with Bob, and then rewriting. I loved fitting words to the music he wrote. I was bitten hard by the theater bug. Our show was selected to be presented. The rehearsal experience was stimulating and exciting. We were like a sports team, flexing our muscles and practicing our moves and getting ready for the big day. My family came up from Atlanta to see the show. I thought it was wonderful. I was deliriously happy. We got panned in the *Brown Daily Herald*. I was monumentally depressed. Those wild mood swings connected with whatever show I am doing have lasted to this day—though Prozac has helped a lot!

Three things changed my life forever during my junior year. First, we wrote another show. It was called *Fiddle De Dee* and it was based on a Chekhov fairy tale. Writing it, rehearsing it, and getting it on left no doubt in my mind. I was going to go into show business. Bob

Waldman and I were going to be the next Rodgers and Hammerstein.

Second, I enrolled in a course called English 23–24. It met four afternoons a week. It was more than a course—it became a way of life. We traced the history of the theater from Greece to modern times. We spent a month on each period and put on a workshop production of plays from each one. It was very detailed. We never got past the seventeenth century, which was fine with me. I was a sponge, soaking up every drop of information and lore fed to me by two remarkable professors, Janice O. van der Water and James Barnhill. So much of what I learned from them became the foundation of my working life.

Sock and Buskin was the name of the theatrical society at Brown. I hear it still is. S & B presented four shows a year. One was invariably Shakespeare. One was a recent Broadway hit, and the two others varied—a Greek tragedy, Shaw, Chekhov, O'Casey. The Shakespeare that year was *As You Like It*. I didn't know the play. Well, I had seen a production of it when I was in high school. At least I saw fifteen minutes of it. It was so boring and incomprehensible to me that I sneaked out as soon as I could. This time it was different. I was the stage manager, so I had to attend every rehearsal. I came to know most of the lines. The words were so lofty and so witty and so beautiful. And the play was so romantic and so funny! Here was this wonderful spunky girl having to pretend she was a guy, and the actual guy she was falling for didn't know she was really a girl. It was all worked out so cleverly. It's still my favorite Shakespeare play.

The third thing that happened that year, the biggest thing of all, was that I fell in love! Her name was Joanna Kellogg. She was also enrolled in English 23–24, so I spent every afternoon with her. She was drop-dead beautiful, with oversize brown eyes and shiny brown hair. She was an actress, too. She played Celia, the second lead in that production of *As You Like It*. There it was. I fell in love with show business, the classic theater, and Joanna all at the same time. I've never fallen out of love with any of them.

*   *   *

Waldman graduated that June and went back to New York to study music composition at Juilliard. I stayed on at Brown for my senior year. We had already decided that after I graduated, I'd go to New York and we would embark upon a professional career. I remember being in New York once during my senior year and realizing that, except for Bob, I knew not one single soul in New York City, let alone in show business. How the hell was I going to do this? I decided not to think about that and charged ahead.

In my senior year I sort of viewed myself as a grand old man, a veteran of two Brownbrokers shows and an authority on musicals. I didn't write another show, but I did chair the selection committee. We chose a piece written by three women—a first in the history of Brownbrokers. Joanna was a year behind me, but we planned to go to New York together upon her graduation. In 1958 that meant marriage—there were no other acceptable possibilities.

When I was looking at those pictures of the class of 1908 on the weekend I graduated, I knew pretty much what I wanted to do with my life: live in New York, write shows with Bob, and marry Joanna. And I did all of those things. Bob and I never became Rodgers and Hammerstein, but we both were and still are working professionals. Bob is still my best friend. Joanna and I were married two weeks after she graduated and we still are. She decided that one showbiz career was enough for one family, so she devoted herself to education. She now holds an EdD and is a long-tenured professor at Fordham University, where she is a world-renowned authority on dyslexia. We became the parents of four daughters and are now the grandparents of six more girls and two boys to boot.

I didn't realize it at the time, but I went from a dreamy, lazy high school kid to a guy with concrete life plans in my time at Brown. In other words, I grew up. Well, more or less. I still haven't completely managed to do that. Where would I be now if I hadn't come to Brown in the fall of 1954? I have no idea.

My Honorary Degree and the Factory Forewoman

EDWIDGE DANTICAT

My mother once offered her boss, a factory forewoman, my first novel—*Breath, Eyes, Memory*—for Christmas, the novel I completed at Brown, the novel that would later be an Oprah's Book Club selection.

My mother planned to tell the factory forewoman, "My daughter wrote this book at university." We said it many times together. "My daughter wrote this book. My daughter wrote this book at university." I still imagine this daughter, not as myself, but as a child my mother and I share—a dream offspring, a graduate and later even an honorary degree recipient from Brown.

I spent an entire day pondering an appropriate dedication for a woman I didn't know, except through a few details my mother had mentioned. She was Chinese. She was fat and rarely impatient. Finally I scribbled, "To Mary, Merry Christmas. Thank you so much for being nice to my mom."

I once went with my mother to another factory from which she had been laid off. I was fifteen years old and we had gone there to pick up some money she was owed for making two dozen purses a day at minimum wage. The room was dim and dusty, the air laden with tiny leather and thread particles, which the large overhead fans spun in a hazy whirlpool above the crammed rows of antique Singers. I couldn't imagine my mother spending every day there, and not getting paid on top of it. But at fifteen, I could only make vows. This would never be my life. I would never work for anyone. I would get my bachelor's degree, then go to graduate school. And in grad school, I would write books.

My parents, it seemed, also silently shared part of this dream. While they believed that daughters should never live far from their parents—I had commuted as an undergraduate at Barnard—they hadn't simply put me on a plane or a bus and wished me well; they rented a van and, bringing along my three brothers, they drove me to Brown from our home in Brooklyn. While I was at Brown, they told people that I was studying to be a teacher—one could teach with an MFA after all. This was what they understood of writers.

Teaching was indeed one of the things I did for the first time at Brown. I had a class full of undergraduates who were hoping to have one of the famous novelists on faculty as their instructor. My students were mostly experimental writers and many of them thought that "But this is what I was trying to do" was a proper explanation for everything they wrote. Somehow we all managed to survive the semester.

While at Brown, I also fell madly in love with the entire canon of African-American literature as it was taught by the brilliant professor Thadious Davis. I joined an African-American sorority—Alpha Kappa Alpha—whose kind and elegant women inspired me to think of more than writing. My two best friends were a poet from California and a novelist from China. I joined a small Haitian church, where I met many people who had fled Haiti in the wake of the violence that followed a US-backed coup d'etat against Haiti's first democratically elected president, Jean-Bertrand Aristide. I wrote an op-ed for the *Providence Journal* about the coup.

I found small pockets of home on my own. I found my voice.

I wish my father could have seen me get my honorary degree from Brown in May 2008. He had died four years earlier. My mom could not make the trip for health reasons. Perhaps this is why, more than anything else, as I received my degree from then-president Ruth Simmons, all I could think of was my mother wanting to give her factory forewoman my book.

Back then, I told myself, maybe my mother's gift had puzzled that factory forewoman. Had she been able to reconcile the fact that my mother would still need to work in a factory even though she had a one-book authoress daughter, newly graduated from a master's program at a fancy school?

Years later, when my father was diagnosed with pulmonary fibrosis, he found a pulmonologist to whom he became quite attached. I had a book of short stories out around this time, and my father asked me to sign a copy for his doctor.

It has taken me some time to decode both my parents' message *to me* in giving away my books—that somehow some of my vows and theirs, concerning my life, were the same after all. Just as they had shown with that family ride to Brown in the rented van, they were totally on board. They believed in me. And even though they valued their privacy so much that they always locked their bedroom door to have even the slightest disagreement, they never complained about anything I wrote while I was at Brown and all those many years after. Neither my misguided "truths" nor my deliberate distortions of the family stories ever bothered them.

They couldn't have known that I would earn the extraordinary privilege of getting an honorary degree from Brown, or that my books would find an audience. All they knew was that I was somewhat on the right path.

Is playwriting teachable?
(the example of Paula Vogel)

SARAH RUHL

People often ask me if I think playwriting is teachable. Making a soufflé, tap-dancing, changing a tire, and making stained glass are all teachable activities—and making a play is not so different from making a soufflé, tap-dancing, changing a tire, and making stained glass all at the same time, but on paper. Why, then, do many see the writing of plays as such a mysterious activity that it cannot be taught? Is it because our culture has such a high regard for individualism that it has such a low regard for teachers? Almost everything in the culture is taught, one way or another, but for originality, which cannot be taught and is therefore judged to have the most value. And yet, in most art forms, the originality of the individual is assumed, whereas the form transmitted through history is taught and teachable. For example: This is Middle C. This is how to point your toes. This is how to sharpen your pencil. (Which I don't take lightly. I remember when a drawing teacher actually showed me how to sharpen my pencil properly when I was twenty and it made all the difference. But I digress.)

Is *playwriting* teachable?

Rather than trying to answer the question in an abstract way, I'd like to tell a story. Paula Vogel begins *How I Learned to Drive*: "Sometimes, in order to teach a lesson, you have to tell a story."

And so. I met Paula Vogel at Brown University when I was a junior. I was twenty. I had just returned from a leave of absence after my father's death. I was very close to him, and he'd died of cancer, in Chicago, the summer of my sophomore year. The first two years of college were a difficult blur, spent mainly studying and racing back to Chicago on a plane at the first opportunity to see my father. He was diagnosed with advanced bone cancer during Thanksgiving of my freshman year. I thought about transferring to the University of Chicago, and even obtained an application, but my father would have none of it. He wanted everything to be as "normal" as possible and didn't want me to live at home among bedpans. Of course nothing was normal, but I tried to be as normal a nineteen-year-old as I knew how, while thinking of death and illness much of the time. I think my heart was broken. I wonder if my father knew somehow that I couldn't leave Providence before I'd met Paula Vogel, or my future husband.

At any rate, I took a semester off from Brown after my father died and spent it back home in Chicago, teaching special education classes by day. At night, my mother and sister and I shared the same house, but each in a private house of grief that could not be shared. I came back to Providence the spring of my junior year and was having trouble concentrating on my studies. It was hard for me to read and hard for me to write. I lived in a blue house on Hope Street. It seemed dark much of the time; the light itself seemed darker, though the seasons were as they always had been in Providence—in winter a damp cold that got inside the bones, and in spring all flowering trees. Regardless of the trees, it looked dark to me. And then I met Paula Vogel. She was teaching my advanced playwriting class.

I could talk about the content of what Paula taught me. All of her students (and these include Nilo Cruz, Quiara Hudes, Lynn Nottage, Dan LeFranc, Jordan Harrison, and Bridget Carpenter, to name a few) speak the same language of Russian formalism (how to make the familiar seem strange) and plasticity (the visual landscape of the stage and how it's created on the page) and stage directions that are impossible to stage. But what strikes me most when I remember Paula's teaching is her *presence* as much as the content of her teachings. I think in this country we have an obsession with content and curriculum, all the while devaluing presence and proximity, which are two teaching values hard to describe or quantify (or, indeed, teach). Paula has a tremendous gaze, a tremendous listening power, and the most intelligent curiosity of anyone I have ever met. She took me seriously.

And so when I was in her class and told her that I was having trouble writing about the things that mattered most to me, Paula gazed at me. She understood grief, and she knew that I'd just lost my father. She said, "If someone asked me to write a play about my brother Carl who died of AIDS, I'd never have gotten out of bed. Instead, I wrote about a kindergarten teacher taking a trip through Europe, which became *Baltimore Waltz*. And I was able to write about my brother." Then I remember her looking at me with that uncanny penetrating gaze she has, the gaze of a brilliant scientist making a diagnosis, but with a nonscientific laserlike empathy, and she said, "Write a play in which a dog is the protagonist."

"Okay," I said. And I did. That was a play called *Dog Play* and it was the first thing I was able to write after my father died. It viewed his illness and death through the eyes of the family dog.

I found in Paula's approach to playwriting a great deal of pleasure, and a great deal of play. It was almost too pleasurable, too decadent. I always thought I'd be a poet, which gave me pleasure, but a solitary ascetic kind of pleasure, not the kind that makes you laugh out loud or stay up late into the night with others. And so I thought her class was a wonderful diversion, and that I would now go back to my chosen path, to be a scholar, and write a slim volume of poetry every once in a while.

I went to study in England for a year and came back a little more mended (baths, tea, grass, and daffodils, I suppose) to my senior year at Brown. I asked Paula to be my thesis advisor. I wanted to write a thesis on representations of the actress in the Victorian novel. Paula said: "No, I cannot advise that thesis. But if you write a play, I will advise your thesis." I felt an almost strangled joy in my chest. I told

Paula that I did have an idea for a play. "What is it?" she asked with that characteristic gleam in her eye.

I stammered, "W-what about a play where this town is playing the Passion Play year after year, and the guy who always has to play Pontius Pilate really wants to play the role of Jesus, played by his cousin?"

I remember again that time slowed down as Paula looked at me in her uncanny way and said: "I think you should write that play." (How many plays has Paula helped conjure into existence, I wonder, by saying to another playwright: *I think you should write that play*? Hundreds or thousands, most likely.)

And so I did write that play, under her guidance. It took me twelve years to finish, and it was called *Passion Play*. My senior year, I met with Paula every week at Café Zog on Wickenden Street. Over coffee and a cookie, she would read my new ten pages, and she would tell me every book I needed to read, and always, she named the exact book I needed to read at the exact time I needed to read it—a kind of psychic superhero librarian. I devoured medieval theater and German expressionism. I finished writing the first act of *Passion Play*.

Knowing that I began my writing life as a rather retiring poet, Paula treated me with much tenderness and guile, sneaking my play into the New Plays Festival at Trinity Repertory Company in Providence, along with plays by her graduate students. (This is one of Paula's chosen teaching methods, which she fully admits. She attempts to make students addicted to the actual dust backstage, that barely-there stuff you have to inhale.) I was elated and terrified. I never thought my little one-act would ever be up on its feet. I wrote it only for pleasure, and for Paula, and for the drawer. She assigned me a wonderful director, Peter DuBois, for my very first production. Big Nazo made the fish puppets. Peter got identical twin girls to play Queen Elizabeth's courtiers.

The night of the opening, my mother flew into town from Chicago to see the play. We were driving down the hill toward Trinity Repertory Company to opening night when we were blindsided, hit by a car going very fast on Hope Street. I wasn't wearing a seat belt in the backseat and I hit my head and blacked out. Before I blacked out, I remember thinking: this is how death comes, quickly.

I woke up and my mom thought maybe we should go to the hospital for an MRI and I said: are you kidding let's go to my play we're almost late. So we went to my play and there was a standing ovation and I remember feeling such an out-of-body sense of rapture seeing the play in three dimensions with actors acting and lights lighting and people watching. I knew then that I would spend my life doing this and not look back. (I got an MRI the following day. It was normal. It did not register the change of vocation.)

When I reflect on all the things Paula taught me—among them Aristotelian form, non-Aristotelian form, bravery, stick-to-it-iveness, how to write a play in forty-eight hours, how to write stage directions that are both impossible to stage and possible to stage—the greatest of these is love. Love for the art form, love for fellow writers, and love for the world.

It is fitting that she and her wife, the eminent biologist and feminist theorist Anne Fausto-Sterling, got frocked for the day and married me and my husband. My husband was a student of Anne's. After years of my mother looking at my course selections and finding only courses in the humanities, and saying to me: "Please, just take one history of science course so that you're educated," I married a historian of science turned doctor.

I never did take a history of science course. My husband (long before he was my husband) and I were both in my beloved David Konstan's class "Ancient Tragedy and Its Influence" freshman year, but it took seven more years for us to actually meet, when we were in graduate school. My husband, Tony, had done an independent study with Anne in the history of science as an undergraduate before going to medical school. Paula and Anne claimed that they used to talk about us over the dinner table before we met, and when we did start dating, they said they held their breath. It seemed fitting that two teachers who were both so life-changing and transformative for each of us would bind us in front of a community.

After we were married, and as I made my first forays into the professional world, it was always Paula I would call first with personal- and theater-related dilemmas. She was one of the first people I called when, slightly panicked, I found out I was pregnant with twins.

"Come to Cape Cod for a week," Paula said. "We'll take care of you."

On Cape Cod, Paula entertained my big girl Anna with making Kleenex into puppets. Anne grilled fish. We swam in ponds. This was the house that Paula had taken me and two other graduate students to, years ago. She had told us to look out on the deck at the view of the Atlantic Ocean and say to ourselves, "This is what playwriting can buy." (She bought the house with the proceeds from *How I Learned to Drive*.)

Now, pregnant with twins and terrified for my writing life, I sat and looked out at the same blue. Anne is a great naturalist and bird-watcher, and a great many birds flew over. In a quiet moment I asked Paula, "Will I ever write again?"

She gave me her penetrating gaze, which I think is almost a form of hypnosis, a summoning. If I were a soldier, Paula would be a general, coaxing me into battle. She said: "Of course you will."

We named our twins Hope and William. Hope Street and Williams Street is the intersection in Providence where my husband and I met. And where we grew up. And that is most of my story.

So, back to the abstract question: Is playwriting teachable? Of course it's not teachable. And of course it is teachable. It lives in a paradox. It is as teachable as any other art form, in which we are dependent on a shared history and on our teachers for a sense of form, inspiration, example, and we are dependent on ourselves alone for our subject matter, our private discipline, our wild fancies, our dreams.

The question of whether playwriting is teachable begets other questions, like: Is devotion teachable? Is listening teachable? Is a love of art and a willingness to give your life over to art teachable? I believe that these things are teachable mostly by *example*, and in great silences. There is the wondrous noise of the classroom, the content, the liveliness of the teachings themselves, the exchange of knowledge, and then there is the great silence of relation. Of watching how great people live. And of their silently communicating: "You too, with your midwestern reticence, can go out into the great world and write. And when we fail, we'll have some bourbon, and we'll laugh." This is all part of the teaching of playwriting over time, and it's unbounded by the classroom. Just as love is unbounded by time.

I find myself thinking of Paula a great deal now that I am teaching playwriting for the first time to graduate students at Yale. I began as Paula's substitute teacher. I wonder what I can possibly give to the students, and whether it will be a dismal fraction of what Paula gave me.

Having young children, I think about preschool a lot. About Maria Montessori, who revolutionized early childhood education by giving children the ability to be independent learners. I think: what would the graduate playwright version of the Montessori classroom look like? It would give playwrights freedom and implements, and would let them direct their own courses of study. In short, it would give playwrights actors. The teacher would be a listener, a first audience. It strikes me that people who are defensive about the teachability of playwriting are uncomfortable with the humble but important position of being a first audience. Or perhaps they worry that if playwriting is teachable it dampens their originality, or the originality of their students. But I believe that humble, anti-guru teaching like Paula's encourages originality by respecting the privacy of her students, never interfering with their unconscious processes.

Speaking of gurus, I am working on a play right now about reincarnation. In the Tibetan Buddhist tradition, when a great teacher or lama dies, the student goes out and looks for his teacher's reincarnation in a baby. The student then brings up this baby, his former teacher, in a monastery and teaches him what he himself was taught. I find this continuity very moving. In the Western tradition, we have no such cyclical tradition that preserves an unbroken chain of knowledge. In the playwriting tradition, many of the transmissions are oral. It is then essential that we get into rooms together and share knowledge, and share presence.

I would be a different person if I hadn't gone to Brown, if I hadn't met Paula. I'm not sure who that person would be. Less brave, I think. And so the best I can do to thank her is to try and encourage other young writers as they test their fragile bravery on the world.

How I Became a Freelance Writer at Brown

MARA LIASSON

I n my sophomore year at Brown I talked my way into a class taught by John Thomas. It was a seminar called "Early Twentieth-Century American Radicals." The title alone was a siren song I couldn't resist, being a self-styled late twentieth-century American radical, junior grade. It was a seminar for upperclassmen. I can't remember what I said to Thomas to get him to let me in but he agreed. And I don't remember much of what we discussed in class, just that the small lecture hall was dim and Thomas smoked cigarettes, which back then made him seem a little tough and hard-bitten—not suicidal.

I wrote a paper for that class about Alfred Stieglitz and the artists he showed at his gallery at 291 Fifth Avenue. I submitted it to a student essay contest at a magazine I had never heard of called *American Art Review*. It got chosen and appeared in July of 1975 as "The Eight and 291: Radical Art in the First Two Decades of the 20th Century." I received $100 in prize money. I was a published writer.

I remember how excited I was as I opened the magazine—it was glossy with full-page illustrations—and then the sick feeling that came over me when I realized the first line of my essay had been rewritten. Instead of a "sea change" there was now the clunkier (I thought) "radical transformation." I was a published writer—with an editor.

In September of that year, my roommate answered a knock on the door of our dorm room and found a man who announced himself as a "dealer" who was looking for Mara. She flipped out and ran to find me at Faunce House, certain that I had gotten involved in drugs over the summer. But he was an *art* dealer from Boston who had read my essay in *American Art Review*. He had asked the Brown registrar how to find me, was told where I lived (something that would never happen today), and tracked me down—at my dorm!—to offer me a freelance writing assignment.

He had bought the entire output of a painter called Gerrit A. Beneker and needed someone to write the catalog essay for an exhibit of Beneker's work at the Vose Galleries in Boston. He would pay me $500, which I thought was a huge fee. Beneker was a kind of socialist Norman Rockwell who painted portraits of factory workers in Ohio. I signed up for James Patterson's psychohistory class, wrote a biography of Beneker, and then turned that into the catalog essay.

Looking back, the whole thing seems so improbable. Everything that happened seemed like a series of happy accidents. Brown was teaching me that this is how the world works. One thing leads to another. I started thinking that maybe I could make a living doing this—or something like this.

Meanwhile, I took every class of Professor Thomas's that I could and in my senior year I wrote my American History honors thesis with him. It had the embarrassing-to-me-now title "The Federal Writers Project and the Folklore of Cultural Pluralism." My husband jokes that I should have called it "The Federal Writers Project and the Single Girl" and left it at that.

The process of writing a thesis with Jack Thomas (everyone knew him as Jack) was scary and sublime. Tacked to the door of his office in the History department was a newspaper cartoon of an old-fashioned bomb (the kind that looks like a bowling ball with a lit fuse) with arms and legs. That was meant, I guess, to illustrate his infamous temper, although I personally never witnessed a Thomas explosion.

Jack Thomas was tall and solid and he had a crushed-looking nose, which, someone told me, he had achieved in a boxing ring. It was a great story—and much too good to check! To me he was larger than life.

He held office hours at four p.m. I can still recall going to see him with a draft of a thesis chapter. He sat behind his desk with his back to the window, the late-afternoon sun streaming in. He was a huge hulking shadow wreathed in cigarette smoke. The chair for students was right in front of the desk facing the window. It was very cinematic—a perfectly lit set for an intimidating academic experience. As he worked his way through my draft there was nothing for me to do but tremble and squint. I still believe that he planned it this way.

Thomas was exacting but also warm and encouraging. He wasn't just interested in my ideas—he expected me to have some. And he marched my thesis down the field and helped me heave it over the finish line, chapter by rewritten chapter. I couldn't have asked for a better teacher, or editor.

In the thirty-five years since, I've thought a lot about what I learned from him about American history: about how ordinary people as well as elected officials make history, how ideas matter and how the intellectual seeds of reform are planted decades before they ever come to fruition. And above all, because Jack Thomas was a great writer of history, how important it is to communicate in simple clear language.

There probably wasn't a straight line from Jack Thomas's American history classes to covering American politics at NPR, but it feels like there was, because Brown gave me the confidence and the freedom to navigate my own ship, even before I had any idea where it would end up.

In Troy There Lies the Scene

MADELINE MILLER

O ne of the phrases I heard most often during freshman orientation was *comfort zone*. And, according to a legion of well-
meaning peer counselors and student leaders, the purpose of Brown
was to get out of it. In that first week we heard inspiring stories about
rugby-playing musicians, biologists who were fencing-team MVPs,
and Egyptologists who had started their own nonprofits. Adventure,
exploration, experimentation! Go forth and change your life with
something new!

I listened, dubious. Yes, I knew that breadth was good, but what I
really longed for was depth: the chance to immerse myself in something I loved. Freed from requirements, I planned to dive into Latin
and Greek literature and not come up for air until four years had
passed.

I did, however, have one interest that was suitably uncomfortable:
since childhood I had harbored a secret love of the stage. A strange
choice for someone as terror-stricken by public speaking as I was, but
the candle continued to burn bright, and I had promised myself that
one day I would give theater a try. Emboldened by my peer counselors, I thought: *Maybe now's the time.*

So I tried, I really did. I lurked by tables at the orientation activity
fair; I picked up audition flyers; I attended information sessions. But
everything seemed hopelessly intimidating. The main-stage productions were run by grown-ups, for god's sake. And Production Workshop, which was supposed to be the friendlier, student-produced
workspace, was populated by terrifying black-clad sophisticates who

could quote Beckett by heart. Acting classes were no easier. The first question on the application was: previous acting experience? Somehow I didn't think my turn as the Little Match Girl in second grade would count.

No matter. My disappointment was quickly forgotten amidst the glories of the classics department: tutorials, lectures, secret libraries, an archaeological dig. In the years that followed, I had the good fortune to find not one but two brilliant mentors, Michael Putnam and Joseph Pucci. Comfort zone? I was in heaven. I decided to stay on and earn my master's as well.

Then, in the winter of my senior year, my boyfriend Doug said, "I'm thinking of codirecting a play for Shakespeare on the Green."

Shakespeare on the Green was a relatively new theater group that performed the Bard's plays outdoors every spring. And thanks to Doug, who'd been with them since freshman year, I had seen every one of their shows. I loved that they were outside, which nicely complemented the loose-jointed directing. I loved their genuine enthusiasm for Shakespeare and that many of the actors were environmental scientists or linguists who just happened to also like acting.

"That's wonderful!" I said.

"And I think you should codirect with us," he said.

I remember being startled; Shakespeare was way out of my field, and directing was even more opaque to me than acting. And anyway, if he already had another codirector, why did he need me?

"Because," he answered, "we want to do *Troilus and Cressida*."

I'd heard of it: Shakespeare's darkly comic retelling of the Trojan War. References to the play used to pop up in the more ambitious footnotes of my classics texts, but I had never sat down to read it. I hustled over to the bookstore and bought a copy.

The Shakespeare critic Harold Goddard called *Troilus and Cressida* an "intellectual twin" of *Hamlet* because it grapples with many of the same themes: corruption and hypocrisy, alienation, the shattering of illusions. In fact, *Troilus and Cressida* is what might have resulted if the melancholy Dane himself had taken up a quill and tried to write the *Iliad*. It's one of Shakespeare's angriest, edgiest, and most problematic plays; it's also one of his funniest. In a single scene, the tone veers from absurdism to scathing satire, from pathos to bathos and back again. I was in.

Except, I didn't have the first idea how to turn the play's brilliance on the page into a performance. Sitting down with my codirectors, Doug and Joy, I became aware of just how much practical stagecraft I didn't know: how many minutes each page of script would take, what a stage manager did, how to run auditions. I spent those early meetings in the background, just listening and trying to follow the new vocabulary: *tablework, sides, blocking.*

Then we started discussing the play. And though I may have been stricken with terror onstage, I learned that backstage, I was the terror. I had opinions, big ones, honed on four years of close-reading classical literature at the feet of my professors. For instance, Achilles and Patroclus. Obviously lovers, I said.

My codirectors raised their eyebrows. After a half-hour lecture on the historical treatment of Achilles and Patroclus's relationship, I finally got to the point: the play says so. Here, I pointed. And here. And I had some further thoughts on the character of Agamemnon. In the Quarto version of the text . . .

I could see my boyfriend wondering if he had created a monster.

Few monsters were ever so happy. The three days of auditions were some of the most intellectually exhilarating of my life to date. My hand ached from writing notes, and we talked ourselves hoarse about who would make the perfect Ulysses, the funniest Ajax. Just as important were the personalities of the actors: we wanted fun people, *game* people, not necessarily the most experienced. NO PREVIOUS ACTING NECESSARY, I had typed on the audition information sheet. And then underlined it, twice.

One of our biggest points of contention was the role of Thersites, Shakespeare's scurrilous, bitter chorus. My top choice was an actor who had come to the audition wearing a torn trenchcoat and huge half-disintegrated flappy sandals, with socks. He ate sheets of seaweed paper straight from a pocket. I thought he was great: eloquent and nastily bitter as the character demanded.

"That dude is weird," Joy said.

"Too weird," Doug said.

Passionately, I disagreed. And though two weeks ago I couldn't have articulated what made someone a good actor, now—after thirty hours of auditions—I was starting to get an inkling. Because he used the language, not just the emotion; because he was naturally responsive; because he could take direction. And thanks to four years of arguing about Vergil with my classics peers, my persuasive ability was at an all-time vehement.

Okay, okay, my codirectors said. If you really feel that strongly.

By the time we got to rehearsals, Joy had to drop out due to other commitments, which meant that I was now officially 50 percent responsible for the play. In a panic, I went to the library and took out everything I could find on *Troilus and Cressida*, and more on Shakespeare besides. But no matter how thoroughly I prepared, when it came time to actually work with the actors, it was always more difficult than I had anticipated. Blocking one simple gesture—Ajax grabbing Thersites's arm—could take half an hour.

"Where should I grab him?"

"There," I said, pointing.

"Sight lines!" the stage manager called out.

"Ouch," Thersites said. "That kinda hurts."

"Actually," Doug said, "I think it works better if he doesn't grab him now at all, but waits until—"

Achilles stuck his head around the door. "When's my cue again?"

Directing was one of the most challenging things I had ever done, harder than translating Aristotle, harder than writing my thesis. I wasn't used to working in three dimensions, nor was I used to working in a group. Everything I had done up to that point—papers, exams, and presentations—had been solo. But in theater, nearly every moment is about collaboration and communication, balancing your own ideas with everyone else's. After I got over the initial shock, it was a thrilling revelation: we were all in this together.

I was also shocked to learn how much ground the title *director* covered in a student production. In addition to running rehearsals, we were also figuring out costumes, props, and sets. In the weeks before the show, I learned what kind of fabric makes the best cape, where to find the cheapest metallic belts, and that if you spray-paint soccer shin guards gold they look kind of like greaves. Thankfully the actor playing Thersites—the one I had insisted upon—stepped in and offered us the entire costume stock from a production of Camus's *Caligula* he'd starred in. You're welcome, I told Doug.

Back in rehearsal, we continued making breathless choices that seemed like the height of brilliance: giving the play's prologue to the doomed seeress Cassandra; cutting the role of Helen; interpreting Achilles's Myrmidons as vinyl-clad dominatrices. (Actually, I didn't think that last one was a very good idea. But Doug swore it would go over well with the Spring Weekend audience, and indeed, he was right.)

As the performance date neared I became a jittery, jubilant wreck. Even when I wasn't on the phone with the sword-rental company or safety-pinning tarps together to make tents, I was so keyed up I couldn't sleep. The same thoughts kept cycling through my head: the play was perfect, the play was terrible, the play was perfect, the play was terrible.

The *Troilus and Cressida* that ran could not be called perfect; this was student theater, after all. But it wasn't terrible, either. It had energy and chemistry and conviction, and a cast that threw themselves into every joke and soliloquy. I remember standing there, transfixed anew by scenes I'd watched two hundred times: we had made this thing, and it wasn't half-bad. Miraculously, the audience seemed to agree. They laughed at the right moments, gasped a few times, and even stayed in their seats through a minor rainstorm. At the end they stood to applaud.

That's still one of my favorite things about theater—the way a show suddenly comes to life when there's an audience, the way cast and crew snap together to make all the moments you've practiced over and over actually work. Seeing it happen was extraordinary and, as it turned out, addictive. I was inspired to direct a second production, and then a third, and eventually ended up founding a Shakespeare theater group (with that same Thersites) that would become one of the great loves of my working life.

Thinking back to those peer counselors, I'm grateful that they encouraged me to try something new: they were right, it did change my life. But I'm also aware that I would never have had the chance— or nerve—to attempt the play without all that time I spent in classics. Having such a solid foundation gave me the confidence to branch out.

The coda to all this is that theater led, in its turn, to a new discomfort: writing my first novel, about that same Achilles and Patroclus. The years I spent directing—telling stories onstage—gave me the experience and courage to attempt one in print. Apparently it's how I work best: one foot comfortably planted, the other one over the precipice.

Giant Steps

AFAA MICHAEL WEAVER 蔚雅風

I play here . . . but let me amend, I assume here
a sepia metaphysics, watch myself emerge in air
breathed twenty-eight years ago, as now nothing
stops me from assembling myself, hair forming
from light, bone tumbling out of tree limbs, skin
making itself a grammar of justice in shadows
along walkways named by seamen, me a newer,
hardier New Englander from southern bourbon.

Learning to love English again, to renew promises
of baptisms as ceremonies in books of rhymes,
a hip-hop not yet sung, one with metric variations
for the opening of *The Tempest*, I now take the role
of Charlie Patton as Prospero, tint the sky with blues
on a stage that waits for us to dance myths that renew,
the clouds now amorphous facts over Brown's gate
looking down to the wooden First Baptist Church
where James Baldwin signed *The Price of the Ticket*.

In this space above time, reassembled, eyes more
a wish than the gel in the socket, I stare into the day
of leaving, graduating, Stevie Wonder being led
to sing to us, after our choral chant for Dr. Seuss,

the green marking what age would do, the toes
that would curl, bright spirits that would leave early,
an abrogation of the soul's treaty, and the rest of us
would live, live to study the currents of being alive,

me the tired John Henry in his Rockefeller carrel,
up north studying the ways language lives, how
                              it makes a poet.

Acknowledgments

Thanks to the unflappable Wendy Strothman '72, LHD '08 hon., P '07, for steering the *Brown Reader* project with keen intelligence and good humor; to David Ebershoff '91 for wearing several hats with astonishing skill; and to Jonathan Karp '86 and Suzanne Gluck '81 for their generous support and guidance. I'm grateful to each of the contributors for their inspiring creativity and dedication to excellence. Working with them has been a great pleasure.

At Brown University, huge thanks to Eve Ornstedt, Christina Paxson, Norman Boucher, Marisa Quinn, Mark Nickel P '09, Katie Vorenberg, Jennifer Betts, Gayle Lynch, C. D. Wright, Christine DeCesare, Kat Schott, Raymond Butti, and Russell Carey. I'm also grateful for input from the following members of Brown's 250th Anniversary Publications Sub-Committee: George H. Billings '72; Nancy L. Buc '65, LLD '94 hon.; Richard Fishman ADE '73 hon., P '89; Odest Chadwicke Jenkins ADE '11 hon.; Carl Kaestle ADE '98 hon.; Karen Newman; Ralph Rosenberg '86, P '17; Clay Wiske MD '16; and Gordon Wood ADE '70 hon., LTD '10 hon., P '86, GP '11.

I'm indebted to Harold Augenbraum, Donnalyn Carfi, Deborah Garrison '86, Erika Goldman, Bret Anthony Johnston, Sean Kelly '84, Rick Moody '83, John Siciliano, and Jean Sternlight for allowing me to pick their brains, and to Abby Weintraub '93 for the beautiful cover design.

Thanks to Simon & Schuster for partnering with Brown University on this special anthology. The terrific S&S team includes Laura Ferguson, Aja Pollock, and Nicholas Greene '10.

Finally, I'd like to thank my parents, Lee and Peter Sternlight, for sending me to Brown. What a gift.

Sources of Quotes

THE BROWN AESTHETIC

1 "The Brown aesthetic": David Shields '78, "How We Are in the World," *Brown Alumni Magazine* (*BAM*), March/April 2009.

1 "Brown remains to this day": Elena Ferrarin '96, "Writing from His Roots," *BAM*, January/February 2012.

1 "I met [Nathanael] West at Brown": Robert Taylor, "S.J. Perelman Takes a Powder," *Boston Globe*, November 22, 1970, reprinted in *Conversations with S. J. Perelman*, ed. Tom Teicholz (Jackson: University Press of Mississippi, 1995), 69.

CAMPUS LIFE

39 "The closest I ever came to an orgy": S. J. Perelman '25, "Cloudland Revisited: Sodom in the Suburbs," *New Yorker*, February 12, 1949, 24.

39 "I loved the fact that": David Corn '81, "You Don't Have to Trust Me," *BAM*, May/June 2013.

ACADEMIC LIFE

87 "As much as we sometimes": Steven Johnson '90, "Kevin Kelly and Steven Johnson on Where Ideas Come From," *Wired*, October 2010.

87 "The semiotics program": Christine Vachon '83, "The Freewheelin' Todd Haynes," *BAM*, November/December 2007.

87 "No matter what I study": Ted Chiang '89, *Stories of Your Life and Others* (East Hampton, MA: Small Beer Press, 2010), 39.

DIVERSITY

137 "I came to Brown": Jaimy Gordon '72, "Providence Baroque: Here Comes Jaimy Gordon," *Gargoyle* 22/23, December 17, 1983.

137 "Though there are no Jewish quotas": Amy Sohn, "Probing Brown's Dark History," *Jewish Daily Forward*, November 10, 2006.

137 "The influence [Augustus A.] White '57 has had": Beth Schwartzapfel '01, "The Doctor of Prejudice," *BAM*, September/October 2001.

SELF-DISCOVERY

183   "I was surrounded by fashion-conscious people": André Leon Talley '73 AM, *A.L.T.: A Memoir* (New York: Villard, 2003), 145.

183   "Senior year I moved into the House": Sam Lipsyte '90, *The Ask* (New York: Farrar, Straus and Giroux, 2010), 51.

183   "My own epiphany": Pamela Paul '93, "Regrets of an Accomplished Child," *New York Times*, November 4, 2012.

POLITICS

219   "On the morning of May 5th": Thomas Mallon '73, "The Year of Thinking Dangerously," *BAM*, May/June 1998.

219   "[At] Brown University, I was always someone": Dimitra Kessenides, "The Execution of Wanda Jean," *Salon*, March 18, 2002.

INSPIRATION

251   "I think one of the most inspirational": Kentucky Educational Television, "A Talk with the Playwright: Lynn Nottage," *American Shorts*, 2013.

251   "Mostly I say, just write": Mary Donnelly, "Kevin Young Interview," FailBetter.com, October 6, 2009.

251   "[What] had the strongest impact on me": Kathleen Potts, "Water by the Spoonful: An Interview with Quiara Alegría Hudes," *Guernica*, July 2, 2012.

251   "[Robert Coover] taught a course": Courtney Eldridge, "Ben Marcus," *BOMB* 89 (Fall 2004).

About the Contributors

Donald Antrim ('81) is the author of three novels, *Elect Mr. Robinson for a Better World*, *The Hundred Brothers*, and *The Verificationist*, and a memoir, *The Afterlife*. He contributes short stories and personal essays to the *New Yorker* and has received fellowships from the National Endowment for the Arts, the Dorothy and Lewis B. Cullman Center for Scholars and Writers at the New York Public Library, the American Academy in Berlin, and the John Simon Guggenheim Memorial Foundation. In 2013, he was named a MacArthur Fellow. He lives in Brooklyn, New York.

Robert Arellano ('91, '94 MFA) is the author of six novels, including the web's first interactive novel, *Sunshine '69*, and the Edgar Award finalist *Havana Lunar*. He is Professor of Creative Writing and a founding faculty member of the Institute of New Writing\Ashland at Southern Oregon University.

M. Charles Bakst ('66) retired from the *Providence Journal* in 2008 after more than forty years as a reporter, editor, and political columnist. He grew up in Fall River, Massachusetts. His late mother, Anna Horvitz Bakst, was a member of the class of 1931. Bakst attended Phillips Academy, Andover, and received a master's degree from the Columbia University Graduate School of Journalism. He and his wife, Elizabeth Feroe Bakst '67, live in Providence.

Amy DuBois Barnett ('91) has shaped the pages and websites of *Harper's Bazaar*, *Essence*, *Teen People*, *Honey*, and *Ebony*, where she is currently editor in chief of the oldest and largest African-American magazine in the country. Barnett has an MFA degree in creative writing from Columbia University. She is the author of the NAACP Image Award–nominated book *Get Yours! How to Have Everything You Ever Dreamed of and More*.

Lisa Birnbach ('78) has published twenty-two books, including *The Official Preppy Handbook* (1980) and *True Prep* (2010). She's written for the *New Yorker, Parade, New York,* and other magazines. She was the Las Vegas bureau chief of *Spy,* and eventually its deputy editor. In addition to being a guest on many talk shows and writing for television comedy programs, Lisa was a correspondent for three years on *The Early Show* on CBS. *The Lisa Birnbach Show,* a daily syndicated radio program, won two Gracie Awards. She tweets at @LisaBirnbach.

Kate (née Al) Bornstein ('69) is an author, performance artist, playwright, and public speaker who has written several award-winning books in the field of women and gender studies, including *Gender Outlaw* and *My Gender Workbook.* Her 2006 book, *Hello, Cruel World: 101 Alternatives to Suicide for Teens, Freaks, and Other Outlaws,* is an underground bestseller that has propelled Kate into an international position of advocacy for marginalized youth.

Sarah Shun-lien Bynum ('95) is the author of two novels, *Ms. Hempel Chronicles,* a finalist for the 2009 PEN/Faulkner Award, and *Madeleine Is Sleeping,* a finalist for the 2004 National Book Award. She lives in Los Angeles and teaches in the Graduate Writing Program at Otis College of Art and Design.

Mary Caponegro ('83 AM) is the author of *Tales from the Next Village, The Star Café, Five Doubts, The Complexities of Intimacy,* and *All Fall Down.* She is the recipient of the Rome Prize in Literature. She has taught at Brown, RISD, Hobart and William Smith Colleges, Syracuse University, and Bard College, where she holds the Richard B. Fisher Family Chair in Writing and Literature.

Susan Cheever ('65) is the author of *E.E. Cummings: A Life* and *Louisa May Alcott: A Personal Biography.* She is at work on a history of drinking in America. She has also published five novels and four memoirs. Her work has appeared in the *New Yorker,* the *New York Times,* and other publications, and she has been nominated for a National Book

Critics Circle Award and won the Boston Globe Winship medal. She has taught at Brown, Yale, Columbia, Bennington, and elsewhere.

Brian Christian ('06) is the author of *The Most Human Human*, which was named a *Wall Street Journal* bestseller and a *New Yorker* favorite book of 2011, and is translated into ten languages. His writing appears in the *Atlantic*, *Wired*, the *Paris Review*, and elsewhere. Christian has been featured on *The Daily Show*, on *Radiolab*, and in *Best American Science and Nature Writing*. He lives in San Francisco.

Pamela Constable ('74) has been a newspaper reporter and foreign correspondent for nearly forty years. Since 1994, she has been on staff at the *Washington Post*, and before that she worked for the *Boston Globe* and the *Baltimore Sun*. She has reported from many parts of Latin America, Asia, and the Middle East. She has written two books on contemporary Afghanistan, Pakistan, and India, and coauthored a book on the Pinochet regime in Chile. She is also the founder of a veterinary clinic and shelter for stray animals in Afghanistan. She lives in northern Virginia.

Nicole Cooley ('88) grew up in New Orleans. She was a Comparative Literature concentrator at Brown and then attended the Iowa Writers' Workshop, where she received her degree in fiction. She has published four books of poems, most recently *Breach* (LSU Press) and *Milk Dress* (Alice James Books), and a novel. She lives outside of New York City with her husband and daughters and is the director of the MFA Program in Creative Writing and Literary Translation at Queens College–City University of New York.

Dana Cowin ('82), editor in chief of *Food & Wine* magazine, oversees all aspects of this lifestyle brand, including books, tablet editions, and the website FoodandWine.com. She is devoted to many hunger-related causes and is on the board of City Harvest, Hot Bread Kitchen, and Wholesome Wave. Cowin lives in New York City with her husband, Barclay Palmer, and their two children.

Spencer R. Crew ('71) has served on the board of the Corporation of Brown University and as president of the Brown Alumni Association. He is Clarence J. Robinson Professor of History at George Mason University. During his more than twenty-five years as a museum professional he was the director of the National Museum of American History, Smithsonian Institution, and president of the National Underground Railroad Freedom Center in Cincinnati, Ohio.

Edwidge Danticat ('93 MFA) is the author of four novels, *Breath, Eyes, Memory*; *The Farming of Bones*; *The Dew Breaker*; and *Clair of the Sea Light*. Her other works include *Krik? Krak!*; *Brother, I'm Dying*; and *Create Dangerously: The Immigrant Artist at Work*. Her numerous accolades include a National Book Critics Circle Award, the Dayton Literary Peace Prize, an American Book Award, being named a National Book Award finalist (twice), and a MacArthur Fellowship.

Dilip D'Souza ('84 ScM) spent years in software before realizing his passion: writing. He has written for *Caravan*, the *Hindustan Times*, the *Daily Beast*, and *Newsweek*; his books include *The Curious Case of Binayak Sen* and *Roadrunner: An Indian Quest in America*. Among his several writing awards is the Newsweek/Daily Beast Prize. Home, with wife Vibha and children Surabhi and Sahir, is Bombay. Cats Cleo and Aziz rule.

David Ebershoff ('91) is the author of three novels, *The Danish Girl*, *Pasadena*, and *The Nineteenth Wife*, as well as a story collection, *The Rose City*. He is an executive editor at Random House and teaches graduate writing at Columbia University. He lives in New York.

Jeffrey Eugenides ('82) is the author of three novels, *The Virgin Suicides*, *Middlesex* (which was awarded the 2003 Pulitzer Prize for Fiction), and *The Marriage Plot*.

Richard Foreman ('59) has directed and designed and often written over seventy plays at major theaters here and abroad. Eight collections of his plays have been published, plus book-length studies of his work in the USA, Germany, and Japan. His awards include a MacArthur

"Genius" grant, a PEN Master American Dramatist Award, and an American Academy of Arts and Letters award for literature, and he is an officer of the Order of Arts and Letters of France.

Amity Gaige ('95) is the author of three novels, *O My Darling*, *The Folded World*, and *Schroder*, which was published by Twelve Books/Hachette in 2013. Named a best book of the year by the *Washington Post*, the *Huffington Post*, and the *New York Times*, among other publications, *Schroder* has been translated into fourteen languages. Her short stories, reviews, and essays have appeared in numerous publications. She lives in Hartford, Connecticut, and is the current Visiting Writer at Amherst College.

Robin Green ('67) is a TV writer-producer who lives in New York City with her husband/writing partner, Mitchell Burgess, amidst shelves full of industry awards for their work on *Northern Exposure* and *The Sopranos*, among other shows. She likes to think that John Hawkes would have enjoyed some of it. If he even had a television . . .

Andrew Sean Greer ('92, '95 MFA) is the bestselling author of five works of fiction, most recently *The Impossible Lives of Greta Wells*. He has been an NEA and New York Public Library Cullman Fellow and received a PEN/O'Henry Prize, a California Book Award, a Northern California Book Award, and a New York Public Library Young Lions Award. He lives in San Francisco.

Christina Haag ('82) is an actress and the author of the *New York Times* bestselling memoir *Come to the Edge*. Winner of the Ella Dickey Literacy Award, she has been published in the *Wall Street Journal*, *Vanity Fair*, and *Hamptons* magazine. She received the Dramalogue Award for Outstanding Actress and continues to work in film, theater, and television. A graduate of Juilliard, she lives in New York City and is currently working on a novel.

Joan Hilty ('89) is the creator of the long-running comic strip *Bitter Girl*; her artwork has also appeared in the *Village Voice*, the *Advocate*, and *Ms.* magazine. As a senior editor at DC Comics, she acquired numerous award-winning graphic novels. She currently develops and packages books as editor in chief of PageTurner Graphic Novels and teaches at the Maryland Institute College of Art. "The Times" is dedicated to Stephen Gendin '89. Special thanks to Louise Sloan '88, Rebecca Hensler '91, and Angela Taylor '88.

A. J. Jacobs ('90) is the editor at large for *Esquire* magazine, an NPR contributor, and the author of four *New York Times* bestselling books, including *The Year of Living Biblically*, *The Know-It-All*, and *Drop Dead Healthy*. He lives in New York with his wife and sons. He asks that you pardon his French.

Sean Kelly ('84) has produced thousands of humorous images on politics, business, and entertainment for the *Washington Post*, the *Los Angeles Times*, *Businessweek*, *Rolling Stone*, and the *Atlantic*, among other publications. His visual commentaries have appeared frequently on the op-ed page of the *New York Times* and he has won top awards from the Society of Illustrators and the National Cartoonists Society.

David Klinghoffer ('87) is a Senior Fellow at Discovery Institute in Seattle. His most recent book, a collaboration with Senator Joe Lieberman, is *The Gift of Rest: Rediscovering the Beauty of the Sabbath*. His other books include *Why the Jews Rejected Jesus: The Turning Point in Western History*, *The Discovery of God: Abraham and the Birth of Monotheism*, and the spiritual memoir *The Lord Will Gather Me In*. A former literary editor of *National Review* magazine, Klinghoffer lives on Mercer Island, Washington, with his wife and children.

Jincy Willett Kornhauser ('78, '81 AM), the widow of Professor Edward Kornhauser, is the author of short stories and novels, including *Jenny and the Jaws of Life*, *Winner of the National Book Award*, *The Writing Class*, and *Amy Falls Down*, all published by St. Martin's Press.

Marie Myung-Ok Lee ('86), author of *Somebody's Daughter*, has a new novel due out from Simon & Schuster in 2015. Her essays have appeared in the *New York Times*, *Slate*, the *Guardian*, the *Nation*, the *Atlantic*, and *Salon*. She was the first recipient of a creative writing Fulbright Fellowship to South Korea and has won the Rhode Island State Council on the Arts fiction fellowship and the Richard Margolis Award for social justice reporting. She has taught at Yale and Brown and currently teaches at Columbia University, where she is the Our Word Writer-in-Residence.

David Levithan ('94) is the author of *Boy Meets Boy*, *The Lover's Dictionary*, *Every Day*, *Two Boys Kissing*, *Nick and Norah's Infinite Playlist* (written with Rachel Cohn), and *Will Grayson*, *Will Grayson* (written with John Green). At Brown, he was an editor of the *College Hill Independent*. He is now a publisher and editorial director at Scholastic, where he started as an intern between his sophomore and junior years of college, thanks to a listing in the Brown career library.

Mara Liasson ('77) is the national political correspondent for National Public Radio. She is also a contributor to the Fox News programs *Fox News Sunday* and *Special Report*. Before coming to Washington in 1985 to work for NPR she was a radio and television reporter in San Francisco and a reporter for the *Vineyard Gazette* on Martha's Vineyard in Massachusetts. She lives in Washington, DC, with her husband and two children.

Lois Lowry ('58) is a mother and grandmother. She has been a journalist and photographer and is currently a writer of fiction, primarily for young people. Of her forty-three published books, two have received the Newbery Medal, awarded each year for the most distinguished contribution to American literature for children. She lives in Maine.

Ira C. Magaziner ('69) is vice chairman and CEO of the Clinton Health Access Initiative and chairman of the Clinton Clean Energy Initiative, both of which he cofounded with former US president Bill Clinton. From 1993 through 1998, he served as senior advisor to President Clinton for policy development at the White House. Prior to his White House appointment, he built two successful international consulting firms, advising governments on economic development and corporations on business strategy. Mr. Magaziner graduated from Brown University as valedictorian in 1969 and attended Balliol College, Oxford, as a Rhodes scholar.

Madeline Miller ('00, '01 AM) concentrated in Classics at Brown University. She also studied in the Dramaturgy department at Yale School of Drama. For the past decade she has taught Latin, Greek, and Shakespeare to high school students. *The Song of Achilles*, her first novel, won the 2012 Orange Prize and was a *New York Times* bestseller. Her essays have appeared in publications including the *Guardian*, the *Wall Street Journal*, *Lapham's Quarterly*, and NPR.org. She lives in Cambridge, Massachusetts, where she teaches and writes.

Christine Montross ('06 MD, '07 MMS) is the author of *Falling into the Fire: A Psychiatrist's Encounters with the Mind in Crisis* and *Body of Work: Meditations on Mortality from the Human Anatomy Lab*. She is an assistant professor of Psychiatry and Human Behavior at Brown University and also a practicing inpatient psychiatrist. She received her undergraduate degrees and a master of fine arts in poetry from the University of Michigan.

Rick Moody ('83) is the author of five novels, three collections of stories, a memoir, and a collection of essays, *On Celestial Music*. He is a music critic at *The Rumpus*, and he teaches at NYU and Yale.

Jonathan Mooney ('00) is a dyslexic writer and activist who did not learn to read until he was twelve years old. He holds an honors degree in English literature from Brown and is the author of *The Short Bus* and *Learning Outside the Lines*. Jonathan is founder and president of Project Eye-To-Eye, a mentoring and advocacy nonprofit organization for students with learning differences. Project Eye-To-Eye currently has twenty chapters in thirteen states, working with over three thousand students, parents, and educators nationwide.

Rowan Ricardo Phillips ('98 AM, '03 PhD) is the author of *The Ground* and *When Blackness Rhymes with Blackness* and has translated *Ariadne and the Grotesque Labyrinth* from Catalan to English. He is a recipient of the PEN/Joyce Osterweil Award for Poetry, the GLCA New Writers Award for Poetry, and a Whiting Award, and has been a finalist for the Los Angeles Times Book Prize and an NAACP Image Award. He is a regular contributor to the *Paris Review* and a writer for *Artforum*. He teaches at Stony Brook University.

Dawn Raffel ('79) is the author of four books, most recently *The Secret Life of Objects*.

Bill Reynolds ('68), a former Brown basketball cocaptain and All-Ivy player, is a longtime sports columnist at the *Providence Journal*. He's also the author of nine books and coauthor of three more, three of which have been on bestseller lists. One became the background for the award-winning ESPN movie *Unguarded*.

Marilynne Robinson ('66) is the author of *Gilead* (winner of the Pulitzer Prize for fiction and a National Book Critics Circle Award), *Home* (winner of the Los Angeles Times Book Prize and the Orange Prize for fiction), and the modern classic *Housekeeping*, which won the PEN/Ernest Hemingway Award for First Fiction and the Richard and Hinda Rosenthal Award from the Academy of American Arts and Letters. Her nonfiction books include *Mother Country*, *The Death of Adam*, *Absence of Mind*, and *When I Was a Child I Read Books*. She teaches at the University of Iowa Writers' Workshop.

Sarah Ruhl ('97, '01 MFA) is a playwright whose plays have been produced worldwide. Her works include *Stage Kiss*; *In the Next Room, or the vibrator play*; *The Clean House*; *Passion Play, a cycle*; *Dead Man's Cell Phone*; *Melancholy Play*; *Eurydice*; *Dear Elizabeth*; and *Late: a cowboy song*. A two-time finalist for the Pulitzer Prize, she also received the Whiting Award, a MacArthur Fellowship, and a PEN Center award. She received her MFA at Brown, where she studied under Paula Vogel. She lives in Brooklyn.

Ariel Sabar ('93) is an award-winning journalist whose writing has appeared in the *New York Times*, *Smithsonian*, and *Harper's*. His debut book, *My Father's Paradise: A Son's Search for His Jewish Past in Kurdish Iraq*, won the National Book Critics Circle Award for autobiography. His second book, *Heart of the City*, was called a "beguiling romp" (*New York Times*) and an "engaging, moving and lively read" (*Toronto Star*). Visit his website at www.arielsabar.com.

Joanna Scott ('85 AM) is the author of eleven works of fiction, including the novels *Follow Me*, *Tourmaline*, *Arrogance*, and *De Potter's Grand Tour*. Her essays and stories have appeared in the *Nation*, the *New York Times*, *Conjunctions*, *Black Clock*, the *Paris Review*, and other journals. She is the Roswell Smith Burrows Professor of English at the University of Rochester.

Jeff Shesol ('91), a Rhodes scholar (Oxford University '93), created the comic strip *Thatch* for the *Brown Daily Herald*. It was nationally syndicated from 1994 to 1998, appearing daily in more than 150 newspapers. Jeff was a speechwriter for Bill Clinton and is a founding partner of West Wing Writers. He is also the author of *Supreme Power: Franklin Roosevelt vs. the Supreme Court* and *Mutual Contempt: Lyndon Johnson, Robert Kennedy, and the Feud That Defined a Decade*. Jeff and his wife, Rebecca Epstein '92, live in Washington, DC, with their two children.

David Shields ('78) is the author of fifteen books, including, most recently, *Salinger*, co-written with Shane Salerno. *Reality Hunger* was named one of the best books of 2010 by more than thirty publications, *The Thing About Life Is That One Day You'll Be Dead* was a *New York Times* bestseller, and *Black Planet* was a finalist for the National Book Critics Circle Award. Shields's work has been translated into twenty languages.

Krista Tippett ('83) is the Peabody Award–winning creator, executive producer, and host of public radio's *On Being*. She was the *New York Times* stringer in divided Berlin and special assistant to the US ambassador to West Germany. She has an MDiv from Yale University. She is the author of *Speaking of Faith* and the *New York Times* bestseller *Einstein's God*.

Alfred Uhry ('58) is one of very few writers to receive an Academy Award, Tony Awards, and the Pulitzer Prize, all for dramatic writing. His plays and musicals include *The Robber Bridegroom* (a musical based on Eudora Welty's story), *The Last Night of Ballyhoo*, *Parade*, and *Driving Miss Daisy* (play and screenplay). His additional screenplays include *Mystic Pizza* and *Rich in Love*. He is a member of the Fellowship of Southern Writers.

Afaa Michael Weaver (Michael S. Weaver, '87 AM) is the author of *The Government of Nature* (University of Pittsburgh Press), his twelfth collection of poetry. He is also a playwright. In 1987, his full-length play *Rosa* was his graduate thesis in Brown's creative writing program. The recipient of Pew and NEA fellowships, as well as a Fulbright, he also has two Pushcart Prizes. He holds the Alumnae Chair at Simmons College.

Meg Wolitzer ('81) is the author of novels including *The Interestings*, *The Uncoupling*, *The Ten-Year Nap*, *The Position*, *The Wife*, and *Sleepwalking*, among others. Her short fiction has appeared in *The Best American Short Stories* and *The Pushcart Prize*. In the fall of 2013, along with singer-songwriter Suzzy Roche, Meg Wolitzer was a guest artist in the Princeton Atelier program at Princeton University.

Permissions

About the Editor

Judy Sternlight ('82) enjoyed a long career in theater and communications, which included teaching and performing improvisational theater with Some Assembly Required in New York City. Passionate about storytelling, she then spent nearly a decade editing books at Random House, Ballantine, and Modern Library before founding Judy Sternlight Literary Services and cofounding 5E, the independent editors' group. She has worked with many acclaimed authors and translators, including Marie-Helene Bertino, Rita Mae Brown, Edith Grossman, Bret Anthony Johnston, Mark Kurlansky, Peter Matthiessen, Daniel Menaker, and Patricia T. O'Conner.